SCHOOL SOCIAL WORK

Its Contribution to Professional Education

Appendix of Eight Illustrative Case Records

Arlien Johnson

*A STUDY BASED IN PART ON THE MATERIAL
PRESENTED AT THE CONFERENCE ON "THE
CONTRIBUTION OF SCHOOL SOCIAL WORK
TO SOCIAL WORK EDUCATION," HIGHLAND
PARK, ILLINOIS, AUGUST 2–8, 1959, SPONSORED
BY THE SCHOOL SOCIAL WORK SECTION,
NATIONAL ASSOCIATION OF SOCIAL WORKERS*

ATIONAL ASSOCIATION OF SOCIAL WORKERS, 2 Park Avenue, New York 16, N. Y.

PRICE: $4.50

The Conference on the Contribution of School Social Work to Social Work Education, and this volume were made possible by a grant from the National Institute of Mental Health.

FOREWORD

This volume represents a milestone in the evolution of school social work; equally important, it serves as a model for postconference publications. This foreword discusses briefly each of these contributions.

The previous writings in school social work have focused almost exclusively on examination and improvement of social work practice in this field. This focus has helped to crystallize practice patterns. Thus, school social work is now able to look beyond the definition of its own practice toward the wider horizon outlined by the juxtaposition of the two professions, social work and education. Dr. Johnson leads the way for us as she interprets the philosophy and practice of the two professions, examines school social work practice as it exists, and looks at the implications of this practice for the training of all social workers. Within a few years we may well see a volume which looks at the welfare of individual communities in light of the combined total potential of school resources and social welfare resources.

The other major contribution of this volume lies in the nature of the book itself, its content and format. When the Conference on the Contribution of School Social Work to Social Work Education was planned, the Conference Planning Committee expected to publish the proceedings in the traditional manner. Later, however, the committee wisely decided that the potential value of the published report of the conference would be much greater if a writer could be found to use the conference material as a base from which to prepare a broad and deep publication.

Interwoven through this book are the presentations and findings of the conference speakers, consultants and participants; wider in scope and more precise in depth is much additional material collected and created by the author. It is hoped that other groups will appropriate this scheme, that is, to entrust their writer with the responsibility of taking from a conference what is most valuable, and combining it with material reflecting his own academic and creative talents. This combination can result in a volume which interprets the things that are and points the way to the things that might be.

That such an ambitious plan can be fulfilled is now clear. For proof one has only to read this book. It is hoped that others will be inspired to emulate what Arlien Johnson has done so successfully.

JERRY L. KELLEY

Assistant Director
National Association of Social Workers
January 1962

PREFACE

This book analyzes the practice of social work in the school and, in conclusion, points out the implications of the findings for social work education. The conference materials on which the book is based were planned by the School Social Work Section, National Association of Social Workers, as a presentation and discussion of the contribution of school social work to social work education; however, the freedom given me to use the conference papers and workshop discussion reports as a point of departure has resulted in a much broader study which emphasizes practice more than social work education.

The study divides naturally into three parts. Part I is an analysis of social work as it is affected by the characteristics of a particular field, that is, by its relation to another profession, education, and to the social institution, the school. Part II relates the practice of social work in the school to the parent body of social work knowledge, value, and method, and discusses the particular characteristics of social work practice in the school. Part III presents conclusions about the contribution that school social work practice has to make to the curriculum of the professional school. Illustrative case material is used throughout the text to make concrete and meaningful the generalizations about practice; reference is also made in the text to the illustrative records in Appendix A.

An analysis of school social work practice is timely in view of the current interest of the profession in studies of practice by fields and what such studies may contribute to the development of social work theory. A method for analyzing practice has been formulated by Harriett M. Bartlett, drawing upon the work of the Commission on Social Work Practice, NASW.[1] The *Working Definition of Social Work Practice* developed by the commission was useful in this study, but Miss Bartlett's work, published in 1961, was not available until after the study had been completed. Miss Bartlett, however, gave me

---

[1] Harriett M. Bartlett, *Analyzing Social Work Practice by Fields* (New York: National Association of Social Workers, 1961); and *Social Work Practice in the Health Field* (New York: National Association of Social Workers, 1961).

The Working Definition of Social Work Practice, 1956 version, conveniently cited in Harriett M. Bartlett, "Toward Clarification and Improvement of Social Work Practice," *Social Work*, Vol. 3, No. 2 (April 1958), pp. 5–8; and March 1961 version (New York: National Association of Social Workers, 1961). (Mimeographed.)

substantial help through her published articles and in correspondence. She responded generously to requests for advice and criticism of certain chapters. I am deeply indebted to this good friend and scholar for her guidance and counsel.

The use made of conference papers and reports of workshop and other discussions should be explained. The six major papers prepared for the general sessions of the conference determined, in part, the content of certain chapters. The first footnote in each of these chapters acknowledges the paper used as source material, but quotations and references to the writer's statements are not further documented in the chapter. This flexible use of the papers enabled me to cull the material that seemed most pertinent to the subject under consideration and to discard the less relevant material. The papers often supplied valuable illustrations of school social work practice. Grateful acknowledgment for the selective use made of their material is made to the authors of the papers—listed in the order in which their work appears: Jane Wille, Robert C. Taber, Elizabeth Keyes, Eleanor Loeb, Mildred Sikkema, and Ruth E. Smalley.

Workshop discussions and the discussions that followed the papers presented at the general sessions were reported by members of the conference who were appointed as recorders. Five workshop groups met following each general session. The recorders' reports enabled me to compare discussion on the same topic in the five groups. Comparison revealed points of agreement and of disagreement, and made evident the ideas that recurred in all of the workshop discussions; it also pointed up areas of confusion and concern about practice. In addition, these reports provided generalizations about certain aspects of practice that emerged from experience. Reference is made throughout the text to content taken from workshop discussions, and often exact phrases and graphic expression of ideas have been retained. The recording of discussions that followed the general sessions was of value chiefly in furnishing the contributions of the five consultants. An effort has been made to include their penetrating and illuminating observations in appropriate context. All the recorders performed their difficult task with discrimination. Their work has made this study more significant than it could otherwise have been.

The audience originally envisioned for this book by the Education Committee of the School Social Work Section was social work educators, including field instructors. But as the material has been developed it seems to have equal value for the student in the school of social work and for the practicing social worker in the school. Teachers, principals, and other school personnel may find certain chapters of interest, especially Chapter 3, "Understanding the School as a Social Institution," and Chapter 4, "Education and Social Work as Professions." Another use for the book, it is hoped, may be to help social workers define more precisely their function and role in the school. As a core of sound practice is agreed upon, it should become easier for the school social worker to interpret to school personnel his role and its relation to the roles of other guidance specialists.

The opportunity to analyze the practice of social work in the school has been a stimulating and rewarding experience for which I am grateful to the School Social Work Section, NASW. The response from the field to a request for case material was most gratifying. Records were received from all parts of the country. Since only selected aspects of practice are illustrated in the text and in Appendix A, some excellent records could not be included. They did serve, however, to give me insight into practice and thus made an indirect contribution. My thanks go to those who participated in the study through submission of case records. Special acknowledgment is made of the work of the Education Committee; the members read the entire first draft of the manuscript and offered constructive criticism. A subcommittee composed of Florence Poole, Joseph P. Hourihan, Jerry L. Kelley, Irene Hobbs, and Rose Green read revisions of the manuscript and also gave invaluable assistance in helping to evaluate case material for its acceptability as school social work practice. The task of selecting case records that will find universal acceptance as good practice is difficult because of the growing and changing nature of the field. I take full responsibility for the final selection of the examples of practice which are found in the text and in Appendix A.

My colleagues at the University of Southern California, especially John G. Milner and Helen Northen, responded generously to my request for comments on certain chapters. Their perceptive criticism and stimulating suggestions helped me keep perspective on school social work as a part of the broader field of social work. I am, as always, indebted to them.

A final word of acknowledgment and appreciation is due staff members of NASW who did much to bring this project to fruition: Jerry L. Kelley, Assistant Director assigned to the School Social Work Section, Beatrice Saunders, Publications Director, and Stella Bloch Hanau, Editorial Consultant. Mr. Kelley acted as liaison between me and the Education Committee, a task he performed with sensitive awareness of problems of communication. His thoughtfulness and his supportive assistance made it a pleasure to work with him. Mrs. Saunders gave encouragement at needed times and places. Mrs. Hanau's skill in perceiving my intended meaning and her ability to clarify organization and expression of thought have contributed much to the readability of the volume. To each of them go my esteem and gratitude.

ARLIEN JOHNSON

Granada Hills, California
January 1962

CONTENTS

Contents

Part 1

The School

As a Field of Practice

for Social Work

HISTORICAL DEVELOPMENT

1

The addition of social workers to public school personnel began in the early twentieth century. This was a period of social ferment and reform in the United States. Among the influences which affected education and social work were new knowledge of behavior offered by psychology and growing social consciousness stimulated by the social sciences.

Education by 1900 was moving from what Cubberley calls the "old knowledge conception" to "education as development." [1] Instead of the assumption that children were alike in needs and capacities and that education was the instilling of subject-matter knowledge, the newer conception was that education was development of the individual capacities of children. It was also seen that this development must be related to the life of the community in which children lived. This conception meant that public education must make provision for children with a wide range of abilities and must be diversified to meet the varying needs of children. While major attention was given to the instruction of the so-called average child, educators were not unaware that studies revealed about 15 percent of the school population to be below average in ability and an almost equal percentage to be above average.[2] Special classes, enriched programs of study, experiments, notably in Winnetka, Illinois, and Gary, Indiana, with highly flexible, individualized programs of education, were widely publicized and by 1920 had affected public school education generally in the United States.

---

[1] Ellwood P. Cubberley, *Public Education in the United States* (rev. and enl. ed.; Boston: Houghton Mifflin Co., 1947), pp. 513–517.

[2] *Ibid.*, p. 520.

Pressure upon the schools for individualized treatment of the child came also from other sources. By 1919 every state had some form of legislation requiring compulsory attendance of children between certain ages, ranging from seven to fifteen years. The battle between those who favored an academic education for a selected number who could best profit from instruction and those who believed that in a democracy every child should be given the maximum amount of education of which he was capable was being won by the latter. This brought into the schools a wide variety of children, some of whom were limited by physical, mental, and social handicaps; it also brought under school surveillance the incorrigible who earlier would have been expelled or allowed to drop out of school. The compulsory attendance laws led the public to expect the school to achieve results with all children, not a selected few. This burden upon the schools caused them to assume, often reluctantly and as a result of outside pressures from parents and other groups, certain programs that formerly had been the province of the courts, welfare agencies, health services, and others. The school was expected to take over responsibility for "the whole child" and for the development of his personality as well as his intellect.[3]

The social worker was one of the specialists, along with attendance officers, nurses, psychologists, and vocational counselors, who was brought into the school system under this expanded concept of public education. His special contribution was in understanding the forces outside the school which affected the child's ability to make use of the educational opportunity provided. Gradually his service has focused as well on the social and emotional problems which interfere with school functioning and achievement, and it is closely co-ordinated with the classroom teacher's work and that of other specialists.

Another influence upon the school in the early twentieth century was the increasing awareness of the importance of children in the future of the nation. The declining birth rate gave added impetus to the conservation of the health and vitality of children and youth. The schools were seen as offering great opportunity for the promotion of child health through diagnostic and preventive services which could be made possible by the addition of school physicians, dentists and dental hygienists, nurses, health educators, and other specialists. The establishment of the United States Children's Bureau in 1912 (now a part of the Department of Health, Education, and Welfare) marked official recognition of the value of research and investigation into aspects of child life which would promote child wel-

---

[3] *See* Chapters 3 and 4 for discussion of the dilemma which these expectations have created for the school and for teachers.

fare. The White House Conference on Children in 1909, which mobilized public opinion in support of such action, was devoted to dependent and neglected children; but subsequent decennial conferences have reflected the shifting interest from selected groups of deprived children to concern with the welfare and maximum development of all children. The school as the social institution having universal contact with children and youth thus became the agency to which many new movements turned for help in realizing social welfare aims. Indeed, many special services were first introduced into schools by organized groups which came to regard the school as "our greatest social agency." [4]

The schools necessarily moved slowly in assuming new duties and in developing new concepts about their place in society.[5] Private groups, therefore, entered into co-operative arrangements with the schools in some cities in order to demonstrate the value of such services as special instruction for the deaf, blind, feeble-minded, crippled. Kindergartens, playground activities, child guidance clinics, and school social work were among other programs that were originally privately financed. By 1924, however, national organizations in the fields of education and social work were setting up joint committees to consider their mutual interests in the deviant child. About that time the National Education Association and the National Conference of Social Work (now the National Conference on Social Welfare) appointed a Cooperating Committee on Behavior Problems of Children. Educators and social workers were again drawn together on many committees of the 1930 White House Conference on Child Health and Protection, and also on the Committee on Relationships Between the School and Juvenile Court, appointed shortly afterward by the National Probation Association.[6] Such co-operative planning has continued with the United States Office of Education and other groups from time to time.

The origin and development of school social work (originally known as visiting teacher work)[7] is perhaps illustrative of the way in which new services become incorporated into the school system.

[4] Edith Abbott, *Social Welfare and Professional Education* (Chicago: University of Chicago Press, 1931), p. 120.

[5] For a development of this statement, *see* William I. Thomas and Dorothy Swaine Thomas, *The Child in America* (New York: Alfred A. Knopf, 1928), pp. 219–227; *see also* Cubberley, *op. cit.*, pp. 564–587.

[6] Lois A. Meredith, "Education and Social Work," in *Social Work Year Book, 1933* (New York: Russell Sage Foundation, 1933), pp. 137–142. Indicative, perhaps, of the mounting interest at that time in social work in the public schools is the fact that an article under this title appears only in the 1933 yearbook.

[7] Other titles sometimes used for school social worker are home and school counselor, visiting counselor, child welfare and attendance supervisor.

A report by the Public Education Association of the City of New York in 1923, states:

> As has frequently happened in other educational experiments, the visiting teacher movement was initiated in some cities by private organizations, and, after the value of the work had been demonstrated, was taken over by the Department of Education. In New York, the work originated [in 1906] in two settlements in which workers with the children felt that they needed to get in closer touch with the teachers of the settlement children. . . . As a result, one resident in each settlement assumed the special work of calling on families of those children who presented serious social or educational problems, and this worker came to be known as the . . . visiting teacher. A committee to extend and develop this work was shortly afterwards formed by the Public Education Association which maintained the work until the Board of Education was convinced of its value and established it as part of the school system. In Boston [in 1907] the work was started by a group of public spirited citizens, whose example was followed by women's clubs and settlements. In Hartford, the third pioneer, the work was undertaken upon the suggestion of the director of the Psychological Laboratory, who realized the need of it in connection with his work with problematic school children.[8]

In Philadelphia the White-Williams Foundation evolved from the Magdalen Society founded in 1800 into a program of counselors in the public schools (1917). The foundation, in co-operation with the Philadelphia School Board, supported an extensive school social work service under the name of school counseling until 1942 when the entire support of the program was assumed by the school board. Rochester, New York, has the distinction of having had the first school social worker (1914) employed directly by a board of education.

The nationwide growth of the movement for the addition of social workers to school personnel has been advanced in several ways. Impetus was given to the movement when in 1921 the Commonwealth Fund inaugurated its Program for the Prevention of Delinquency. One section of the program was for demonstrations of "visiting teacher services" in thirty communities throughout the United States, in co-operation with local school boards.[9] Another influence

---

[8] Thomas and Thomas, *op. cit.*, pp. 228–230. The Public Education Association was a voluntary organization affiliated with the Commonwealth Fund, set up to promote visiting teacher work in the Program for the Prevention of Delinquency. The program also included support of child guidance clinics on a demonstration basis, scholarship aid for the training of psychiatric social workers, visiting teachers, and probation officers.

upon the expansion and standardization of school social work has been the organization of workers in such positions. The first professional association was formed in 1919 under the name of the American Association of Visiting Teachers; its lineal descendant is the School Social Work Section of the National Association of Social Workers. Two scholarship programs have helped to increase the number and to improve the quality of school social work personnel. The first program of scholarship aid was offered by the Commonwealth Fund as part of its Program for the Prevention of Delinquency (1921–1930). More recently, the National Institute of Mental Health has extended its educational grants program to include preparation of school social workers.

An important national influence upon social work in the schools has been the United States Office of Education. Under its auspices a group, made up of school social workers, school administrators, state commissioners of education, and representatives of schools of education and of social work, were called together in 1945. The purpose of the meeting was to formulate qualifications and to define functions of school social workers. In 1959, United States Commissioner of Education Lawrence G. Derthick created the position of specialist in school social work on the staff of the Office of Education. A well-qualified person was appointed who is available for consultation to school systems requesting information or advice about school social work services, and who in other ways endeavors to represent and extend this important service for children.

The number of social work positions in the public schools and the number of school jurisdictions with such service are not accurately known. Some indication of the spread of the movement is evident, however, in the fact that in 1944 school social work services were in operation in 266 cities, and since that time several states and Puerto Rico have passed and implemented legislation for service on a statewide basis.[10] In Illinois alone, in 1959–1960, 117 school districts employed 197 social workers. The membership of the School Social Work Section of NASW, which has membership standards based on professional education, was 1,100 in July 1960 and had increased during the year.

---

[9] Communities comprised three rural counties: Boone County, Mo., Huron County, Ohio, and Monmouth County, N.J.; and twenty-seven cities: Berkeley, Calif., Birmingham, Ala., Bluefield, W.Va., Burlington, Vt., Butte, Mont., Charlotte, N.C., Chisholm, Minn., Coatesville, Pa., Columbus, Ga., Detroit, Mich., Durham, N.C., Eugene, Ore., Hutchinson, Kan., Kalamazoo, Mich., Lincoln, Neb., Omaha, Neb., Pocatella, Idaho, Racine, Wis., Richmond, Va., Rochester, Pa., Rock Springs, Wyo., San Diego, Calif., Sioux City, Iowa, Sioux Falls, S.D., Tucson, Ariz., Tulsa, Okla., Warren, Ohio.

[10] Florence Poole, "School Social Services," in *Social Work Year Book 1957* (New York: National Association of Social Workers, 1957), p. 510.

GOALS AND VALUES
IN PUBLIC SCHOOL EDUCATION

2

To understand the school as a field of practice for social work it is essential that social workers understand the goals and values of education in the United States.[1] Familiarity with public school education through one's own attendance is not sufficient—and, indeed, may be a deterrent—for understanding the school today. In any society, education is one of the major transmitters of culture. Education both reflects and interprets a nation's basic philosophy—social, political, economic. To study the history of education in the United States is to study important stages of development of our nation. A recent report (1959) sponsored by the Fund for the Advancement of Education states:

> In all history, no nation has had a greater commitment to the value of education for all its citizens than has the United States. No other nation has depended so heavily on education for its economic progress and the achievement of its ideals. No other nation has made greater demands on its school and its educators.[2]

The fact that the United States is a democracy sets the framework of goals and values for education as, indeed, it does for other profes-

---

[1] This chapter is based in part on a paper by Jane Wille, "Goals and Values in Education: Their Implications for Social Work Education," presented at the Conference on the Contribution of School Social Work to Social Work Education, Highland Park, Illinois, August 2–8, 1959, and published in *Social Work*, Vol. 5, No. 3 (July 1960), pp. 97–103.

[2] *The Efficiency of Freedom,* Report of the Committee on Government and Higher Education (Baltimore: Johns Hopkins Press, 1959).

sions.[3] Democracy is more than a form of government; it is also an attitude of mind, a prevailing set of assumptions about individual and group rights and duties. The individual, it is believed, should have freedom and opportunity to develop his full potentialities as a person and as a citizen without regard to differences in religion, race, class, or sex. But he is also a part of a community, that is, of a group of people living in organized association who have responsibility collectively for one another's welfare. The goal of education, in general terms, is the realization of the values relating to the individual and society which are inherent in a democracy. It has been well said:

> ... education's responsibility to society is to guide and encourage each child and adult to work for the full development of his intellectual, physical, spiritual, and social endowments. No education is adequate which neglects any of these needs. The ultimate strength of our country depends on the moral strength, economic competence, and social responsibility of the individual citizen.[4]

Within this broad framework of democratic aims and ideals, great diversity exists in educational programs. Values and goals are not static but change with the times. As Wille notes, the examination of educational goals is particularly pertinent today when many critics assert that the educational system on the whole is suffering from "obsolescence," that educators should be teaching children *how* to learn as well as *what* to learn. Technological changes demand leadership from those who can think creatively and independently.

If social workers are to understand the problems of educators and are to make their contribution toward the establishment of valid goals for the public schools, they need to appreciate some of the reasons for the present diversity in educational goals.

First, the public school in the United States has evolved from local efforts with all the heterogeneity of traditions and customs found in this country. It was 1850 before the principle of public school education for *all* children was generally accepted, and this occurred after heated controversy over the merits of tax-supported, publicly controlled and directed, nonsectarian common schools. Little more

---

[3] Wille quotes M. F. Ashley Montagu on the meaning of value: ". . . the maintenance of a set toward the attainment of a goal" is defined as a value. "The person learns to want many goals. When these goals are remote and strived for, value obtains." In brief, we place a value on what we strive for.

[4] John Nebo, ed., *Administration of School Social Work* (New York: National Association of Social Workers, 1960), p. 13.

than a century ago, surprising as it now seems, this issue was arousing bitter feelings and antagonisms, second only to those associated with the battle for the abolition of slavery.[5] Even in 1961 the fear of loss of local self-determination in education is an obstacle to federal aid for education. The heterogeneity of cultures and subcultures also affects specific values held by communities with respect to the support and aims of education, and leads to the statement frequently made that we have fifty state systems of education rather than one American system.

A second reason for diversity is the rate of social change in recent years. Material inventions such as those affecting transportation, communication, replacement of manual labor by machines have made vast changes in ways of living. Old values have been displaced and new ones have not been firmly established. Standards of conduct are often an incoherent mixture of old and new without clear-cut mandates to guide and control. Education as the transmitter of culture is, therefore, often caught between holding to old, outmoded activity, or advancing ideas which local supporters of the schools, the taxpayers, view with alarm as departures from "reading, writing, and arithmetic." Certainly, the continuous change in American society, in the past half century especially, has made for inconsistency in values as expressed in behavior and has complicated the task of the educator.

Finally, the acceleration of inventions and demands for skilled labor to help supply armaments for defense and to satisfy consumer demands for goods has brought to the fore the persistent questions, should education be primarily in the "liberal" tradition and cultivate the person, or should it prepare directly for a vocation, with strong emphasis on subject-matter content. Under the influence of so-called progressive educational theories, some schools have given major emphasis to "life-adjustment" education which has been described as "less intellectual, less specialized, and more personal, more social" than traditional education.[6] On the other hand, some schools have stressed intellectual training and subject matter as the essentials of education. Between these extremes are many schools which have undertaken to strike a middle ground, to take into consideration the whole child and the totality of his interests as well as his need to learn facts and values.

In spite of these factors making for diversity in educational values and goals, an "American" system of education has evolved in three

---

[5] Ellwood P. Cubberley, *Public Education in the United States* (rev. and enl. ed.; Boston: Houghton Mifflin Company, 1947), p. 164.

[6] Bernard Mehl, "Political and Social Cohesion in Secondary Education in the United States," in *The Secondary School Curriculum, Year Book of Education 1958* (Yonkers, N.Y.: World Book Company, 1958) p. 137.

centuries. Although influenced by European theories, it is said to be a "sturdy native development." [7]

characteristic goals
and values in american education

Many individuals and many social forces have helped to give form and philosophy to American education. One student of the subject states:

> The present-day idea of the common school can best be viewed as a social theory which synthesizes at least five great strains in American educational thought: the *practicalism* of Benjamin Franklin, the *republicanism* of Thomas Jefferson, the *moralism* of Horace Mann, the *individualism* of G. Stanley Hall, and the *reformism* of John Dewey.[8]

The influence of these and other educators was cumulative. Each added to, and deepened, the permanent values that came from his predecessor; and each, in turn, was influenced by the climate of the period in which he lived and worked. Out of conflict and debate have come lasting values that have given some unity of form and philosophy to education in spite of influences making for diversity. A summary of basic principles would include the following:

1. *Public education must be public; i.e., universal and compulsory.*
The doctrine proclaimed by the Constitution that "all men are created equal, and endowed by the Creator with certain inalienable rights" gave basis to the argument that in a democracy education must be universal and compulsory. Only a system of free, tax-supported, nonsectarian schools could adequately prepare the child of today to be the responsible citizen of tomorrow. To insure democratic control of the school system it was held that local boards of citizens, serving with only nominal compensation, should administer specific programs. Over the years, state supervision and state aid to local communities were accepted. By 1957 some 60,000 school districts with local boards of citizens were responsible for the education of the children enrolled in the public schools; these represented about 90 percent of children of school age.

2. *Education should provide common ideals of citizenship and of individual rights and duties in a democracy.*
From the beginning, education was seen to have a twofold pur-

---

[7] Cubberley, *op. cit.,* p. 471.

[8] Lawrence A. Cremin, "The American Common School in Theory and Practice," in *Education and Philosophy, Year Book of Education 1957* (Yonkers, N.Y.: World Book Company, 1957), p. 243.

pose. It must be "practical" and include knowledge that would help a man to earn his living; at the same time, it must teach moral and spiritual values so that common ideals of the general welfare would be formed. Education was at once a conserving and a reforming force in society. In the United States, public education has, indeed, served to mold a heterogeneous population into a nation with definite characteristics called "American." At the same time, education has been held by some to be a force for social change and for the improvement of society. Conformity is required to give stability, and creative individuality is necessary for change and progress. Confusion over these aims is frequently discernible when they are not seen as interacting and reciprocal.

3. *Education must be individualized in order to provide for the varying capacities and abilities of children.*

The growth of psychology, European and American, as a science has had a marked influence on education in the twentieth century. The approach to education is now child-centered in contrast to the earlier knowledge-drill for all alike. The school must provide a differential type of education to suit the varying capacities—or handicaps—and abilities of students. As previously pointed out, this approach has led to special classes, enriched curricula, attention to health, including social adjustment, and to the services of specialists such as the social worker, in order for each child to make maximum use of the educational opportunity and thus to develop his potentialities to the fullest extent.

4. *Education must be socializing if it is to further democratic ideals and nurture individual development.*

From philosophy and sociology another dimension was added to education in the early twentieth century. John Dewey was, perhaps, the chief synthesizer of these streams of thought and the interpreter of their importance to educational theory. Education is seen as "a freeing of individual capacity in a progressive growth directed to social aims." [9] All living contributes to, or blocks, learning. A child learns from his associates, takes his values from the groups of which he is a part, and is dependent upon the school to help resolve contradictions in standards and values. The school, in turn, is a part of the community and interacts with the standards and values which are represented in it. But the school also has responsibility to serve as an agent for social change, to improve the quality of community life. Emphasis is upon a child-centered curriculum in a community-centered school.

In summary, it is clear that goals and values are not static but are vital parts of the life of the times. Lerner states that the Amer-

---

[9] John Dewey, *Democracy and Education* (New York: Macmillan Company, 1916), p. 115.

ican public school system historically is "the product of impulsions that have come from within instead of having been imposed from without," and he adds that if American education looks like a "crazy quilt" in that it lacks a consistent philosophy, it is "an organic expression of American life and character." [10] Belief in the value of education and perhaps over-reliance on its efficacy to solve all kinds of problems are inherent in American traditions. Combined with this view is an anti-intellectual attitude toward an education that trains the intellect but does not show results in earning power and practical use. In the twentieth century, the growth of psychology, social sciences, and philosophy has had an influence on educational theory. The wide range of needs and abilities of individual children has been recognized; at the same time, the importance of influences outside the school in affecting standards and conduct has led to the increasing assumption by the school of responsibility for helping to relate the total child to his total learning environment. John Dewey and his followers influenced education tremendously by seeing personal growth and development as an integral part of the growth and development of society. Dewey's ideas have doubtless done most to give American education some common ideology in spite of many variations in practice.

some common aims of the
teacher and the social worker

The broad basic goals of education and social work are similar. Both professions reflect the dominant currents of thought of the first half of the twentieth century. While educators were affected primarily by Dewey and his followers, social workers were greatly influenced by Sigmund Freud, other psychoanalysts, and psychologists of the period. Both Dewey and Freud are generally recognized as having had a pervasive influence upon many areas of twentieth century thought. The former approached the study of behavior from an analysis of normal responses; the latter began with the study of the abnormal. Both men were engaged in a problem-solving approach to the understanding of human nature and both were incorporating into their thinking the scientific findings of the day.[11]

---

[10] Max Lerner, *America As a Civilization* (New York: Simon and Schuster, 1957), p. 733.

[11] Dewey was said to be one of the makers of the twentieth century. *See* Henry Steele Commager, *The American Mind* (New Haven: Yale University Press, 1950), p. 100: "So faithfully did Dewey live up to his own philosophical creed that he became the guide, the mentor, and the conscience of the American people: it is scarcely an exaggeration to say that for a generation no major issue was clarified until Dewey had spoken."

After a period in which critics relegated Dewey's work to a past era, a fresh evaluation has recently been taking place. *The Saturday Review*, November 21,

Some of the insights they have provided are a part of the professional knowledge of both education and social work. The use made of them, however, is different in education and in social work.

Three important ideas, selected from the literature of the two professions, are presented without any attempt to analyze the underlying philosophical or scientific frameworks. These ideas are: (1) the *individual* and his power to grow, (2) the *group* and the social nature of conduct, and (3) the *community* and co-operative endeavor as an expression of democracy.

the individual and his power to grow

The teacher recognizes that education is a process in which the child is helped to find inner motivation for growth. Ideally, the teacher sees the child as an individual with his own specific capacity for development and with his own interests, and he understands the child in relation to environmental forces that impinge upon him. When subject matter is presented by a teacher with this kind of understanding, it enhances both intellectual and emotional development of the child. He is stimulated to tackle problems and to learn how to solve them so that other problems can be solved in the future. The teacher's objective is to help the child develop ways of thinking and of utilizing experience so that he can continue throughout life to master new knowledge and solve new problems with the strength that comes from disciplined achievement. In short, the aim of education for the individual is learning how to learn.

1959 issue, contains a special section on Dewey. Francis T. Villemain, one of the contributors states: "A conception of education that is relevant to our civilizational needs grows out of the thoughts of John Dewey; however, that conception has been largely obscured by widely circulated myths. . . . Dewey held that any given philosophy, despite all claims to the contrary, was in fact a reflection and criticism of the society in which it was developed. Dewey's philosophy—*in context*—turns out to be an unqualified rationale in support of behavior-patterns and institutions that promise to solve the prevailing problems of men." p. 26.

Sigmund Freud came to the United States in 1909 to deliver a series of lectures in connection with the twentieth anniversary celebration of Clark University. *See* Albert Deutsch, *The Mentally Ill in America* (New York: Doubleday, Doran, and Company, 1938), pp. 470–471: "His visit here aroused tremendous interest in his theories, which was reflected in the large output of literature on psychoanalysis at that time. . . . Assuming an ever-expanding scope, it has influenced not only psychiatry, but such diverse disciplines as philosophy, psychology, sociology, anthropology, criminology, pedagogy, art and social work."

Ernest Jones, in his biography of Freud, attempts to estimate the effects of Freud's influence, direct and indirect, on psychiatry, education, psychology, philosophy, anthropology, sociology, religion, art, literature, criminology, and social life. *See The Life and Work of Sigmund Freud* (New York: Basic Books, 1957), Vol. 3, Chapter 17, pp. 432–441.

While the teacher strives to see each child with his individual needs, his primary task is to keep in mind the child's relation to the class or group of which he is a part. And for the class, there are norms of achievement, excellence, and co-operative endeavor, set according to the age-grade of the students. A child is evaluated by these norms; and he is expected to conform to certain standards of neatness, cleanliness, and behavior as well as academic achievement. The progress of the class as a whole in their learning is necessarily a primary goal of the teacher. He can most effectively free children and enable them to learn if there is not too wide a range of ability or of behavioral problems within the group. With thirty or more children in a class, he must aim at some median of instruction.

The social worker, too, believes in the power of an individual to grow and change. His goal is "the enhancement of social functioning wherever the need for such enhancement is either socially or individually perceived." [12] The child or adult who comes to his attention is usually one who is experiencing some obstacle to normal functioning. He stands in need of help to become self-directing and self-dependent so that he can live at harmony with himself and others and realize his capacity for growth. In a sense, the task of the social worker is re-education. To this task he brings knowledge of personality structure and of environmental forces that produce deviations in behavior. According to Perlman, "The structure and functioning of personality are the products of inherited and constitutional equipment in continuous interaction with the physical, psychological and social environment the person experiences." [13] Like the teacher, the social worker must find the key to motivating the person to want to change and find new satisfactions in living and learning; at the same time, he must be alert to those external realities that limit such opportunities. His chief tool is the individual interview during which a relationship that involves both intellect and feeling is gradually developed.

The social worker in the school focuses on helping the child to make use of the educational opportunity to grow through learning. His function includes help to the child to perform his role as a student and help to the school personnel to provide suitable educational resources and opportunities so that the obstacles that hinder learning are modified. He accepts the child whose feelings may be expressed through a wide range of variation in behavior, encourages

---

[12] Werner W. Boehm, *Objectives of the Social Work Curriculum of the Future* (Social Work Curriculum Study, Vol. I: New York: Council on Social Work Education, 1959), p. 46.

[13] Helen Harris Perlman, *Social Casework: A Problem-solving Process* (Chicago: University of Chicago Press, 1957), p. 17.

expressions of feelings of difference as the child is able to move toward change, however small. Wille points out:

> The social worker in the school does not have responsibility for specific achievement of the individual child nor of a group. His help is focused on the individual child as he works, through a relationship with this child, to enable him to take some responsibility for his participation in the student role. . . . The social worker, who has knowledge of the values of the child's family, understands the conflicts which the child experiences because of differing teacher values. Such values as cleanliness, orderliness, and not fighting or swearing may represent an entirely different value system for the child. The social worker views the child's difficulty in accepting and adhering to such values in the context of his family and neighborhood pattern. His goal is to help the child attain an appreciation of school values based on more than superficial conformity.

The ultimate aim is the restoration and/or the enhancement of the child's social functioning as a person and as a student.

the group and the social nature of conduct

One of the aims of education, as previously stated, is the transmission of the culture of a society so that common ideals of citizenship in a democracy can be carried forward. The teacher has responsibility to impart ethical and spiritual values as he teaches specific subject matter. He does this through the give-and-take of group discussion, through helping children experience a feeling of group cohesion and mutual interdependence in the classroom. Part of his competence is ability to understand and guide group interaction toward social ends. For the power of an individual to grow depends, in part, upon his need for others and the ability to utilize experience gained in association with others. Thus, in addition to other skills, a teacher needs to know both theoretically and practically how to work with groups. Only then can maximum returns be expected from group association as an aid to education.

Moreover, the classroom is being increasingly regarded as an aid or a hindrance to good mental health. A survey of mental health programs in the school reveals that there is a growing conviction that many of the minor behavior and learning problems of children can best be managed in the classroom.[14] As a result, some teachers are seeking in-service training to gain understanding of the dynamics

---

[14] William G. Hollister, "Current Trends in Mental Health Programming in the Classroom," *Journal of Social Issues*, Vol. 15, No. 1 (1959). The entire issue is devoted to the topic, "Mental Health in the Classroom."

of groups and more knowledge of the factors that affect the emotional climate, morale, and work-centeredness of classes. This trend places additional expectations upon teachers, and they need the supportive and consultative help that other disciplines such as social work, psychology, and the health specialties can give them.

The social worker also believes in the importance of group association as a force in the development of personality. The group work specialist has knowledge of group interaction and process, and thus he is able to help groups function in such a way that activities contribute to the growth of the individual and toward desirable social ends. Dewey's ideas about the inter-relatedness of personal and social development undoubtedly early affected the thinking of social workers. Other sources of insight have been psychiatric concepts of growth and development, sociological research on group process, and anthropological materials relating to class and cultural differences in behavior.[15] All social workers are now expected to have some knowledge of the dynamics of group interaction and to be able to apply this knowledge as they see the individual as a member of a family, play, work, or social group.

The social worker in the school has many opportunities to make use of knowledge about work with groups. The classroom is one kind of group experience for the child. If he cannot take his place in it, the social worker may be asked to help the teacher find a solution. Furthermore, the school itself is a social system within which are many groups and subgroups, natural and formed in composition. The social worker, usually only one among personnel from several disciplines, must be able to analyze the situation and find his place. If he has sufficient knowledge and experience he may be helpful as a consultant to teachers and others when problems arise about group interaction.

community co-operative endeavor

Education not only helps to form national ideals, but it also reflects the values held by a particular nation. Essential to a democracy is the idea of the common welfare, the need for co-operative endeavor. Learning is thus affected by the kind of community a child lives in, for he learns outside as well as in school. One of Dewey's contributions to education was his development of the concept that education has continuity through all kinds of experience. The school, therefore, needs to be related to the community in which it is located. He stated:

It is true that the aim of education is the development of indi-

---

[15] Grace L. Coyle, "Social Group Work," in *Social Work Year Book 1951* (New York: American Association of Social Workers, 1951), p. 47.

viduals to the utmost of their potentialities. But this statement in isolation leaves unanswered the question as to what is the measure of the development. A society of free individuals in which all, through their own work, contribute to the liberation and enrichment of the lives of others, is the only environment in which any individual can really grow normally to his full stature.[16]

The end of education, thus conceived, is social and "the criterion to be applied in estimating the value of the practices that exist in schools is also social." [17] In brief, education should be directed toward producing students who can work for the improvement of democratic institutions because they have learned to *act* with and for others while, through disciplined intelligence, they have learned to *think* and judge for themselves.

The duties of the teacher with respect to the community are described in the Code of Ethics of the National Education Association. The third principle states:

The teaching profession occupies a position of public trust involving not only the individual teacher's personal conduct, but also the interaction of the school and the community. Education is most effective when these many relationships operate in a friendly, cooperative, and constructive manner. In fulfilling the obligations of this third principle, the teacher will—

1. Adhere to any reasonable pattern of behavior accepted by the community for professional persons.

2. Perform the duties of citizenship, and participate in community activities with due consideration for his obligations to his students, his family, and himself.

3. Discuss controversial issues from an objective point of view, thereby keeping his class free from partisan opinions.

4. Recognize that the public schools belong to the people of the community, encourage lay participation in shaping the purposes of the school, and strive to keep the public informed of the educational program which is being provided.

5. Respect the community in which he is employed and be loyal to the school system, community, state and nation.

6. Work to improve education in the community and to strengthen the community's moral, spiritual, and intellectual life.[18]

The question might be raised whether the kinds of community responsibility outlined above help the teacher make community life

---

[16] Quoted in *The Saturday Review, op. cit.,* p. 25.

[17] *Loc. cit.*

[18] Conveniently cited and discussed in Myron Lieberman, *Education As a Profession* (Englewood Cliffs, N.J.: Prentice-Hall, 1956), pp. 430–434.

a part of the learning of students in the classroom. Indeed, one critic maintains that the "teacher of six classes a day with forty students in each class, who also has to sponsor school activities, take tickets at athletic contests all year, attend PTA meetings to satisfy the principal, live and teach according to the prejudices of the local community or the most powerful members thereof, and perform janitorial, clerical, and non-professional services" is distracted from his main business of teaching.[19] Suffice it to say that the ideas that the school has close ties with the community of which it is a part and that teachers are expected to participate responsibly in community affairs as representatives of the school are well established American traditions.

Social work, like education, is rooted in the community. For many years the bulk of professional social workers were employed by voluntary agencies which were founded and supported by citizen groups. With the growth of public social services since 1935, the majority of professional social workers are employed in these services. To help guide public policy, local and state governments and the national government frequently appoint boards of citizens to serve in administrative or advisory capacities. The social worker believes in such citizen participation as part of the democratic process of co-operative endeavor.

The Code of Ethics of the National Association of Social Workers recognizes the community implications of social work practice. It states:

Social work is based on humanitarian, democratic ideals. Professional social workers are dedicated to service for the welfare of mankind; to the disciplined use of a recognized body of knowledge about human beings and their interactions; and to the marshaling of community resources to promote the well-being of all without discrimination. . . .

This Code of Ethics embodies certain standards of behavior for the social worker in his professional relationships with those he serves, with his colleagues, with his employing agency, with other professions, and with the community. In abiding by this code, the social worker views his obligations in as wide a context as the situation requires, takes all the principles into consideration, and chooses a course of action consistent with the code's spirit and intent.[20]

Social work aims to bring about improvement in the social institutions of society. One expression of this aim was the adoption of a series of public policy statements by the Delegate Assembly,

---

[19] *Ibid.*, p. 213.
[20] *NASW News,* Vol. 6, No. 2 (February 1961), p. 14.

NASW, in May 1958.[21] In general, their purpose is to further public policy which will protect people from certain hazards that result from the imperfect functioning of the basic social institutions, and to increase opportunities for more abundant living for all. The social community organization method in social work is particularly concerned with planned social change and with the co-ordination of co-operative endeavors; this method is the special skill of some practitioners. Increasingly it is recognized that all social workers should have some preparation in the use of this method if they are to be able to realize one of the goals inherent in social work: the improvement of community life.

The social worker in the school has need of such knowledge and skill. While his primary function is work with individuals, he also has the responsibility for knowing the social welfare resources of the community so that he can bring them appropriately into use on behalf of the school. In his work with children, he becomes aware of gaps in community services and can help the school call these to the attention of the relevant planning bodies. Frequently he is asked to represent the school before local organizations, to interpret the services of the school on behalf of children with problems, and to engage the co-operation of these organizations.

concluding comments

As indicated in the foregoing discussion, the teacher and the social worker have similar ideas about the power of individuals to grow and change, about the social nature of conduct and its importance in personality development, about their responsibility to understand, and relate to, the communities in which they are employed. The use they make of such ideas, however, is shaped by the specific tasks before them. The teacher is oriented generally toward so-called normal behavior and has as his task the aiding of children in groups to learn subject matter which makes up the curriculum and constitutes "education." Norms of achievement and conduct are expected. His training has been less influenced by dynamic psychology than has that of the social worker. The latter supplements the major purpose of the school and the teacher by helping the individual child who has difficulty in engaging constructively in the school program. This he does by helping the child to overcome environmental or emotional obstacles which interfere with his learning. The social worker is accepting of difference in the child and through individual interviews is able to evaluate and treat, or refer to a community agency, the child who needs such help. His aim is

---

[21] *Goals of Public Social Policy* (New York: National Association of Social Workers, 1959).

to enable the child to function more effectively so that he can learn and grow.

The school cannot achieve its goal of "helping each child to become as good and capable in every way as native endowment permits"—the goal defined in the final report of the White House Conference on Education held in April 1956—unless it has partners. Other professions and organized groups must help. Social work as an influential force in our society must relate to the basic institution of education in a significant way. Social workers need to have knowledge of the broad aspects of education, its philosophy, and developments in the context of changing needs in society. These are the subject of the next chapter.

UNDERSTANDING THE SCHOOL
AS A SOCIAL INSTITUTION

3

The social institution through which
the goals and objectives of formal education are imparted in the
United States is the school.[1] Taber states:

> Other than the family, no social institution plays a more vital role
> in the development and growth of our children than do our
> schools. Education, once restricted to the favored few, is now a
> vast and complex process with multiple functions and new respon-
> sibilities. No other institution holds such a strategic place in our
> social fabric and no other institution plays such a vital part in
> moulding the future of our nation.

The social worker must understand the school as a particular type
of social organization if he is to make his services effectively a part
of it. An analysis of some of the organizational behavior characteristic of the school is therefore pertinent.

the school social system

An educational sociologist has referred to the school figuratively
as a "social organism" and states that a characteristic mode of social
interaction must be established for a school to come into existence.[2]

---

[1] This chapter is based in part on a paper by Robert C. Taber, "The Con-
tribution of Social Work to the Social Planning Aspects of the School as a Social
Institution," presented at the Conference on the Contribution of School Social
Work to Social Work Education, Highland Park, Illinois, August 2–8, 1959.
(Unpublished.)

[2] Willard Waller, *The Sociology of Teaching* (New York: John Wiley and
Sons, 1932), Chapter 2.

Other sociologists speak of the school as a *social system* or a network of relationships between people in a certain setting; these people have defined status or position, and defined roles or patterned behavioral expectations which are associated with the status each occupies. Merton maintains that an array of associated roles (role-sets) accompanies a particular social status. He gives as an example the teacher:

> The status of the public school teacher has its distinctive role-set, relating the teacher to his pupils, to colleagues, the school principal and superintendent, the Board of Education, and, on frequent occasion, to local patriotic organizations, to professional organizations of teachers, Parent-Teacher Associations, and the like.[3]

Similarly, the administrator has a number of associated roles such as "middleman" between teaching staff and school board, line official who sees that policies are executed, consultant to the board on policy formulation, consultant to teachers and other staff members on special problems. His is also a position of institutionalized leadership or one where powers and duties inhere in the office, regardless of the person occupying the office at a particular time. The person may enhance the office or detract from it, but certain leadership activities are expected from whomever the person may be. In addition to his official role-set, as social workers well know, the administrator carries for some adults an unofficial role of authority; *i.e.*, they may relate to him as they have related, or now do, to other authorities in their lives—as a person to be liked or disliked, to be obeyed or resisted, emulated or discounted.

The role-sets of the specialists within the system must also be defined and related to those of the teacher and administrator. The particular problems with respect to the social worker as specialist are discussed in the concluding section of the chapter.

activity of central concern: teaching and learning

The functions of any organization help to determine the structure or the form which the network of relationships takes to carry out the organization's purpose. In the school, the giving and receiving of instruction—teaching and learning—are central to the interaction that characterizes the school as a social system. The teacher-pupil relationship is at the heart of the social structure, but modifying it

---

[3] Robert K. Merton, *Social Theory and Social Structure* (Glencoe, Ill.: The Free Press, 1957), p. 369.

is a hierarchy of positions, some superordinate and some subordinate. The effectiveness of the teaching-learning relationship is greatly affected by the actions and relationships of the school board, superintendent, principal, supervisor, other teacher colleagues, specialists from outside education, and by the composition of the student body itself. Also affecting the social climate of the school are those employees, called by Waller the "fringes of the school," the janitor, clerical staff, cafeteria workers, and others.[4] Within the school as a social system, there is specialization in terms of function and differentiation in terms of authority that goes with each function. A system of positions emerges; each position carries with it certain symbols that rank it in the system and this rank is the person's status (position) in the organization. In other words, a status system is a set of value judgments that ranks individuals and groups in relation to one another, as higher, lower, equal. This serves to give regularity and order, it imposes and fixes responsibility among the members of the organization, and it establishes rules of conduct. Merton states:

> Each of these offices contains an area of imputed competence and responsibility. Authority, the power of control which derives from an acknowledged status, inheres in the office and not in the particular person who performs the official role. . . . The system of prescribed relations between the various offices involves a considerable degree of formality and clearly defined social distance between the occupants of these positions. . . . Formality, which is integrated with the distribution of authority within the system, serves to minimize friction by largely restricting (official) contact to modes which are previously defined by the rules of the organization. Ready calculability of other's behavior and a stable set of mutual expectations is thus built up. Moreover, formality facilitates the interaction of the occupants of offices despite their (possibly hostile) private attitudes towards one another. In this way, the subordinate is protected from the arbitrary action of his superior, since the actions of both are constrained by a mutually recognized set of rules.[5]

An illustration of the expectations of the teacher in the public school may make this theoretical statement clearer. Interviews by a sociologist with sixty Chicago teachers revealed their attitudes toward, and expectations with respect to, parents, principals, and colleagues.[6] The teacher was found to wish to avoid any dispute

---

[4] Waller, *op. cit.,* Chapter 7, pp. 80–92.

[5] Merton, *op. cit.,* p. 195.

[6] Howard S. Becker, "The Teacher in the Authority System of the Public School," *Journal of Educational Sociology,* Vol. 27, No. 3 (Nov. 1953), pp. 128–140.

with parents over his authority in teaching. To this end, he believed that parents should not get involved in the operation of the school any more than absolutely necessary. He accepted the principal as the "supreme authority" in the school regardless of how poorly he filled the position; he saw the principal as representing the office and its authority in terms of the same principles of professional education and experience that he felt gave him authority over parents. Expectations of the teacher were that the principal would provide a defense against parental interference and student revolt against the teacher, by supporting and protecting him whenever his authority was challenged. In fact, the teacher preferred that the principal be regarded by the students as "tough," and not a friendly court of appeal which might weaken the teacher's control. As to colleagues, certain understandings prevailed; for example, that one teacher would not challenge another's grades, would not visit another teacher's class. The investigator concludes:

> ... that the relations of institutional functionaries to one another are relations of mutual influence and control and that outsiders are systematically prevented from exerting any authority over the institution's operations because they are not involved in this web of control and would be literally uncontrollable, and destructive of the institutional organization, as the functionaries desire it to be preserved, if they were allowed such authority.[7]

An institution like the school is described as a small, self-contained system of social control which creates a stable and predictable work setting. Persons outside the professional group who are not involved in the network of mutual understanding and control, such as parents, may have very different values from those by which the teacher legitimates his authority. When the social worker in the system includes the parents in planning for their children, he may seem to the principal or teacher to be threatening the self-containment of the system.

Since wide variation in educational philosophy and practice can be found in the United States, as previously pointed out, this study of the attitudes and expectations of a sample of Chicago teachers may not be universally representative of teachers. But it does seem clear that in an institution such as the school certain positions carry defined responsibilities and expectations and that these are maintained through authority inherent in each position, by social distance between the members of the system, and by mutually recognized "rules of the game." This kind of framework within which teaching and learning take place has its effect in formalizing relationships between pupils and school personnel.

---

[7] *Ibid.*, p. 141.

internal organization
of the school: constant factors

The structure of the school, according to Waller, is typically autocratic in some degree and it must be so in order to carry out its function. Variation in the degree of autocracy depends upon how good
is the rapport between administrative authorities, teachers, and students.

> Where there is not a cordial rapport between school executives
> and teachers, control becomes more autocratic. A despotic system
> apparently becomes necessary when the teaching staff has increased
> in size beyond a certain limit. Weakness of the school executive
> may lead him to become arbitrary.... The relationship between
> students and teachers is in part determined by intrafaculty rela-
> tionships; the social necessity of subordination as a condition of
> student achievement, and the general tradition governing atti-
> tudes of students and teachers toward each other, set the limits of
> the variation. But this variation is never sufficient to destroy the
> fact that *the schools are organized on the authority principle, with
> power theoretically vested in the school superintendent* and radi-
> ating from him down to the lowest substitute teacher in the
> system.[8]

Waller describes the despotism of the school as in a constant state
of "perilous equilibrium," maintained by that "ever-fickle equilibrium which is discipline."

The common pattern for the organization of public schools in the
United States is division into elementary, junior high, and senior
high schools. Although the public school system in this country is
complex and diversified, it has, as previously noted, characteristic
goals and values. Constant factors present in the internal organization of the school, as it seeks to realize educational goals, include:
(1) the curriculum, (2) the daily schedule, (3) promotion, (4) activities
and ceremonial occasions, and (5) students as a sub-culture.

curriculum

A curriculum or planned program of activity is divided into segments called subjects. In the secondary schools, the curriculum is
usually divided into "college preparatory" courses of study and specialized (vocational) courses of study. Important to the child in
making the transition from family to school is the fact that in the
elementary school, especially in the first three grades, he has one
teacher who is most often a woman. In the junior and senior high

---

[8] Waller, *op. cit.*, p. 9.

schools the child moves from one class to another, each taught by a different teacher. Whereas he often had at least one main teacher in the first six grades, he now has several different teachers of both sexes.

The kind of learning expected of him is described by Parsons as (1) cognitive learning—the mastery of knowledge and its uses, and (2) moral learning, or responsible citizenship, designated as "deportment" in an earlier generation.[9] In the elementary grades these are not sharply differentiated and the pupil is evaluated in general terms such as "bright," "responsible," and so on. In the secondary schools, however, the focus is on the quality of a student's achievement and where this may lead in the future for him as an adult. He must make a choice between the part of the curriculum preparatory for college, and the part leading more directly to occupational training.

daily schedule

The daily schedule is something to which the child must learn to conform. Every person in the school is expected to be at a certain place carrying on defined types of activity and behaving in accordance with prescribed rules at every hour of the school day. Failure to be at the appointed place must be accounted for. Teachers as well as students are subject to the demands of the daily schedule. Release of a child for an appointment with the social worker, for example, interferes with his planned program; and it is often difficult to arrange appointments with teachers during school hours. Corroboration comes from a group of school social workers:

> We need to know how to get around in a school building. Schedules, bells, and regulations have to be learned. The principal may be extremely busy until after the tardy bell. Some teachers have free periods when they either welcome or resent conferences with us. After school on Wednesday, for example, there may be a stampede of the entire staff to go bowling. To ask for an appointment at that time would be downright detrimental.[10]

Brookover and associates state that little is known about the effect of the relatively rigid school schedule on the behavior of the child;

---

[9] Talcott Parsons, "The School Class as a Social System: Some of Its Functions in American Society," *Harvard Educational Review*, Vol. 29, No. 4 (Fall 1959), p. 314.

[10] Minutes of the Portland, Oregon, School Social Work Section, NASW, as reported by Mrs. Julia K. Hoffman, Chairman, July 1, 1960. The writer is indebted to this Section for a thoughtful discussion of what kinds of knowledge social workers need about education and the school.

but that it has been justified "on the ground that the child in America must learn to be where he is supposed to be at the proper time if he is to succeed in a work situation." [11]   Actually, in some elementary schools today there is flexibility in allocation of time to various subjects, at the teacher's discretion, when interest and productive activity seem to warrant.   Such flexibility is more difficult to arrange, however, in the secondary schools where students move from one room to another each period, to a different teacher.

promotion

An important aspect of school life is promotion from grade to grade or subject to subject.   The teacher or teachers evaluate each child's level of achievement in relation to the norm expected of one of his age-grade.   Failure to achieve the norm means retention in the same grade and loss of association with a group (class) and this may affect the child's motivation to "pass."   For this reason, some schools occasionally promote the child even when he is below the desired norm of achievement.

Certain privileges frequently attach to specific grade levels, such as membership in school societies and attendance at social events. Especially in the junior and senior high schools, many extracurricular activities are organized.   Athletics become of great importance not only to the participants but also to the school as a whole as a symbol of strength and unity of purpose.

The extent to which a teacher is able to help his students achieve the desired norm of performance in the classroom is considered one measure of his ability as a teacher.   With most schools coeducational, the teacher tries to treat the sexes alike in "all crucial formal respects" and to be fair and impartial in his judgments. Parsons points out that the structure of the school class and the number of students, as well as their similar age range, means that the teacher has much less chance than a parent to give "particularistic favors" to any one child.[12]   The school social worker, on the other hand, provides "particularistic" attention for the child who is not competing successfully and is a problem to the teacher and the school as well as to himself and his family.   His services within the school become increasingly important for the child as classrooms and schools increase in size.

That there is a relation between normal progress in learning and good mental health is an assumption developed out of experience of the School Mental Health Service of the St. Louis (Missouri) County Health Department.   The department provided a number of school

11 Wilbur B. Brookover, Orden C. Smucker, and John Fred Thaden, *A Sociology of Education* (New York: American Book Co., 1955), p. 162.

12 Parsons, *op. cit.*, p. 303.

districts in the county with services of psychiatric social workers. In one school district where the case load increased too rapidly to be covered, an experiment was undertaken. Since the largest common denominator in the school referrals was learning difficulty, an evaluative tool was developed, the Academic Progress Chart, which used already available educational data to trace the course of any individual child's educational growth. It was found that the chart also gave an index to the child's mental health. The underlying theory upon which this approach was based is described in these words:

> Learning, in the organized, school sense of the term, is a function of healthy ego development; and academic achievement can be seen as, in part, a product of this faculty that recognizes the demands made of the individual by the world around him, that motivates him to try to meet these demands, and that enables him to harness and direct his energies so as to achieve his aim and find due satisfaction in having achieved it. Learning difficulty can be expected in the child who fails to recognize the demands, or who lacks motivations to meet them, or who is unable to channel his energies into reaching his chosen goal, or who—having reached his goal—is unable to find due satisfaction in his attainment. Any functional learning difficulty may thus be attributable to either (a) faulty or inadequate ego development, or (b) the disorganizing effect of severe stress on previously adequate ego strengths. The child's learning performance in school then should reflect, in part, his personality structure and its functioning efficiency, as well as any organic limitation that may be present.[13]

Promotion from grade to grade, therefore, becomes a primary objective of teacher, student, parents, and community; it is an indication that the school is fulfilling the function expected of it. But in the fast-moving world of today, many stresses and strains fall upon families and children and interfere with normal progress in learning in school. For these children the social worker is a school resource to help evaluate the problem and to do something about it.

activities and ceremonial occasions

In order to fulfill its task of socialization, of development of the "commitments and capabilities which are essential prerequisites of their future role-performance" as adults, Parsons believes that the

---

[13] Lorene A. Stringer, "Academic Progress as an Index of Mental Health," *The Journal of Social Issues,* Vol. 15, No. 1 (January 1959), p. 16. For a discussion of learning in relation to the dynamics of personality development, *see also* Mary S. Kunst, "Learning Disabilities: Their Dynamics and Treatment," *Social Work,* Vol. 4, No. 1 (January 1959).

school must "internalize" these commitments and capacities in its students. How can this be done? The teacher, of course, makes every effort to accomplish this end. His is an institutionalized role; that is, he is viewed by students as a person with individuality but as one who is also typical of other persons, namely, teachers. The effective teacher often is able to serve as an ego-ideal for the student, a representation of those values and virtues to which the student aspires. But Waller asserts that certain cultural conflicts are necessarily at the center of school life. One of these revolves around teachers and students as the former try to represent the wider culture of society while the children cling to the culture of the locality. Another conflict, more universal perhaps, arises from the fact that the teachers are adults who try to impose adult attitudes and behavior upon children as part of the growing-up process, while the children cling to the culture of childhood. "Teachers have always known that it was not necessary for students of strange customs to cross the seas to find material. . . . There are, in the school, complex rituals of personal relationships, a set of folkways, mores, and irrational sanctions, a moral code based upon them." [14] The problem of the school, then, is how to ameliorate this conflict and how to condition the environment so that socialization develops.

One means, supplementary to formal instruction, is the development of activities and ceremonies that tend to weld the students together, to produce a "we" feeling for one another and for the school, and that lead eventually to acceptance of certain ways of behaving in, and feeling toward, the school and its adults. Children are usually willing to move gradually into the adult world if they have confidence in the adult leaders and if what is prescribed squares with the child's comprehension of what seems appropriate and practical in the light of his life experience to date.

Activities commonly found in most schools include athletics, work on the school paper, glee club or other musical organizations, literary societies, and dramatics. Ceremonial occasions include assemblies with community singing, pledge of allegiance to the flag, awards for academic or athletic achievement by individuals or groups of students, speeches that help to inculcate common goals and standards. Ritualistic symbols are exemplified by school songs, yells—especially in connection with athletic events—class pins, and emblems.[15] Teach-

---

[14] Willard Waller, "The Separate Culture of the School," in Alfred McClung Lee, ed., *Readings in Sociology* (New York: Barnes and Noble, 1959), p. 102.

[15] An amusing example of a school song written a half century ago by the teacher of a rural elementary school was given to the Highland Park Conference by Dean Milton Chernin:

"If you want an education, just come along with me,
Cannonsville, Cannonsville, is the place where to learn!"

ers participate as leaders or sponsors for various activities and students are given varying degrees of responsibility, depending upon the philosophy of the administration, for taking initiative in development of "school spirit." In these ways the school tries to lead the young into the world of adult culture. Waller concludes:

> The journey from the world of the boy to the world of the man is rarely smooth and continuous. But it has fewer sharp corners to turn if the members of the adult world are able to project themselves back into the psychic world of childhood. . . . Though an enlightened pedagogy may ameliorate the conflict of adults and children, it can never remove it altogether. In the most humane school some tension appears between teacher and students, resulting, apparently, from the role which the situation imposes upon the teacher in relation to his students. There are two items of the teacher's duty which make it especially likely that he will have to bring some pressure to bear upon students: he must see to it that there is no regression from the complexity of the social world worked out for students of a certain age level, and he must strive gradually to increase that complexity as the child grows in age and approximates adult understanding and experience. Activities may reduce conflict, but not destroy it.[16]

The social worker in the school also tries to lead the child toward maturity. His methods are different from those of the teacher but he supports the teacher in his role while helping him to understand the reasons that may be hindering the child from making progress toward learning and growing up.

students as a subculture

Not all learning takes place in the adult-child relationship. Children also learn and grow or are influenced through association with their peers. Here, the child selects the association he wants to make with others and is free, to a degree, of adult supervision. Identification with a peer group, approval and disapproval of others, capacity to influence one's peers—all these help the child to develop independence and further the growth process. The peer group's segregation by sex in the latency period is important as a process of reinforcement of sex-role identification. In the secondary school, the cross-sex relationships become of primary concern in peer association and are preparatory for adult roles of marriage and family life. Inability of a child to form peer relationships is often a cause for referral to the school social worker. It is sometimes the basis on which group treatment is instituted.

The strength and influence of an adolescent culture upon educa-

---

[16] Waller, "The Separate Culture of the School," *op. cit.,* p. 106.

tional achievement, or lack of it, is reported by Coleman. His study over a period of two years was of the "climate of values" which existed among students in nine public high schools of the Midwest. These included schools typical of America with a range in social class, size of school, type of community, and parental economic status. His conclusion is:

> . . . that the interests of teenagers are not focused around studies, and that scholastic achievement is at most of minor importance in giving status or prestige to an adolescent in the eyes of other adolescents. . . . In short, despite wide differences in parental background, type of community, and type of school, there was little difference in the standards of prestige, the activities which confer status, and the values which focus attention and interest. In particular, good grades and academic achievement had relatively low status in all schools. . . . In fact, there is a good deal of evidence that special effort toward scholastic success is *negatively* valued in most teenage groups. Scholastic success may . . . add to a student's status among his fellows; but the success must be gained without special efforts, without doing anything beyond the required work.[17]

Important values to the boys were athletic prowess, cars, social success with girls. The girls valued social success, including personality, beauty, clothes, and, of course, dates with boys. It was found that not all students gave in to the group pressure; in large schools scholastically oriented subgroups did form. But for most students it seemed that social activities, sports, dates, and cars took precedence over intellectual activities.

Coleman suggests that the school structure of competition is partly the cause of the anti-intellectual attitudes. At an age when group associations are at their peak, educators have built an interpersonal competition with continuous grading of the student's performance in every subject. He advocates group effort for intellectual attainment as for athletic events, and the substitution of intergroup competition for so much interpersonal competition.[18]

Milner, another student of teen-age culture believes that, as a group, teen-agers do want to learn. They are interested in a curriculum that will help them achieve what they are aware they need

---

[17] James S. Coleman, "Academic Achievement and the Structure of Competition," *Harvard Educational Review*, Vol. 29, No. 4 (Fall 1959), p. 338. The complete report is available in Coleman, *The Adolescent Society* (Glencoe, Ill.: The Free Press, 1961). *See also* Brookover *et al., op. cit.,* Chapter 12, "Socialization and Personality Adjustment in the School: I. Social Climate."

[18] Coleman, *op. cit.,* p. 349. Coleman's findings led John G. Milner, Professor, School of Social Work, University of Southern California, to make the observation presented in the following paragraph in a letter to the writer, August 1, 1960.

at this period of life; that is, how to (1) relate to the opposite sex, (2) find a place in a peer group, (3) determine how they can earn a living, and (4) find emancipation from parents and other authority figures of childhood. They respect knowledge but not grades. This point of view raises the question whether the present educational curriculum in a fast-changing world meets the needs of youth. Much learning takes place outside school and youth may feel the obsolescence of school curricula, an obsolescence charged by some critics of education, as reported earlier.

Research into the operation of small groups, their structure and process, has significance. The classroom provides opportunity for application of some of the principles of work with groups, even though the average of thirty or more children to a class may seem too many for a "group." Studies made at the University of Michigan and elsewhere indicate that the "socially unaccepted" child, whatever the reason, is handicapped in learning and that:

> . . . the major barriers to changing his behavior may be in the classroom, rather than or in addition to forces within the child. . . . In addition, sociological analysis strongly suggests that the attitudes and behavior of the individual are strongly linked to those groups to which he belongs or aspires. . . . For the classroom teacher, the important consequence of this observation is that to deal effectively with a child may require isolating group forces that are constraining his behavior and inducing changes in clique norms and groups.[19]

Social work has incorporated some of these findings as well as others from social psychology and psychiatry into the method of social group work. The social worker who has had instruction in the dynamics of group behavior as well as individual behavior— and increasingly schools of social work provide such instruction for all students—is able to apply such knowledge in his work with children and with teachers. He often serves as consultant to the teacher to help him work with the child in the group. The social worker may never see the child but may work only with the teacher.

external environment of the school: sociocultural attitudes

The school has been described as a "microcosm that mirrors the macrocosm." [20] A universal educational system necessarily covers widely divergent geographical, social, economic, and cultural areas.

---

[19] Neal Gross, "Some Contributions of Sociology to the Field of Education," *Harvard Educational Review*, Vol. 29, No. 4 (Fall 1959), p. 281.

[20] Waller, *The Sociology of Teaching, op. cit.,* p. 16.

To understand the educational system within the larger social structure, we need to understand some of the changing value systems, demographic movements, and the class and stratification problems that impinge upon the educational system as a whole and upon specific neighborhoods and communities in particular. As a further aid in understanding the external environment of the school, the place of the board of citizens—the school board—in serving as the official link between the school and the community is discussed.

Taber has analyzed some of the current social changes and resultant problems that affect children and schools. These include: (1) mobility of population, (2) mothers working outside the home, (3) family instability, (4) employment of youths, and (5) rapid industrialization.

Mobility of population tends to make for instability and tension. Movement of families from rural to urban living, from segregated living in the South to the greater freedom of the North, and from congested city dwelling to the more open suburbs with, paradoxically, their overcrowded schools are well-known phenomena. Not uncommon is the example of the child in the sixth grade who has had thirteen changes of address since entering the first grade. Families and children, under these conditions, often lack a sense of belonging to a community, and children have little opportunity to form lasting associations with peer groups.

A second change affecting the family is the increasing number of mothers working outside the home. Women now make up one-third of the labor force, and the number of mothers in this group who have children under eighteen years of age is reported by the Department of Health, Education, and Welfare to have doubled since 1950. Unless provision is made for supervision of the children after school hours, problems frequently arise, as school social workers can testify.

Family instability is evident in the number of arrests for child neglect, the divorce rate, and the apparent increase in births out of wedlock, especially among teen-age and young adult women. Cases referred to school social workers frequently reveal boys without fathers in the home who have no male adult figure with whom to identify. Early marriage of young people ill prepared for the responsibility of marriage and family life is another factor that affects the welfare of society. The school finds teen-agers often continuing in school after marriage because of limited job opportunities. This sometimes raises questions about relationships between married and unmarried students.

Employment of youths is becoming restricted. Most states now have compulsory school attendance laws to 17 or 18 years of age unless a job can be found at 16, when a work permit may be issued. With the declining market for young workers—only one-third as many 16- and 17-year-olds were employed in Philadelphia, for example, in 1959 as in 1945—many youths of marginal ability remain in school without profit because they have no other choice. Automation and the high degree of job specialization needed because of technical advancement means that the young person of today must have early and wise vocational guidance to fit into the labor market.

Finally, rapid industrialization and urbanization, as well as world tensions and uncertainties, affect the social and moral climate. Community norms of behavior become disorganized. Old values have become weakened and new ones have not taken their place sufficiently to be authoritative. Relationships—economic, political, social—have not kept pace with the wonders of scientific inventions that have displaced old ways of living with new ones. Compulsory military training affects both boys and girls by interrupting life plans. Unless the family can provide the child with a consistent framework of values, he frequently flounders and lacks that interpenetration of habits that Dewey calls character. Even the most stable family today becomes puzzled about priorities in values when conflicts arise.

the school and the community

When we examine the microcosm, the school within a specific community, in this macrocosm, the larger society, we can discern the effects of these conditions upon the school. The up-grading of mass education is evident in enrollment statistics. In 1890, less than 7 percent of boys and girls between the ages of 14 and 17 were enrolled in high school; 60 years later about 80 percent attended high school. Attendance at college has also increased 57-fold since 1870 although the population has increased fourfold. The sociologist Arnold Rose suggested at the Highland Park Conference that perhaps the school may not continue to be an expanding institution, that public pressure will be for intellectual training rather than so many activities that have been added to make education "well rounded." Parents then will have to take more responsibility for the socializing aspects of education and the job of school social workers may be to help them in this task.

Three case examples of contrasting communities may help to illustrate the differences in family stratification and class, parental problems that reflect community problems, and school response to the needs of children.[21]

---

[21] For these examples and other illustrative material, the writer is indebted to Dr. Peter Geiser, Assistant Professor, San Fernando Valley State College, Northridge, California, and to some of his students in Sociology 459 who wrote term papers on "The School as a Sub-Culture." They have given permission to quote from the analyses of their experiences as teachers.

Community A. The elementary school with which I am associated has a student body of 1,300 pupils, a faculty of 35, and an administrative staff of principal and vice-principal. The local community is made up mostly of middle class families who have established themselves in owned or rented homes. Most of them own their homes. The people are primarily white Protestant; in the school are only one Japanese, ten Mexican, ten Italian, and eight Armenian children. Approximately twenty-five percent of the student body are of the Jewish faith.

To support my impressions, I made a survey of an A-6 grade classroom of 31 students. This class was an average group of students whose parents might be considered typical community residents. Findings were that the average number of children per family was 2.2; the largest number of children in one family was five; seven families had an only child. The majority of the children were born in this area. Their families had not moved frequently although the children averaged 1.8 schools attended other than their present school. Almost one-half of the mothers worked outside of the home. This may account for the large attendance in the after-school playground program which has an average of 100 children who play there daily. Fifty-eight percent of the children belonged to a youth group. The most popular were YWCA, Boy Scouts, Girl Scouts, Camp Fire Girls, Indian Guides, and Woodcraft Rangers. With both parents working, it was not surprising to find that the families had an average of 1.7 cars and 26 percent had swimming pools at home.

The educational level of the community is average and above: a high school education is the general rule and over half of the parents had had some college education. They are "education conscious." Parents respond promptly to teacher conference requests, report card evaluations and discussions, and visiting day attendance. During the beginning of the school year, the PTA has its membership drive. It is not unusual for rooms to have 200 percent of the parents joining; that is, both parents join. This high proportion is more common in the primary than in the upper grades. The PTA organization is very active in the community. The principal has made a strong effort to establish a cooperative, working relationship between the home and school. Over the nine year period since this school was established, the school has held a monthly parent visiting day program which has not varied in its purpose: to enlighten the community about the school's life and to promote mutual understanding of the curriculum, teaching practices, and to acquaint them with the personnel involved in the school program. Over the nine month school period the major portion of the curriculum is presented in class demonstrations by each teacher for the parents of the children in her class.

This community is fairly stable, its families are homogeneous on the whole, and although many mothers are employed outside the home, provision has been made for leisure-time activities for the children.

In contrast is Community B. Both schools are in the same school district.

Community B. I teach in an elementary school located in a community in which are representatives of many ethnic groups. These include Negro, Oriental, Mexican, Eastern and Western European cultures. Many of these parents are now in what would be termed secondary heterogeneity. They have retained the patterns of the former culture, speak the language and follow the customs and ideals of "the old country." Their children are often torn between the old world culture of the home and the demands of the community outside the home. The bulk of the community can be classified into Lower Middle, Upper Lower, and Lower Lower classes. Only a limited number have more than a high school education and it is not uncommon to find parents with an elementary school education only.

A sampling of occupations as shown on the school cumulative record cards reveals a predominance of manual laborers, gardeners, unskilled workers, with a meagre sprinkling of engineers, salesmen, and one or two in the field of fine arts. A number of records show an unemployed father with the mother as the sole support of the family. In some instances the whereabouts of the father is recorded as unknown. A number of families are on Aid to Dependent Children; the PTA provides lunch money and clothing for others. In contrast, there are within the community a number of families with financial means to provide for necessities plus some "extras" (a few of the children have been to Disneyland). There is also a large segment of transient residents although migration into and out of the community has been declining for the past five years and the area seems to be becoming stabilized.

There are some families who own their own one-family dwellings; the majority of these are Caucasians or Orientals with a sprinkling of Mexican families. Many children, however, come from families who live in a big multi-family public housing project consisting of perhaps thirty buildings. Even in the largest apartments, several children are often crowded into one bedroom. Most of the instability in the community seems to come from "The Project" as the children refer to it. The majority of occupants are Mexican, Negro and Caucasian but almost no Orientals, an interesting contrast when compared with the homeowners' group. Pride of occupancy varies considerably with some families giving attention to curtains, flower boxes and the like, and others not even putting forth the effort to keep the rooms clean. The many children in the project seem to lack adequate controls. They are often poorly clothed and seem constantly hungry. The children play on the streets until late at night. Fights among teenagers erupt suddenly and violently. There seems to be little parental discipline; their lives appear disorganized and present a real problem to the school. Teachers find themselves disciplining and instructing children about matters that should be handled in the home. Occasionally a father is discovered to be in jail for stealing.

Despite the generally modest financial condition of members of the community, practically every family, including those in the project, seems to have a television set. The children are avid fans, often watching the screen until very late hours. Most of the children come to the first grade with little experience with books and little readiness for learning to read. The school has tried to fill the gap with books, records, trips, and other experiences.

One of the school's major problems is winning the parents' interest in school affairs. At a typical night PTA meeting will be found a handful of parents, usually the same parents who have for some time maintained a spark of communication between the school and the community. It is not uncommon at such a meeting to find that the faculty outnumbers the parents by a wide margin. This "core" of parents who attend come from the more stable, financially comfortable, homeowning segment of the community.

This community illustrates the discrepancy between the goals of the school and that of lower-class parents; a number of them speak a "minority" language and have customs different from the majority, and their energies go to providing the necessities of life. The teacher must assume some of the responsibility usually belonging to the family if the child is to be able to absorb the ideals and values which the school represents.

Community C. This community and school situation were reported by a teacher in a union high school in a town of 35,000, located in a rural agricultural county, currently affected by in-migration and social change. From school records and by means of a questionnaire distributed to all 10th grade pupils (about 400 in number), this teacher undertook a study of the family backgrounds of the children and of their school adjustment.

He found that about one-third of the children were of Mexican origin, about six percent were Negro; the majority, slightly over one-half, were of so-called white stock. Examination of the records of education of the parents showed that 30 percent had some elementary school education (one-half of this number had completed elementary school); almost 50 percent had some high school education (about two-thirds had graduated); and more than one-fifth had attended college. The employment of the father ranged from skilled work (47 percent) to no employment (4 percent). One father was in the penitentiary. Almost 40 percent of the mothers were employed outside the home.

An analysis of the ability level of the children revealed that about one-half had I.Q. ratings of 100 or above. Of this number, 12 percent had I.Q.s from 115 to 129, and two boys had I.Q.s over 130. These were the gifted children. At the other end of the scale were almost one-fifth of the group which rated below 85. This distribution of ability takes on added meaning when replies are examined to the part of the questionnaire which asked: "Are you in the same program (college preparatory or non-college) that you were in at the beginning of the 9th grade? Are you satisfied with the program you are presently in? Why did you enroll in the course originally?" Forty-four percent of the boys and girls were in the college preparatory course. About one-third of the children had changed their programs since the 9th grade. Sixteen percent of the children were dissatisfied with their present programs. Most of these were in the college preparatory course and felt the work was too difficult for them. Furthermore, the ability groupings of the dissatisfied students were low normal to below average so that the work was probably beyond their ability. Even though they had been counselled to take the non-college courses, parental pressure and that from their peers had made them continue in these courses even when they had little achievement.

The teacher draws these conclusions: "With the launching of sputniks many parents felt that they must pressure their children into going to college; thus there was a tendency to register a student in the academic program even though the counselor indicated that the student might have difficulty. Academic success in the present and a college education in the future is a goal common to many of the parents. If the child's ability makes this a realistic goal, most of the teachers give special time and effort in helping the child to this end. Conflicts frequently arise when the child's ability is only average and the parents are pressing for better grades. Few of these parents are willing to accept the idea that their child is doing as well as can be expected: the teacher, the system, or both are at fault."

The problem here is the difference in expectations of parents and schools when children have varying abilities with parents bringing pressure on the school for achievement beyond the ability of the child.

school board

Another aspect of the external environment of the school is the school board. It is the official link between the school and the community. In many respects the school board functions like a board of directors of a corporation. It, in effect, employs the super-intendent, teachers, and other staff members of the school; it makes the policies that guide the school program, or at least gives approval to policies recommended by the superintendent. The fact that members serve without compensation for the most part, and that they are elected or appointed to the position, gives them prestige. It is extremely important that the members have the confidence of the community so that their recommendations as to financing and policies be supported. It is equally important that the school board and the superintendent concur upon educational objectives and means of working toward them.

From what sections of the community are school board members likely to be selected? Brookover and associates report that studies show members of school boards are drawn almost exclusively from professional and business groups in towns and cities, and from high-status farm representatives in rural areas.[22] Motivations of school board members studied in Massachusetts were found to include desire for political patronage and for representation of a segment of the community. Constant vigilance on the part of voters is recommended as necessary if the best people of the community are to serve as board members. When a school system becomes obviously mismanaged and inadequate, parents and other citizens have been found to organize to improve the situation.

Many community groups bring pressure upon the school board to incorporate material into the curriculum. The school board can be the first line of defense against such pressure if the members are educationally oriented to what is relevant for such inclusion. Many well meaning groups see the school as the channel through which their special interests can be furthered. A 1959 report states:

> In view of some of the nation's most respected organizations, it *is* the schools' job to advance their cause. The American Automobile Association, for instance, thinks more schools should teach more students to drive. Temperance organizations want schools to indoctrinate students in the evils of drink. Local Chambers of Commerce believe that schools should find curriculum time for on-the-job training; labor groups wish the schools would devote time to the rights and history of labor. The National Council of the Churches of Christ in the U.S.A. feels that every student should be given time off each week (at the request of parents) for

---

[22] Brookover and associates, *op. cit.*, p. 63.

out-of-school religious instruction. . . . In Portland, Oregon, a high school principal recently calculated that 2,155 class periods had been devoted to the city's annual Rose Festival.[23]

Some states have yielded to pressure groups to the extent of requiring by law the teaching of certain subjects. In California, for example, state law requires elementary schools to teach nineteen nonacademic subjects, including safety, fire prevention, conservation of natural resources, "training for healthful living," manners, and morals. In some communities, such as New Britain, Connecticut, the fund drives in the schools have become so numerous that only those approved by the Board of Education are permitted. Attempts to eliminate any of the "extras" always bring storms of protest from groups with vested interests.[24]

The school board has a vital place in the school social system. Closely allied to its effectiveness is the position of superintendent of schools. He is, in effect, the executive officer and educational leader, the education specialist. As previously pointed out, he serves as the middleman between the school board and the teaching staff. He must represent the community point of view to the principals and teachers; and he must represent the educational expertise of the teaching staff to the school board and general community. The literature of educational sociology contains interesting discussions of the conflicts, real and potential, which exist because of lack of agreement and understanding of organizational goals of the school system and of lack of consensus on the role definitions associated with educational positions.

Gross states that studies have shown "striking disagreement" between principals and school boards in regard to certain educational objectives. Furthermore, principals and teachers frequently do not have the same ideas about educational values and objectives. He reports the findings of a study of approximately 50 percent of superintendents and school board members in Massachusetts which revealed basic lack of agreement between them over their division of labor. On the selection of textbooks, nearly nine out of ten superintendents felt that the school board should always accept their recommendation, but less than half of the school board members agreed with them. And on the employment of new teachers, seven out of ten of the superintendents preferred [25] that the school board

---

[23] Phillip Reeves, "They're Stealing Time from Our Schools," *Coronet*, Vol. 46, No. 6 (October 1959), pp. 102–103.

[24] *Loc. cit.*

[25] Gross, *op. cit.*, pp. 276–279. *See also* Gross, *Who Runs Our Schools?* (New York: John Wiley and Sons, 1958); Myron Lieberman, *Education as a Profession* (Englewood Cliffs, N.J.: Prentice-Hall, 1956), especially, "The Local Community as a Source of Moral Authority," pp. 55–58.

act only on their nominations but only one out of five of the school board members agreed with them. Such disagreements create many stresses in the social system of the school and hinder smooth operation toward major goals. The Massachusetts study revealed "room for improvement" in the kind of educational leadership desired from superintendents. Improvement of the professional training programs for administrators is currently under study in several universities with the aid of grants from the W. K. Kellogg Foundation.[26]

the social worker as
specialist in the school social system

The larger a school system grows, the more necessary it becomes to differentiate certain functions and to make them the responsibility of specialists. A number of educational specialists are employed in elementary and secondary schools. In addition, as already noted, the school has added specialists from professions other than education—notably medicine, psychology, nursing, and social work. Students of the sociology of organization point out the problems which the administrator and specialist encounter in working together. The problems arise from the fact that the specialist is a person who brings into the organization competence for a specific task that supplements or improves the "main-line" job.

The problems include: (1) the "trained incapacity" of the expert, his focus upon the importance of his specialty so that he fails to appreciate the total operation of the organization and his place in it, (2) his strong identification with fellow specialists or professionals which may hamper his identification with the work of colleagues in the organization, (3) his aversion to modifying the "systematic ideas of a field of specialization" or, in other words, his hesitancy to be flexible in adapting his skills in an unfamiliar situation such as the organization may present to him, and finally (4) his tendency to "confuse knowledge with wisdom," and hence not recognize his own limits or respect the contributions of the nonspecialist to the solution of a problem. Moreover, the specialist may feel that he is "the stranger" or outsider, not fully accepted because he has not belonged to the organization from the beginning; he may feel that his point of view is not understood by the group with which he works, that he is regarded as "not organically connected" with the organization, and that he has only more general qualities in common with colleagues.[27]

26 Gross, *Who Runs Our Schools?* *op. cit.,* pp. 140–142.

27 Robert Dubin, *Human Relations in Administration* (Englewood Cliffs, N.J.: Prentice-Hall, 1951), Chapter 8, "Specialists," pp. 113–127.

The social worker in the school often exemplifies the characteristic behavior of the specialist described above. Testimony as to the social worker's problems in finding his place in the school social system comes from a group of school social workers:

> Difficulties come in walking a tight rope between identifying ourselves as members of a school staff and as social workers, members of a social agency. Just who are we? We have two (or more) bosses: our own casework supervisor and the principals to whose schools we are assigned. They all make periodic evaluations of our work and our probationary reports. . . . Being "on the team" is complicated by our being "different." Teachers have feelings about social workers. They have questions about what we say in our conferences with principals. They may feel that we have an "inside track" with the principal or that we carry more weight with him than they do. They wonder whether it is safe to express to us their feelings. Sometimes there is a cleavage between a principal and his teachers or there are sub-groups within the teacher group. We can but try to be identified with the majority in order to work effectively with the largest number.[28]

The school administrator, in turn, has the problem of relating the social worker's function to that of other units of the organization. Alleviation of this administrative problem depends upon: (1) the administrator's ability to understand the services represented by the social worker, so that he can provide the type and kind of structure that will permit a maximum of collaboration and efficiency, (2) his ability as leader to help facilitate collaboration and co-operation of human beings throughout the system, whose interactions he can foresee and deal with, and (3) the social worker's ability to accept and fulfill his role-set in the organization.

The literature on social work in the school contains a number of guides to the building of understanding and good relationships. A publication on administration of school social work summarizes some of the ways by which the social worker can become a part of the school social system. These include:

1. Understanding the role of social work as it operates within an institution whose primary function is to educate children and focusing his goals on this educational function;

2. Understanding the over-all educational philosophy, practices, and policies of his school district and of the individual buildings he serves;

3. Understanding, respecting, and using lines of authority, re-

---

[28] Minutes of the Portland, Oregon, School Social Work Section, NASW, *op. cit.*

sponsibility, and communication as they operate within the school district and within individual buildings;

4. Working closely with teachers, principals, and other school personnel on individual cases, sharing appropriate information with them and utilizing their knowledge and skills;

5. Maintaining co-operative relationships with representatives of other special services within the school and, with administrative leadership, participating with these representatives in a mutual delineation of each person's responsibilities and in a recognition of overlapping elements in their roles;

6. Understanding the function, policies, and procedures of community agencies and interpreting them to the school, and interpreting the school's functions, policies, and procedures to the community;

7. Attending faculty meetings, serving on committees, and assuming other appropriate responsibilities which will promote his integration with the faculty.[29]

It will be noted that reference is made above to the social worker's understanding and working within a school district and "within individual buildings." In large cities, a worker may have from five to ten schools as an assignment. In reality, each building or school is a sub-cultural group within the total system, dependent upon leadership of the principal to set the climate or tone for administration of the particular school. Thus, the social worker may need to understand several sub-cultures and to be flexible in adapting his services to the requirements and stages of acceptance which exist in each. Here is the statement of a group of experienced school social workers on this point:

We need to know the physical plant and customs within a particular building. Certain hours only men or only women, only smokers, or only non-smokers, are welcome in this teacher's room or that one. We need to know the administration of a particular school so that we can talk to the principal *first,* so that we properly recognize his authority and that of the school secretary, so that we fit in with their procedures and structure, especially with regard to telephone calls, mail and messages, checking in and out of the building, etc. . . .

We need to know the educational philosophy of the school system and of the particular school. What is their thinking about discipline, report cards, promotion and retention of pupils, exclusions, parent-teacher conferences and relationships? How do they teach reading? Do they feel our responsibility ends when a child

29 John C. Nebo, ed., *Administration of School Social Work* (New York: National Association of Social Workers, 1960), p. 35.

has been told to stay out of school due to academic or disciplinary problems? How do they view themselves within the system? Some feel "I'm here to teach." Others feel "I'm here to aid in all of the child's individual relationships."

We need to know how to see strengths and weaknesses of teachers and schools—not just from the social worker's point of view, but from education's point of view and from that of the community. These things are all necessary in order to translate dynamic, psychological concepts into terms that are practical and applicable by the teacher with her particular vocabulary and concepts.[30]

Following are two contrasting examples of the situations in which the social worker may have to function, as reported by teachers.

example 1

Thirty teachers comprise the faculty, six men and twenty-four women. . . . In national backgrounds, the majority are from northern European stock; a handful are native Californians; and some come from distant sections of the United States. Religious affiliations include six Jews, five Christian Scientists, two Catholics, one Mormon, one Seventh Day Adventist; the others are Protestants. . . . As a group the teachers seem to enjoy one another's company and social functions are well attended without evidence of coercion. . . . This is the third year the school has been open, and while the faculty has increased in number, many of its original members are present. Nearly half of them live on the fringes of the school community; they are for the most part those who have no trouble in living the kind of restrictive life which the community puts upon the teacher: a dignity that results from a restricted role and the restricted but well defined status which goes with it.

The school administrator (principal) is a woman: single, gray haired, petite, and much a lady. While she is too considerate to criticize, close association with her makes it fairly easy to decide of what she approves and disapproves. She is conservative but tasteful in dress, has a low pitched quiet voice, and gentle manner, and a pleasant smile at all times. . . . This is her first year as an administrator. She has told the faculty that she would back them in absolutely anything they did with the exception of corporal punishment. And she has been as good as her word. . . . From conversation with various faculty members, it appears that the reaction to the principal is good. They report less tensions and demands than in previous years, more thoughtfulness about demands upon teachers' time and outside obligations, and genuine understanding and consideration as well as helpfulness with classroom problems.

---

[30] Minutes of the Portland, Oregon, School Social Work Section, NASW, *op. cit.*

example 2

There are thirty-five teachers on the staff. They represent many cultural distinctions. Almost two-thirds of the teachers grew up in Eastern, urban communities; the others are from a mixture of small towns and farm areas. . . . They have various religious and political preferences that tend to make for "cliques". . . . Within the teacher group there is a marked tendency for these groups to turn into conflict groups. There are degrees of rank in the teaching group of our school. Some who hold master's degrees train student teachers from a local college, and they tend to be attracted to one another because of this common interest. They have more status within the school than the non-supervising teachers.

The role of the principal is autocratic. . . . His attitude as a former teacher changed when he was given his present assignment. He is now concerned with up-grading instruction, and in some instances he has used devious methods to gain status among the leaders in the school district. Therefore, his relationship with teachers is questionable. He strives to maintain a dignity befitting his superior position. . . . He gains status by title and takes on a different set of values. . . . He has a dual role in relation to his staff. . . . Smiles and gestures of approval are weapons he must use to gain favor from his staff, whether meant sincerely or not. In short, he is different from the teachers. . . . He can play golf once a week during school hours if he pleases. He is more curriculum minded, and more community minded than the teachers.[31]

The school social worker, like the faculty, is directly responsible to the principal. Referrals of children needing the social worker's attention are usually channeled through the principal, and his approval is generally needed for contacts with children or parents which the social worker and the teacher might wish to initiate. The worker's acceptance as a member of the school staff will depend in large measure upon the principal's conviction about the efficacy of social work service for children having trouble in school, and his ability to transmit this conviction to his teachers. It has been well said, "The interprofessional relationship between the school social worker and the principal of a school is the key to effective performance of school social work in that school. The interprofessional relationship between the worker and the teacher is the key to effective casework for a school child in difficulty." [32]

The school social worker, then, must be able to establish a relationship with the principal and the teachers before he can help children most effectively. His task in doing so is not made easier by the fact that he may spend only a day or half a day a week in

---

[31] Geiser and students, *op. cit.*
[32] Nebo, *op. cit.*, p. 28.

each school. Under these conditions, he may find it difficult to become part of a specific faculty group and may be regarded as an "outsider" until he is able to demonstrate his common objective with the group, that is, helping children to learn. When he is recognized as having special competence with the child who has social and emotional problems and when the teacher is able and willing to share responsibility, his role is clarified, and acceptance develops. His progress in becoming a part of the school will depend upon his knowledge of the social system which it comprises, upon his ability to demonstrate his special competence in relation to his place in the system, and finally, upon his skill in translating knowledge into practice. As the representative of a profession other than education—and often the only one in a school—the social worker should also be aware of the importance of being accepted as a person before he can expect to be accepted as a professional colleague.

summary

The school as a social system has a network of patterned relationships of people, each category of whom has distinctive role-sets or a group of associated roles. The form these relationships have taken in the public school are the outgrowth of its purpose, *i.e.,* the giving and receiving of instruction or the teaching-learning objective. The classroom teacher is therefore at the heart of the social system but is surrounded by those above and below him in status. These statuses carry authority inherent in the responsibilities attached to them. They also result in a system of prescribed relations such as social distance, formality in communication, thus giving stability and predictability to behavior and mutual expectations. The structure of the school tends to be hierarchical with power vested in the superintendent and, in turn, in the principal. The larger the school, the more likelihood of autocratic administration; the better the rapport between the members of the system, the less likelihood of autocratic administration.

A number of forces affect the equilibrium of the social system. Consideration was given to three major factors: (1) the internal organization of the school, (2) the external environment of the school, and (3) the social worker as specialist in the school social system.

Within the internal organization of the school, adults are primarily responsible for the curriculum, the daily schedule, promotions, and activities and ceremonial occasions through which social control is maintained. But the students also have an influence upon learning through association with their peers. They have their own sets of values, mores, and attitudes toward the school, and they can facilitate or retard the efforts of adults to lead them into the adult world of values and responsibilities. So significant are these self-directed activities of groups of students, that increasing attention is being given to group interaction in the classroom as a means of helping students in their social and intellectual adjustment and learning.

The external environment of the school necessarily molds it. The social problems of the larger society impinge upon individual and group development. Communities vary greatly in class and racial composition, in family stability, in mental endowment of children. Under these conditions, the educational goals of parents and citizens in general may or may not coincide with the goals of the school. The school board which is the official link between community and school may also vary in its strength from community to community. And the leadership and administrative ability of the superintendent, as the executive officer of the school board, may affect the extent to which education is effective or inadequate.

The social worker as specialist was discussed in the context of the problem inherent in any social system where specialists are intro-duced. The specialist's function is partial; that is, related to a specific service which is intended to improve or supplement the "main-line" job of the organization. The administrator must be able to understand the role of the specialist and his place in the system if the latter is to perform with maximum efficiency; the specialist, on the other hand, must recognize his limitations within the system and be able to identify with the main purpose of the organization. Special problems for school social workers were noted: numbers of schools to serve, each one having its own sub-culture; numbers of principals or administrative officers who vary in their understanding of and ability to make use of the social worker's services to the best advantage; isolation in the sense that the school social worker may be the only one of that profession working in a particular school.

The school as a social system is a complex phenomenon. The social worker in the school must be cognizant of its general out-lines, able to accept his place in the system, and well enough oriented to discern what aspects of his experience are characteristic of the social system and what aspects are peculiar and perhaps modifiable. Such knowledge lends consistency and purposiveness to the service he is in the school to render. Of importance also is more definitive agreement among social workers on what comprises the role-set of the school social worker.

EDUCATION AND SOCIAL
WORK AS PROFESSIONS

4

The social worker in the school uses
the same body of knowledge, values, and method that is used by
social workers wherever they practice, but his primary focus is upon
the psychosocial problems that interfere with a child making full
use of learning in school. In performing his function of helping
the child to overcome environmental and emotional obstacles to
learning, he works with members of other professions found in the
school but most closely with teachers, who carry the central function of education. What is specific to the practice of social work
in the school, therefore, is the activity that grows out of understanding how to help children and parents when working with
another profession which has its own constellation of knowledge,
values, and method, and when working within the school as a
social system which has definite values and goals in interaction
with those of the teaching profession.

In analyzing social work and education as professions, three areas
will be considered. First, some of the problems that these professions face as they move toward full professional status in our society;
second, the content of social work practice as currently conceived;
and third, some of the issues and trends in education as a profession.

background and problems of
education and social work as professions

Teaching and social work are ancient occupations but they have
become professions relatively recently. Industrialization wherever
it occurs furthers the growth of professions because associated with

it are specialization, emphasis upon science as a basis for professionalism, growth in scale and complexity of social organizations, and setting of standards for regulation, by the profession, or by the state, or by both. All of these factors enhance awareness of common bonds among practitioners and lead them to strive for recognition of their work as a profession, with the concomitant hope of prestige, security, and income.[1] These influences are seen in the development of education and social work.

The fact that education is universal and compulsory in the United States has meant that large numbers of teachers are employed by local school boards, their salaries paid from tax funds; the standards or qualifications for teaching show wide variation from one community to another. As the level of general education has risen in this country from elementary to high school, more specialized preparation in subject-matter content has been required of teachers. And as urbanization has increased, the size and complexity of local school organizations have grown. Educators employed in the elementary and high schools total almost one and one-half million persons, of whom 1,366,884 are classroom teachers, about two-thirds of them in elementary schools.[2] The national professional organization is the National Education Association. For the year 1959–60, it had a membership of 713,994 persons, or approximately 50 percent of those eligible, *i.e.*, "actively engaged in the profession of teaching or other educational work."[3] A total of 5,708 delegates from local and state associations attended the 1960 NEA annual meeting.

Social work grew out of local community recognition of the need to provide services for various groups; and this recognition has gradually come to require, in varying degrees, that these services should be provided by "practitioners trained to understand the

---

[1] Harold L. Wilensky and Charles N. Lebeaux, *Industrial Society and Social Welfare* (New York: Russell Sage Foundation, 1958), pp. 283–287.

[2] Figures are based on latest available estimates from the U.S. Office of Education and the National Education Association, as reported in *Saturday Review*, September 17, 1960, p. 71.

[3] Myron Lieberman, *Education as a Profession* (Englewood Cliffs, N.J.: Prentice-Hall Inc., 1946), pp. 267, 260–261. An antecedent organization of NEA was the National Teachers Association, formed in 1857 at the call of the presidents of ten state educational associations; women were excluded from membership. A unique feature of NEA is that it was chartered by Congress in 1907; its constitution can be changed only with the consent of Congress, something that has been done twice, in 1920 and 1937. Membership figures are from NEA *Addresses and Proceedings of the 98th Annual Meeting* (Washington, D.C.: NEA, 1960), p. 331.

[4] "Working Definition of Social Work Practice," conveniently cited in Harriett M. Bartlett, "Toward Clarification and Improvement of Social Work Practice," *Social Work*, Vol. 3, No. 2 (April 1958), p. 6.

services, themselves, the individuals, and the means for bringing all together." [4] Voluntary agencies, incorporated by interested citizens or organizations to provide services for individuals or groups that have need of them, were, in part, the product of urbanization. Social problems multiplied as people crowded into cities. Specialized services were therefore set up around such interests as children, aged, sick, neighborhood improvement. Employment of social workers in large numbers by governmental agencies has occurred since the passage of the Social Security Act and other social legislation following the depression of the 1930's. The total number of persons filling all types of positions classified as social work is estimated to be around 100,000.[5] A national professional organization that combined five separate associations was organized in 1955 as the National Association of Social Workers. Its membership in 1962 was about 34,500; the number qualified for membership but not belonging is unknown. Membership requires the two-year master's degree in social work but many members of the predecessor organizations were "blanketed in" with less than full professional preparation. NASW had 158 chapters (as of 1961) throughout the United States.

With these dimensions and sanctions of social work and education in mind, the question might now be asked to what extent these occupations meet the criteria of a profession. Members of each group show great self-awareness with respect to certain areas in which the group falls short of full professional stature; but the majority of each group believes they deserve to be considered members of a profession. Criteria against which to measure a profession usually include these attributes: (1) special competence that rests upon a systematic body of knowledge organized as theory and continuously added to from findings of science and practice, (2) transmission of this knowledge through education and training which imparts skill and gives authority to ideas and judgments of the professional person, (3) sanction of the community which confers certain powers and duties, (4) responsiveness to the public interest which finds expression in a regulative code of ethics and in expectation of ethical behavior and conduct on the part of members, and (5) formal association of practitioners within and around which values, norms, and symbols develop, thus forming a "professional culture." Both education and social work seem to meet these criteria in greater or less degree.[6] Common problems that to some ex-

---

[5] John Kidneigh, "Social Work as a Profession," in *Social Work Year Book 1960* (New York: National Association of Social Workers, 1960), p. 564.

[6] Many social work practitioners do not qualify under (2) and (5); they are "untrained." Discussion here relates primarily to social workers who meet the criteria of professional training (2) and NASW membership (5).

tent reflect the stage of development of these professions are discussed below. These include occupational selection factors such as sex differential, class origins, motivation, turnover and recruitment; and organizational factors affecting professionalization, such as community demand and expectations, certification, and standard setting for educational preparation.

occupational selection factors

Education and social work are said to be shortage professions; that is, there are many more positions open than there are qualified candidates to fill them. Since other professions also face serious personnel shortages, competition exists for recruitment of the best possible candidates for admission to each profession.[7] Education and social work have the disadvantage at present of being marginal or middle in prestige as rated in studies in which people have been asked to assign a rank order to a list of occupations in terms of their prestige.[8] What are some of the reasons for this status?

Sex differential. Doubtless one factor that has affected prestige and professionalization is sex differential. In both professions, from three to four times as many women are employed as men. The number of men has been increasing since World War II, however, and their advance to administrative and supervisory positions has been rapid. The large majority of women in both professions are in practitioner positions, as classroom teachers and as social workers who give direct service to clients (caseworkers or group workers). The higher up the position is in the hierarchy, the higher is the salary. A problem for both professions, therefore, is how to retain and reward the teacher or social worker who does an above average job as a skillful practitioner.

Class origins. In the two professions, class origins seem to be similar and have implications for recruitment and for professional education. Studies cited by Lieberman and by Wilensky and Lebeaux indicate that both teachers and social workers have been coming from progressively lower class origins. Military service and veterans' educational benefits opened up new horizons and opportunities for many lower class men who might not otherwise have attended college or aspired to enter teaching or social work. Since

---

7 "Other Professions Face Serious Personnel Shortages," Council on Social Work Education, *Social Work Education*, Vol. 8, No. 1 (February 1960), p. 3.

8 Wilensky and Lebeaux, *op. cit.,* p. 310. For an exhaustive analysis of the prestige question in social work, *see* Alfred Kadushin, "Prestige of Social Work—Facts and Factors," *Social Work,* Vol. 3, No. 2 (April 1958), pp. 37–43.

people in the lower and middle classes in the United States out-number the upper classes, it is to be expected that all of the professions would recruit a number of persons from these classes. Of interest here are effects of class position upon attitudes and behavior, such as upward mobility-striving with the uncertainty and anxiety about status that accompany it and the tendency to conform and identify with the values and customs of the class toward which one strives.

Motivation. Motivation for entering any profession is a complex phenomenon. Those entering education or social work are said usually to have "people-oriented values"; *i.e.,* they prefer to work with people rather than things and like to think of themselves as "helpful" to others. A study based on a sample of 7,150 beginning teachers made by the U. S. Office of Education in 1957 confirms this statement.[9] Lieberman points out, however, that questionnaire studies of the characteristics of teachers have many limitations. He questions the conclusion that teachers as a group are highly moti-vated to "serve society" or to "help children." Rather, such factors as a desire to enter a respectable white-collar occupation or an interest in teaching a particular subject may be the important con-siderations. He cites the results of the Kuder Preference Record to show that on the social service scale of the test, the scores of teachers varied considerably. On the other hand, the scores of social and welfare workers, clergymen, and nurses showed a con-sistently high interest in helping others.[10] Kadushin refers to sev-eral studies of social work as a career choice which confirm selection because of an interest in people. He notes, however, that motivation may vary according to differences in background. Intrinsic satis-factions such as personal fulfillment may attract persons from pro-fessional middle-class families; extrinsic satisfactions associated with upward mobility, such as the white-collar nature of the occupation, may attract persons from minority or lower-class groups.[11]

Two conclusions might be drawn. Motivation in entering a profession is related very often to its occupational prestige among established professions and to the extent it offers personal rewards; and as a profession becomes institutionalized and as large numbers

---

9 Ward S. Mason, Robert J. Dressel, Robert K. Bain, "Sex Roles and the Career Orientations of Beginning Teachers," *Harvard Educational Review,* Vol. 29, No. 4 (Fall 1959), p. 380.

10 Lieberman, *op. cit.,* Chapter 8, "Teachers and Their Characteristics," es-pecially pp. 216–221.

11 Alfred Kadushin, "Determinants of Career Choice and Their Implications for Social Work," Council on Social Work Education, *Bimonthly News Publica-tion,* Vol. 6, No. 2 (April 1958), pp. 19–20.

of people enter it, the range of motivations widens, with self-interest often taking precedence over altruistic considerations.

Recruitment and turnover. The two factors, recruitment and turn-over, are closely related and are considered together. Education and social work, along with other service professions, have had a decline in the number of highly qualified applicants at a time when the need for teachers and social workers has grown steadily with population growth. Both professions have had nationwide recruitment programs. Obstacles to recruitment are said to include these factors:

1. The marginal occupational status of these professions, combined with the large number of women in them, make salaries relatively low. In the words of one economist, "In all occupations, men receive 50 percent higher incomes than women; in the professions, two-thirds more." [12]

2. Graduate education beyond the bachelor's degree which is required for full qualification makes preparation expensive, especially when compared with financial returns.

3. The number of untrained people in teaching and social work positions is confusing to the college student selecting an occupation; careful interpretation of the standards toward which the professional organizations in the respective fields are working is needed, if well-qualified persons are to be recruited.

Turnover in education and social work is so high that it has been said that the problem of recruitment may be more a problem of retention. The study of 7,150 beginning teachers, to which reference has been made, points up some of the reasons for high turnover. Most women (70 percent) expected to leave teaching at some time in order to become homemakers; only 16 percent planned to teach continuously until retirement, and 58 percent hoped to teach again after a period of homemaking and child-bearing. Of the 36 percent of men in the sample, about one-quarter wanted to remain classroom teachers, one-half aspired to move into some other area of education, and one-fifth expected to use teaching as a stepping-stone to some other occupation.[13] Although this study was of beginning teachers and does not represent the actual rate of turnover in the profession, it highlights the large number of women who regard teaching as a temporary occupation until marriage.

Social work has a similar problem. Among welfare agencies' staffs where large numbers of untrained workers are employed, the separation rate has been found to be as high as 35 percent annu-

---

[12] Seymour Harris, "Who Gets Paid for What?" Council on Social Work Education, *Bimonthly News Publication*, Vol. 6, No. 2 (April 1958), p. 31.

[13] Mason *et al., op. cit.,* pp. 373–374.

ally.[14] But even graduates of schools of social work also leave the field. One study showed that 25 percent of 505 graduates had left the field within ten years, most of them (70 percent) within five years after graduation. Marriage and family responsibilities were given as the chief reasons.[15]

organizational factors affecting professionalization

The five occupational selection factors discussed above indicate that education and social work have many similar problems. A brief examination of certain organizational factors will further elucidate the status of these professions.

Education and social work are needed services that have been sanctioned by local communities; and as state and federal governments have given financial support, they have added their authority to that of the local community. Boehm points out that a profession operates as an organ of society. Problems arise when the values and the expertise growing out of the knowledge and method of the profession do not precisely coincide with the demands and expectations of the community. He states:

> It is as an *organ of society* that social work, like other professions, operates. This means that the goals it seeks must not be incompatible with the values held by society. It also means that the functions delegated to it by society impose a twofold responsibility: to determine the professional activities through which it seeks to attain its socially sanctioned goals and modify them as necessary in the light of changing social needs and to exercise discipline and control over practice that will insure its professional accountability. In sum, the responsibility of a profession derived from its sanction by society is to insure that its goals are compatible with the values of society, while its functions and methods are held to professionally determined standards and controls.[16]

Community demands and expectations. It seems inevitable that there will always be points of difference between the professions and the public. The scientific bodies of knowledge on which the various professions rest are constantly growing and changing, but public understanding of these advances does not always keep pace.

---

14 Kadushin, *op. cit.*, p. 21.

15 Helen R. Wright, "Employment of Graduates of the School of Social Service Administration" (University of Chicago), *Social Service Review*, Vol. 21, No. 3 (September 1947), p. 317.

16 Werner W. Boehm, "The Nature of Social Work," *Social Work*, Vol. 3, No. 2 (April 1958), p. 11.

Furthermore, a professional group seeks autonomy as it develops specialized knowledge and skill, while society seeks to control it. Education and social work are particularly vulnerable to public opinion and pressures because (1) they involve relations about which the average person feels he has familiarity, and (2) they are only beginning to delineate their respective bodies of knowledge, theory, and method that support their claims for special competence.

Certification. Whether certification is by a profession or by law, it has a two-fold purpose—to protect the public from the incompetent and to give the profession control of its practice.[17] The state intervenes and requires some form of licensure when it is convinced that the public welfare demands such protection. The profession often requests such state regulation to achieve public recognition of its importance and to help it control the standards for practice. It then co-operates in the administration of the law. A profession may also undertake certification of its members in order to raise standards.

Although social workers in several states have tried to secure some form of legal sanction, they have succeeded in very few states. The California form of voluntary registration has allowed those social workers who have completed at least one of the two years required for the master's degree in social work to take an examination to qualify as "Registered Social Worker" and to place the letters RSW after their names. The program is under the direction of the Board of Social Work Examiners which is made up of seven persons appointed by the Governor, at least three of whom must be Registered Social Workers; at least two others must be lay persons. In 1961 Rhode Island passed a similar restriction-of-title law but use of title "Registered Social Worker" is restricted to persons who hold the two-year master's degree.

The National Association of Social Workers supports its members' efforts to secure state legislation to regulate practice, preferably of fully qualified social workers. In the meantime, NASW has begun a program of national voluntary certification. This established, as of December 1, 1961, an Academy of Certified Social Workers within the association, admittance to which is membership in NASW and two years of practice experience; use of the initials ACSW is evidence of competence.[18] Through such a program of certification NASW hopes to define its own standards more clearly and to

---

[17] NASW has distinguished five types of legal regulation: (1) restriction of title, (2) restriction of title and function, (3) restriction of title or function, with exemptions for allied professions, (4) restriction of function, and (5) agency licensure. *NASW News,* Vol. 5, No. 2 (February 1960), p. 14.

[18] *NASW News,* Vol. 6, No. 2 (February 1961), p. 2.

strengthen them, while making progress toward definition of practice that some day may make possible the licensing of practice and not merely of title.

Certification of teachers and other educators is overlaid by tradition and is hampered by the public image of the teacher. Great variation exists.[19] By 1955, authority for certification of teachers was vested exclusively in state agencies in forty-five states. In some states wide diffusion of authority is found. Two of the problems of concern to educators are the composition of state boards of education, and the multiplicity of educational certificates that are issued. As of 1951, ten states expressly excluded professional educators from membership on the state board of education; but two states (Arizona and Indiana) required that a majority of the board should be engaged in educational work. The National Education Association has always held that a lay board is desirable; and the U. S. Office of Education has stated: "It is improbable that anyone would advocate that a board of education should be composed mostly of educators." [20] Unlike most professions, therefore, educators do not have a direct voice in entry and expulsion of members from the profession, nor do they regulate requirements to be met to practice the profession. The problem of multiplicity of certificates is currently under discussion in many places, and proposals have been made to reduce the number from as many as fifty certificates to five or six. By 1955, thirty-one states required the bachelor's degree for an elementary teaching certificate. Over-all academic requirements for secondary teachers are usually greater than for elementary teachers. According to a study by the U. S. Office of Education, the median preparation of secondary teachers is about five years of college.

In summary, with respect to certification, education has been recognized by the public as requiring some kind of standard-setting for teaching. The profession, however, has not had control of such standards; lay boards of education with the help of educational administrators have acted in each state. The result has been a wide range of qualifications for teaching. Social work, on the other hand, has had more practitioner influence in defining qualifications in terms of educational preparation; the national professional organization has made a beginning with certification on a national basis; and social workers in the various states are working toward public recognition through some form of legal regulation of social work practice.

Standard-setting for educational preparation. The function of standard-setting for professional education is of great concern in

---

[19] Lieberman, *op. cit.* Remarks on certification are based on Chapters 4 and 5.
[20] *Ibid.*, p. 106.

any profession because it is closely related to what constitutes the basic or core content of practice. The extent to which practitioners influence educational preparation is different in education and social work.

Impetus for the professional education and training of social workers came from practitioner groups themselves and led to the establishment, early in the twentieth century, of independent schools of social work in half a dozen large urban centers. The school in Chicago led the way to university affiliation about 1920 when it became a part of the University of Chicago. Gradually, by 1940, all schools were required to have such affiliation; many universities organized schools of social work. Standard-setting for curricula and accreditation were strongly influenced by associations of practitioners, the American Association of Medical Social Workers, the American Association of Psychiatric Social Workers, and other groups.

The American Association of Schools of Social Work, first organized in 1919, aware of pressure from practitioner groups for special courses, agreed upon a so-called basic curriculum about 1932; and the schools have continued joint effort to define curriculum content. The Council on Social Work Education which absorbed the AASSW in 1952 has a standing committee on curriculum.[21] The present policy statement on curriculum is regarded as a guide for the sixty-three graduate member schools and permits flexible use and experimentation within three prescribed major subject areas: (1) human growth and behavior, which includes knowledge and understanding of the normal life cycle of the individual and deviations from this norm, (2) social services, which includes a comprehensive knowledge and understanding of social welfare policy, structure, programs, and the existing organizations created to administer them, (3) social work practice which includes the professional methods (casework, group work, community organization, and supplemental methods such as administration and research), and the way these methods are used in carrying out social work functions. Field instruction, usually in casework or group work, is considered essential

---

21 The Council on Social Work Education which came into existence July 1, 1952, had represented in its structure, in 1960, the 63 graduate schools of social work in the United States and Canada, 108 undergraduate departments in colleges or universities which offered an organized sequence of courses "with social welfare content," 40 national employing agencies (voluntary and official), 18 representatives designated by NASW, and 18 representatives of the general public. A semi-autonomous 15-member Commission on Accreditation is responsible for formulation of standards for the two-year master's degree and for policies governing the accreditation of professional schools. The Council acts as the national spokesman on all matters relating to social work education. *See* Ernest F. Witte, "Education for Social Work," in *Social Work Year Book 1960* (New York: National Association of Social Workers, 1960), pp. 225–229.

in the development of skill and occupies from one-fourth to one-half of the student's time in different schools. Less formalized standards for the relatively recent development of post-master education exist for the fourteen of the sixty-three schools which offer advanced programs, although discussion of third-year and doctoral programs has been possible through the Advanced Curriculum Committee of the Council on Social Work Education.

In summary, social workers have participated through self-organized bodies in the development of standards for education. These have included requirements not only for curriculum content but also for the standing of the university, and standards for faculty selection and for internal organization of the professional school. Co-operation of the national professional association in development and support of standards has been an important influence in the growth of professional education; membership requirements are in terms of professional education, and a one dollar per member contribution from dues to the Council on Social Work Education has helped support that organization.

Standard-setting for the professional education and training of teachers is a more complex problem than it is for social workers, first, because of the number of practitioners, and second, because of the public nature of the profession which allows many different groups to demand a voice in standard-setting.

The spread of compulsory education laws created a need for teachers and led to the organization of two-year state normal schools, the first at Lexington, Massachusetts, in 1839. Public secondary education meant that teachers had to have more specialized knowledge of subject matter and this need helped to transform the normal schools into four-year, degree-granting institutions. A study of 180 state colleges in 1958 by the U. S. Office of Education showed that more than one-third of them were primarily teacher preparatory institutions. The balance offered liberal arts and other "terminal-occupational" programs in addition to teacher training. Since World War II the trend has been toward adding master's degree programs.[22] Universities began to include education among the professional schools as Dewey, Hall, Thorndike, and others offered a philosophical and scientific approach to education that provided a better theoretical base for teaching.[23] In 1954, 1,209 colleges and universities were approved for teacher education by 48 state departments of education.

---

[22] Karl William Meyer, "The Passing of the Teachers College," *School and Society*, Vol. 87, No. 2160 (October 24, 1959), p. 416.

[23] John S. Brubaker, "Resolving the Conflict between Academic and Professional Training of Teachers," University of Michigan *School of Education Bulletin*, Vol. 30 (March 1959), p. 82.

Accreditation for teacher education on a national scale was begun in 1927 when the American Association of Teachers Colleges set up accreditation procedures. In 1948 this association merged with two others; and in 1954 accrediting functions were assumed by the National Council for Accreditation of Teacher Education (NCATE).[24] At that time the council specifically accredited 284 of the 1,209 colleges and universities for teacher education. By 1960, NCATE had accredited 333 colleges and universities from which 70 percent of the new teachers were graduating.[25]

Although accrediting standards of NCATE include "the existence of an integrated pattern of subject matter and professional courses" and "the combination of laboratory and abstract experiences which are necessary to ensure that prospective teachers will have a good understanding of the functions they are to perform as teachers," Lieberman criticizes the lack of designation of any particular courses or even subject matter to be included, as well as the lack of any minimum amount of general or professional education which must be offered.[26]

The National Commission on Teacher Education and Professional Standards (NCTEPS), created in 1946, is the part of the National Education Association which has the major responsibility for working on problems of professionalization; *e.g.*, "recruitment, selection, preparation, certification, advancement of professional standards, including standards for institutions which prepare teachers." [27] Similar commissions have been established in state education associations and are an important influence in standard-setting.

To summarize, education of teachers was initiated by training institutions rather than by practitioners as in social work. The universal nature of public education and its control by lay boards of education have been influences that have retarded control of professional standards by teachers. As with social workers, educators have shown a heightened sense of professional awareness in the past three decades and have accordingly strengthened their national professional activities through mergers of functions; *e.g.*, the single national accrediting body since 1954 and the Commission on

---

[24] Lieberman, *op. cit.*, p. 163. At the time of organization (1954), NCATE was made up of 21 members appointed by the following organizations: 6 by the American Association of Colleges for Teacher Education, 3 by the Council of Chief State School Officers, 3 by the National Association of State Directors of Teacher Education and Certification, 6 by the National Commission on Teacher Education and Professional Standards (a commission of NEA), and 3 by the National School Board Association.

[25] *NEA Addresses and Proceedings, op. cit.*, p. 362.

[26] Lieberman, *op. cit.*, p. 177.

[27] *Ibid.*, p. 273. NCTEPS reports goals for the teaching profession in Margaret Lindsay, ed., *New Horizons for the Teaching Profession* (Washington, D.C.: National Education Association, 1961).

Teacher Education and Professional Standards within NEA since 1946. Confusion in what is the primary function of the school is reflected in confusion in the primary content of educational preparation of teachers.

content of social work practice

Social work in the school has as the foundation of its practice the same constellation of *value, purpose, sanction, knowledge* and *method* that characterizes social work practice generally.[28]   While the profession of social work may be said to be comprised of those individuals who have come to hold the value commitments and to possess the knowledge and methodology of social work, the practice of social work focuses on the use of such a body of value, knowledge and methodology.   In short, practice is the practitioner in action. Practice might be described as interventive action of a practitioner when that action is guided by specified value assumptions, knowledge, and technique directed to specified purposes, under appropriate sanctions.   Before undertaking to discuss the adaptations of practice that are made by the social worker in the school setting, it seems desirable to set out some of the assumptions that are emerging which help to delineate the meaning of practice in social work wherever it occurs.

value

Value commitments arise from the philosophical concepts which a profession holds as convictions or fundamental beliefs; they are guides to the individual practitioner's actions and are shared by all who call themselves "social worker."   While not necessarily peculiar to social work, they may have some uniqueness in the way they are used in professional practice.   Values in social work would seem to derive from this primary assumption:

---

[28] Sources for this section on "Content of Social Work Practice" are primarily materials being developed by the Commission on Practice, NASW. Although only in process of formulation, the *Working Definition* is helpful in providing a frame of reference from which specific social work practice can be analyzed. *See* Harriett M. Bartlett, "Toward Clarification and Improvement of Social Work Practice," *Social Work*, Vol. 3, No. 2 (April 1958), pp. 3–9, in which the *Working Definition* appears as formulated in December 1956. A progress report, dated February 17, 1961, in mimeographed form, has also been used as a reference. *See also* Bartlett, "Ways of Analyzing Practice," National Conference on Social Welfare, *The Social Welfare Forum, 1960*, pp. 194–205; and Bartlett, "Responsibilities of Social Work Practitioners and Educators Toward Building a Strong Profession," *Social Service Review*, Vol. 34, No. 4 (December 1960), pp. 379–393; Werner W. Boehm, *Objectives of the Social Work Curriculum of the Future* (New York: Council on Social Work Education, 1959), pp. 43–45.

It is good that every individual set and persistently seek his own goals in life to the limit of his capacity, and that he balance this self-seeking with an essentially equal effort to help others set and seek their own goals to the limit of their capacity.[29]

The application of this assumption in practice is expressed in such phrases as belief in the dignity and worth of each individual, faith in the capacity of an individual to grow and change, and belief that society has the obligation to help the individual reach whatever his maximum capacity is for self-realization, and that in turn he has responsibility to contribute to the welfare of others and of society. In order to apply this assumption effectively, the profession must continuously strive for more and better knowledge about human behavior and about the efficacy of the instrumentalities that have been created to meet social welfare needs.

purpose

Purpose, or that which social work practice aims to accomplish in accordance with its values, is expressed through more immediate or specific goals such as "(1) the modification of human and environmental conditions which at any time or place inhibit maximum self-realization of individuals and their contribution and (2) the creation of conditions which facilitate individual self-realization and contribution." [30] Boehm states that the goal of social work is "the enhancement of social functioning wherever the need for such enhancement is either socially or individually perceived." [31] The social worker may intervene toward these ends in processes in which an individual, a group, or a community planning committee is engaged in problem-solving activities.

knowledge

Knowledge that underlies social work practice comes from several sources. It can be described under three main categories: (1) theoretical knowledge about human development and behavior, (2) generalized knowledge about social welfare programs and agencies that have been created for people when they are unable to function without help, and (3) knowledge derived from social work practice experience. A few comments about each kind of knowledge are offered.

---

[29] "Report of the Subcommittee on Working Definition of Social Work Practice," Commission on Social Work Practice (New York: National Association of Social Workers, February 1961), p. 3. (Mimeographed.)

[30] *Ibid.*, p. 4.

[31] "The Nature of Social Work," *op. cit.*, p. 13.

Knowledge about human development and behavior rests upon the social and biological sciences. Social psychology and psychiatry have had a marked influence on social work thought; more recently, anthropology and sociology have provided concepts for application. In transmuting knowledge into use, the social worker keeps the whole person in view. Bartlett states: "Social work deals with whole persons and whole groups, not with 'pieces' of their behavior. It is consistently concerned with the psychic and the social, the inner and the outer, aspects of social functioning. There is emphasis upon the growth of the individual, rather than on objectively defined goals." [32] Verifiable assumptions about human development and behavior give the social worker insight and provide principles to guide his actions.

Knowledge about social welfare programs and agencies is generalized to give the social worker an understanding of why and how social resources develop to meet human need. In addition, he has specific information about what such resources are in the locality in which he will use them. With such generalized knowledge he is also able to help develop new resources when the need is indicated.

Finally, knowledge derived from experience in the practice of social work—that is, practice wisdom—is conceptualized for use in the major activity of social work, namely, intervention in social relationships. Some of the concepts here are: professional relationship, consciously used with the client as a means of helping; the psychology of giving and taking help from a person or source outside the individual; and the disciplined use of oneself with full awareness of one's own emotions and attitudes as they affect professional functioning. Another area of practice wisdom is related to the assessment of the critical, controlling elements in the social situation or process and the choice of the professional actions that will affect a change in them.

method

Method includes what is usually described as casework, group work, and community organization. The Committee on Working Definition of Social Work Practice of NASW in 1956 proposed to follow the trend in practice and to regard as method the "responsible, conscious, disciplined use of self in a relationship with an individual or group." Method puts into action all that the social worker knows of value, purpose, sanction, and knowledge in its various forms. By means of the professional relationship the practitioner "facilitates change: (1) within the individual in relation to his social environment; (2) of the social environment in its effect upon the individual;

---

[32] "Ways of Analyzing Practice," *op. cit.*, p. 199.

(3) of both the individual and the social environment in their inter-action." [33]   The worker is guided by professional judgment which stems from systematic observation and critical appraisal of the process engaged in and its effects upon participants.   The practitioner makes use of techniques (regularized and patterned actions) that have developed from experience. He develops skill as he uses method and techniques with due regard for the material or situation with which he is working, so that maximum results can be obtained.

In concluding the discussion of the content of social work practice it should be pointed out that social work is undertaking to improve its service as a profession through research in several directions. The Commission on Practice, NASW, under the able chairmanship of Harriett M. Bartlett, began in 1955 its pathfinding efforts to develop a working definition of social work practice.   Even in its present tentative stage of development the definition offers a point of reference for study of practice by setting out the content of practice wherever found under a constellation of factors; *i.e.,* value, purpose, sanction, knowledge, and method.   At the same time that NASW is undertaking to make its own contribution to social work services through clarification of practice, the Council on Social Work Education has been concerned with the improvement of social work education.   A study of the curriculum was begun in 1956 under the direction of Werner Boehm and eventuated in a thirteen-volume report, published in 1959.   With these two types of effort and their interrelationship in application, social work should advance in professional competence.

some issues and trends
in education as a profession

The social worker in the school needs to understand not only another profession, education, but also the social system, the school, in which education takes place.

Learning and teaching, the basic work of the school, takes place in the classroom.   The teacher is central to the educational trans-action and operates in a small social system.   Smith defines teaching as "a succession of acts by one individual intended to bring about learning (of particular aspects of the culture) on the part of other individuals." [34]   To do this the teacher must observe the individual student's reactions, diagnose his feelings and interests, and follow as best he can the progress of the student's understanding—for "the

---

[33] Bartlett, "Toward Clarification and Improvement of Social Work Practice," *op. cit.,* p. 7.

[34] B. Othanel Smith, "On the Anatomy of Teaching," *Journal of Teacher Education,* Vol. 7, No. 4 (December 1956), p. 339.

light in his mind shows up in the light in his face." At the same time the teacher communicates by means of signs, symbols, and language what is being taught. He is at once the observer, listener, and participant. The complexity of the teacher's task is described in this way:

> Suppose a teacher is instructing a science class by means of a demonstration. . . . He must pay attention to what he is doing and at the same time talk about what he is doing. But he must do even more. He must pay attention to the entire class and choose words and ideas appropriate to the capacities of his students. This three-way intellectual performance is seldom found outside of a teaching situation. It is not an easy one to learn. . . . Even the experienced teacher is seldom well enough aware of his performance to tell the beginner what to do and how to do it.[35]

Incorporated in the method and techniques of teaching is a constellation of value, purpose, sanction, and knowledge that constitutes the profession of education. But a number of forces and factors that are outside the control of the teacher affect what he can do, and hence affect both the profession of education and the operation of the school. Education is universal, it is an experience shared by practically the entire population, and consequently many stereotypes of the school and of teachers produce diverse expectations. Furthermore, everyone feels, in greater or less degree, a claim upon education to meet his individual needs; and organized groups want the school to include content in the curriculum that they individually favor. Finally, tradition has placed the over-all direction of the school system under lay boards of education which determine not only purpose but also content, and sometimes even methods of teaching.[36] Under these conditions, the teacher in the classroom may not always have a clear mandate as to the "particular aspects of the culture" to be taught. His performance as a teacher is

[35] *Ibid.*, p. 343.

[36] In Los Angeles in the spring of 1961, twenty-eight candidates filed for three positions on the board of education. Among the statements of platforms were: "I support vocational guidance and educational counseling in high schools, but I hold that counseling on personal and emotional problems should be handled first by parents, then by regular classroom teachers," and "I am concerned about the inroads on patriotism in our schools, specifically insofar as the flag has been removed from classroom and the Pledge of Allegiance abandoned." Other statements had to do with sex education "which was assigned ten years ago to parents has been surreptitiously re-introduced" in the counseling-guidance program; "increased emphasis on phonics instruction in the elementary grades"; criticism of current testing methods as not properly measuring student skills; and need for curriculum revision.

inevitably influenced by the conflicting values and purposes of the school administration and of the community.

If the board of education, as the representative of the community, decides upon the purpose or functions of education, should the professional educator then decide *what* and *how* functions are to be carried on? This is one of the issues in education. One critic is reported to have said "Excessive local control is not our historic tradition. This is one of the nostalgic images that we need to replace." [37] Such control, he contends, results in unequal standards among schools over the country. Another educator contends that if education is to be a profession, certain matters should be decided by educators. Among them are:

> The subjects to be taught and the material (such as textbooks) to be used in teaching them; the criteria to be used in deciding who should be admitted, retained, and graduated at all levels; the forms to be used in reporting pupil progress; school boundary lines and the criteria for permitting students to attend schools outside the boundary lines. . . .[38]

Another issue upon which educators as well as the public disagree is *how* the objectives of education are to be realized. Should the teacher be an expert in subject matter, especially in the high school, or should he be skilled in method of teaching? This touches a basic problem in all professional education—whether function is more important than knowledge of the subject for which the function is performed. Education has been accused of too great preoccupation with form and not enough attention to content. The trend now seems to be toward a balance between content and method.

Lay control of education has blocked professionalization in another direction, that is, in the extent to which educators determine membership in, and expulsion from, their profession, standards for professional education, and regulation of the conduct of members. The national professional organization, NEA, with three-quarters of a million members, has not defined standards for membership beyond the stipulation that the person be actively engaged in teaching. Since the various states decide who is qualified to teach, NEA has taken the position that such certification constitutes a minimum standard even though wide variation in requirements may exist. Closely related to membership standard are educational qual-

---

[37] Harry D. Gideonse, President of Brooklyn College, in an address before the National Congress of Parents and Teachers in Philadelphia, May 24, 1960, as reported in the *Los Angeles Times,* May 25, 1960, Part II, p. 1. He was reported to have drawn "rounds of applause from the PTA delegates" when he blasted the "so-called sacred American tradition of local control of schools."

[38] Lieberman, *op. cit.,* p. 91.

ifications for certification. Here the states show wide differences. Similarly, the schools of education in colleges and universities seem to have considerable variation in the requirements for general and special education in preparation for teaching. Since teaching is an art as well as a science, practice teaching is quite generally a part of preparation. Lieberman concludes, however: "We have already seen that the professional as well as the non-professional portions of teacher education curricula vary to such an extent that one can question whether there is any common body of knowledge, skills, and techniques in the teaching profession." [39] This critical opinion may not take into account certain "stirrings" in education which seem significant for the future.

Four developments that seem to point toward changes in education are coming in part from within the profession and in part as a result of public pressures since educational competition with Russia has been publicized. They are: (1) the trend toward limitation of functions of the school, (2) mental health awareness that has brought increased demands for attention to classroom mental health, (3) experiments in teacher-training that are in the direction of the development of the professional self and clearer definition of the role of the teacher, and (4) application of automation to learning through use of teaching machines and other devices. These developments are selected as "straws in the wind" with respect to trends in education. They have implications for the role of social workers as they relate to teachers and to the school administration.

Limitation of school functions. The trend toward limitation of functions is the reaction to the overloading of the school with too many expectations. One educator, for example, asserts that the school must transfer to community agencies some of the functions it has performed. He states: "The institution that has been asked to do everything . . . is drawing away and finally . . . admitting there are certain tasks it cannot assume . . . the omnicompetence of education is giving way at the present time to some rather cold-hearted and hardheaded reality recognitions. The school is looking to other agencies and looking to them with not pleas but with a demand that community agencies accept responsibility." [40] Since the role of the teacher is closely related to the functions of the school, new developments are found in teacher training.

Mental health awareness. The public's awareness of mental health has spread as community mental health education has been sup-

---

39 *Ibid.*, p. 190.
40 George W. Goethals, "The Role of the School in Mental Health," in Arthur J. Bindman, ed., *New Developments in Mental Health,* Proceedings of a Conference, Lenox, Mass., November 2–4, 1959, p. 55.

ported by governmental and private foundation funds. The work of Anna Freud and others is said to have been one of the influences which called the attention of teachers to psychotherapy and the use of some of its concepts in education.[41] Interest in child development in teacher training, begun by Dewey, was furthered by Ryan, Prescott, Havighurst, and many other educators. Use of the knowledge was not explicitly developed, however, and led sometimes to confusion of role. Small group theory (group dynamics) has been made known through such research on classroom relationships as that carried on at the University of Chicago's Human Dynamics Laboratory.[42]

Teacher-training. This seems to be moving from subject-centered training, through pupil-centered training, to teacher-centered training. Biber and others are calling attention to the need for more orientation to personality dynamics and to development of the relationship process in the education of teachers.[43] The understanding of one's self is essential in such education. One educator states:

> The best teacher training now imparts not only matters relating to subject matter and strategies of presentation (methods), not only something to do with the development of the child, but further skillful training in helping the teacher to understand her own motivational system in relation to that of the child. Believe me, I am not suggesting that all teacher training at the present time encompasses such a broad range, I am speaking here about the best. And although this best is rare, it is having an equally profound effect upon schools and upon community mental health.[44]

Automation. Automation is having an effect on education as well as on other areas of life. Perhaps the most spectacular development is the teaching machine. Developed by a behavioral psychologist, it provides "programmed learning" which is believed to hasten learning and to aid retention of what is learned.[45] Both the Ford

---

41 Percival M. Symonds, "Mental Health in the Classroom: Historical Perspective," *Journal of Social Issues,* Vol. 15, No. 1 (1959), p. 3.

42 *Ibid.,* p. 4.

43 Barbara Biber, "Teacher Education in Mental Health," in M. Krugman, ed., *Orthopsychiatry and the School* (New York: American Orthopsychiatric Association, Inc., 1958).

44 Goethals, *op. cit.,* p. 58.

45 B. F. Skinner, "Teaching Machines," *Science,* Vol. 128, No. 3330 (October 24, 1958), pp. 969–977; Charles I. Fotz, *The World of Teaching Machines, Programmed Learning and Self-Instruction Devices* (Washington, D.C.: Electronic Teaching Laboratories, 1961). For a popular account, *see* "Programmed Learning," *Time,* March 24, 1961, p. 36.

Foundation and the Carnegie Foundation have given grants of funds to the Manhattan Center for Programmed Instruction for the writing and testing of programs for public schools. Educators, too, have been devising new ways of hastening learning through placing more responsibility on the student, and leaving the teacher free to be of help to more children, more effectively. One educator says of these trends:

> New staffing patterns will be required and team teaching will come into its own. With team teaching will come different-sized groups of students for different learning purposes. More use will be made of teaching machines, motion pictures, television, tape recorders and language laboratories. These innovations will require new school buildings that provide flexible use of space.[46]

concluding comments

Social work and education have a number of common problems as they grow in professional stature in society. But they also have important differences.

The knowledge base of practice is under examination very actively in social work. With the discontinuance of educational preparation for the so-called specializations, practitioners through the national professional organization are engaged in examining and undertaking to test what is the core content of practice and what are the specifics. A similar movement to find the generic base in education is evident in efforts to reduce the number of certifications, but here the initiative seems to have come from boards of education and administrators rather than from the teachers themselves.

Social workers, in addition to examining their own practice for knowledge, are reaching out to the social sciences, particularly anthropology and sociology, for new concepts to test through use. Social psychology, and particularly psychoanalysis, have already supplied many useful working concepts to social work. An enlargement of purpose can be discerned: from a preoccupation with pathology, social work is also stressing concern for the so-called normal range of behavior in which preventive intervention may strengthen individuals and groups at times of crises so that breakdown will not occur. Teachers, at the same time, are becoming interested in understanding not only normal behavior but also deviations with a view to using such insight, first to evaluate children's behavior, and then to understand their own reactions. This should lead to better definition of the teacher's role and help him to use referral to

---

[46] Harold Howe, 2nd, "Needed: A Radical Change," *Saturday Review*, September 17, 1960, p. 74.

specialists with discrimination. The beginning noted above of teacher training institutions helping the teacher to develop a professional self, characteristic of training of social workers and psychiatrists, is a sound development.

The over-all status of social work and education as professions in our society is similar enough to be a cause sometimes for friction in co-operative endeavor. Such factors as women predominating in both professions, class origins, high rate of turnover, and similar salary schedules tend to make for competition in recruitment and other areas. Neither profession "halos" the other; each aspires to raise its status. If, however, social workers and teachers are informed about one another's profession they may find that their common bonds outweigh their differences.

Because of the importance of the school as an institution second only to the family in society, and because of the conflicting claims of the community upon teachers and school administration, the social worker needs to understand education as a profession and the school as a setting for his practice. This chapter has endeavored to look at the teacher and the social worker as members of professions.

The background material in Part 1 provides the base from which the specific functions and activities of the social worker in the school are analyzed in subsequent chapters.

Part 2

Functions and

Activities of the Social

Worker in the School

BASIC TASKS: AN OVERVIEW

5

The basic activities of the social worker in the school have the same goal as do those of social workers in any field of practice, *i.e.,* "the enhancement of social functioning wherever the need for such enhancement is either socially or individually perceived." [1] To achieve this goal, the social worker has a distinctive method of practice that, resting on a foundation of value, purpose, sanction, and knowledge, comprises his profession (*see* Chapter 4). While the various fields of practice make use of elements common to all social work, each has a specific function which determines the emphasis given to, and the adaptation in use of, the common elements.[2]

The social worker in the school shares the three general functions of social work—*restoration* of impaired social functioning through identification and control of those factors which have caused impairment or breakdown in social relationships, *provision of resources* through mobilization of capacities in the individual and resources in the community, and *prevention* of social dysfunction. His specific function, however, is to add his professional competence

---

[1] Werner W. Boehm, *Objectives of the Social Work Curriculum of the Future* (Social Work Curriculum Study, Vol. I; New York: Council on Social Work Education, 1959), p. 46.

[2] Boehm defines *function* as "specific categories of socially sanctioned aims that social work seeks to achieve. . . . The *methods* of social work are conceived as the means whereby the functions of social work are discharged, and the *functions* of social work are conceived as the means whereby the ultimate *goal* of social work is attained." *Method* is further defined as "a systematic ordering of certain characteristic activities grouped according to their appropriateness for use in given types of situations which require professional service." *Ibid.,* pp. 46–47.

to that of other specialists in the school in order to help children who are not learning or are not achieving expected educational goals to make maximum use of the opportunity to learn and to develop into social beings in society.

In carrying out his function, the school social worker is engaged in two kinds of activities: those which focus on a particular child, and those which focus on the welfare of school children generally. Each of these is outlined in this chapter as a background for discussion of adaptations in social work practice which have significance for all social workers and for social work education.

activities focusing on a particular child

In the school, the child is the primary client of the social worker. To help him, however, the social worker may need to work with adults within and outside the school, who are a part of the total situation affecting the child. His activities can be described under four headings: (1) casework service to children and/or their parents, (2) group work service for selected children, (3) collaboration with other school personnel, and (4) consultation to teachers, principals, and others on behalf of a child.

casework service

Casework service to children and/or their parents may be needed because of certain interrelated major problem areas which children and parents have with respect to the school. These are most often problems related to authority, to achievement expectations, and to shared responsibility between parents and school personnel for the over-all development of the child. The symptoms of these problems take many forms, including learning difficulties, absence from school (due to social, emotional, environmental factors), disturbing behavior ranging from unusual aggression and defiance of authority to extreme withdrawal and fearfulness. In kindergarten and elementary schools children are most often referred to the school social worker because of behavior and personality difficulties; in the secondary schools attendance problems seem to be the most frequent reason for referral.[3]

The social worker in giving casework service is an integral part of the school as a social institution, with all the connotations it carries for the child and his parents. As in other fields of practice, the social worker represents this setting of which he is a part. The

---

[3] Mildred Sikkema, "An Analysis of the Structure and Practice of School Social Work Today," in Grace Lee, ed., *Helping the Troubled School Child* (New York: National Association of Social Workers, 1959), p. 104.

school is legally obligated to enforce children's attendance, a reality which the social worker must accept. He must be able to help the child and/or parents understand, and make constructive use of, the school's purpose, opportunity, and authority. The focus of the casework relationship is on the problem and the situation which are impeding the child's intellectual and social development. In working with parents, the social worker endeavors to help them as parents of a child in school. His aim is to help the child and the parent accept, and make use of, all that the school offers. When problems demand resources outside the province of the school, he helps the family to use the agencies in the community. An analysis of the distinctive features of casework service in the school is given in Chapter 6. (*See* Appendix A, Record 1, Typical Example of School Social Work Service, p. 177.)

group work

Group work as part of a school's program of social service is not yet well established. Scattered experiments, however, show great promise for this form of service in helping children with certain types of personality and adjustment problems. Furthermore, the rapidly expanding school population may require new ways of providing social services so that the professional personnel available can reach larger numbers of children. Social group work has already proved effective alongside of casework services in institutions for disturbed children, in hospitals, and in community centers as a method of treatment of social relationship problems.

An example of social group work in the schools is an experiment conducted co-operatively by the Champaign Public Schools and the School of Social Work of the University of Illinois, from February 1949 to June 1951. Fifty-one boys from elementary schools who had problems of getting along with peers and/or teachers were invited to join small club groups. Participation was seen as an adjunct to casework or other services the boys might already be receiving. A report of the project describes the behavior in the beginning:

> In early meetings, many of the activities showed aggressive or withdrawn behavior and lack of capacity to get along with each other. The tusseling on the mat frequently ended in arguments. Table games involving minimal cooperation between two boys were at first easily disrupted. Some would retreat to reading comic books. The group worker sought to encourage pair friendships at the start and to develop an understanding relationship with each boy. Limits were used at the point where the aggressive behavior threatened to erupt into fights but otherwise very few

were used. Stories were always of interest and this was one spot at which group members, relating primarily to the worker, were able to act as a group. Refreshments were served, usually consisting of soft drinks and cookies, and some formality was arranged here by the worker, again calling for a minimum of group cooperation.[4]

Group conversation during activities, such as crafts, games, dramatics, art projects, gave opportunity for ventilation of feelings. School and teachers were often the subject of discussion. At one session when the group was painting, a principal was a visitor. The group worker reported:

> Meanwhile a discussion about school had been started. Henry said that he hated school. (I looked at the principal. She winced and could not conceal her perturbation but said nothing.) Albert said he shouldn't hate school. Henry insisted that he did not like school. I asked him why. He said that he had to read all the time. He said he wanted to have fun. He said in response to my question that fun meant drawing and painting. I asked him if he did not do this in class. He said he did. . . . Later . . . the principal said I really had my hands full.[5]

No formal evaluation of this project was made, but the consensus was that almost every boy had shown some improvement in school relationships. The report on the project states that it was not a "group therapy project" or a recreational project but "was conceived as a means through which social relationships could be learned, with whatever capacities or limitations the boy brought to the group, and through which the wise relationship of an understanding group worker might help the member in his specific social adjustment to his peers and teachers in the school situation." [6]

In 1959, the School Social Work Section, NASW, through its Practice Committee, made an inquiry of its members by questionnaire to "extract important questions concerned with the practice of school social work." Of the 336 responses, 239 were applicable to various aspects of the inquiry and were analyzed. In respect to work with groups, the consensus from 197 usable responses was that such work should be a function of the school social work program and that it should be carried on by existing staff members. About one-fourth of the 197 respondents reported that school personnel make requests of social workers to work with groups.[7] When groups

---

[4] Paul Simon, "Social Group Work in the Schools," *Bulletin* of the National Association of School Social Workers, Vol. 31, No. 1 (September 1955), p. 5.

[5] *Ibid.,* p. 7.

[6] *Ibid.,* p. 10.

are formed, frequently the parents of members are also invited to meet several times for discussion of common problems. Few social group workers are employed by the schools; the casework staff sometimes have brief in-service training, most often by a psychiatrist or psychologist, or occasionally they have social group work consultation. Three excerpts from replies to the questionnaire, as summarized by the School Social Work Practice Committee's Subcommittee on the Questionnaire Studying Certain Aspects of Social Work Practice, illustrate the wide range of group activities:

1. There have been occasional requests from school personnel to work with groups of children, for purposes of economy of time. Since no one on the staff has had group work training or experience, the department has resisted such requests. I consider the request a valid one.

2. I have been interested in trying next year to form a few groups as an experiment. This is largely because in accidental situations (unplanned) I have seen things happen which have had better results than I could have had in working with one youngster directly. . . . I feel I need to know more about this—and especially what kinds of children can benefit the most from this kind of experience.

3. It would seem to me that the purpose of the group would basically determine who should handle the groups that are created. Children with deep emotional problems who are placed in groups for a therapy purpose would better be guided by persons who have had this specific training. . . . I use groups with such problems as peer difficulties, poor attitudes toward school and home, etc. Most of my parent groups have been designed to give information and work through feelings which came about as a result of parent-child conflicts. There is a point, however, beyond which I feel the need for special help and into which I do not delve.

These excerpts show the diversity of attitudes and practice with respect to social group work in the schools. They range from "resistance" to requests from school personnel for group work because of lack of training and experience, through trial and error efforts, to appreciation of the need for both casework and group work knowledge and skills. The findings of the questionnaire as a whole would seem to point up the importance of all students in schools of social work having more preparation in understanding the dynamics of group formation and interaction. The responsibilities of school social workers for work with groups are not limited to parents and children but extend to teachers, principals, and school personnel.

---

[7] *NASW News*, School Social Work Section, Vol. 5, No. 3 (May 1960), pp. 17–18.

collaboration

Collaboration with other school personnel on behalf of a child is an essential activity of the school social worker. Since his service is supplementary to that of the teacher in helping children to learn and to grow emotionally, he works with children who are selected by the teacher, principal, or other member of the staff as being in need of his services. He undertakes to understand the total child in his total situation. This means that he must also take into consideration other school personnel and their activity as it affects the child. He regards himself as part of the school team. As a specialist in the enhancement of social functioning, specifically as it applies to children in school, part of his skill is in creating an interprofessional relationship with the other specialists in the school. As he comes to have an understanding of the child and his situation, he may need to take responsibility for integrating the parts that make up the whole—the services of the nurse, the psychologist, the counselor, and other specialists, as well as the roles played by teacher and parents. The following record illustrates this activity of the social worker.

The school nurse asked the social worker to see the mother of Jimmy, a nine-year-old boy who persistently remained home from school or asked to be permitted to go home from school because of illness. Whenever the school nurse examined him the child showed no elevation of temperature or other symptoms of illness. Both mother and father were employed. The social worker confirmed the referral with the teacher who said that Jimmy was not working up to capacity, that he lacked ability to plan his work and to follow through on it to completion. The record states:

> After the first interview with the mother, with the approval of the principal, the school social worker arranged a joint conference with the teacher, the school nurse, and the principal, to plan for treatment of Jimmy within the school.
>
> The teacher, who had had Jimmy's mother as a student of this school a number of years ago, could not recall much about her school adjustment. But all agreed that this mother was a perfectionist, that she was of high intelligence, and that she either expected or implied greater expectations of Jimmy than he felt he was able to perform. It was agreed that we might have difficulty in getting Mrs. B. to arrange time for or to want counseling help for Jimmy. The school social worker pointed out that her impression of the mother was based on only one interview; but other members of the group with longer experience with the mother confirmed this impression. The social worker felt that Mrs. B. had a need to be employed outside the home and to be

very busily engaged in church and community activities, and that it was doubtful if this could be modified so that she would spend more time at home with her son. However, should Mrs. B. be able to arrange appointments, every effort would be made to make this as easy as possible for her, with the goal of some modification in her treatment of her son and her expectations of him.

In the meantime, in order not to fixate psychosomatic symptoms, the school staff would treat Jimmy as follows: Whenever the school nurse was at the school she would treat the boy's physical complaints on a reality basis, such as taking his temperature, giving him honey and water or treatment which would appear satisfying to the boy; then, rather than send him home, she would have him rest in her office until he was ready to go back to the classroom. It was felt that in this way the gain of going home and escaping feared school failures would be reduced, thus avoiding strengthening the neurotic pattern. The principal said he would treat the boy in the same manner when the school nurse was not scheduled at the school. The teacher said she would modify her academic expectations of Jimmy. She would lower attainment goals in the classroom but would be exacting in requiring that he reach those goals; she had noticed that he was very pleased whenever he was able to complete an assignment. The social worker would try to gain the mother's cooperation and would continue to try to draw the father into counseling although this had been discouraged by the mother. All agreed to confer from time to time on the progress of these approaches in the treatment of Jimmy; regardless of parent participation, the school staff would follow the plan made in conference.[8]

The school social worker is often able to facilitate communication between members of the school staff who are each aware of some aspect of a child's problem. This increases the effectiveness of the school's efforts to restore a child to normal functioning or to help him use his potential capacities to the best advantage. The social worker frequently takes the initiative in strengthening such collaborative efforts, as in the case of Jimmy.

consultation

Consultation to teacher, principal, or other school personnel on the problems of a particular child is another activity of the school social

---

[8] A record exhibited at the National Conference on Social Welfare, May 11–16, 1958, Chicago, Ill., by the School Social Work Section, NASW. For an excellent summary of teamwork, *see* John C. Nebo, ed., *Administration of School Social Work* (New York: National Association of Social Workers, 1960), Chapter 6, "Interprofessional Relationships," pp. 36–41.

worker. Replies to the NASW School Social Work Section questionnaire, however, show that this activity is not well established. Consultation can be distinguished from collaboration by the difference in responsibility carried by the social worker for what happens as a result of the information or knowledge which is imparted. His purpose in working with the consultee is to help the latter perform his own role better. The worker's authority rests with his knowledge and skill in communicating with the consultee so that the latter gains fresh insight into his own activity in behalf of the child. The social worker may have no direct contact with the child or perhaps only brief contact.

An example of a conference between a teacher, principal, and school social worker illustrates the consultation process. The request from the school was for help with Joey, a hyperactive 7-year-old boy in second grade. He was described as crying easily, demanding constant attention, seeking love and affection, and accomplishing only when given such attention. He threw his lunch away and took food from other children; he left the room when the teacher's back was turned. This child lived in a foster home with a 9-year-old sister. The parents were divorced and both were remarried. The record states:

> Both the principal and the teacher emphasized the great appeal of this child. I quickly became aware of their strong child identification and accompanying rejection of both the mother and to a lesser extent of the foster mother. The teacher had been absent three days the past week and felt part of the reason for her illness was that she was so upset about Joey. So much emphasis was placed on the child's need for love and affection that it was several minutes before I became aware of what a difficult problem he was to handle in the classroom. . . . Joey evidently put on real temper tantrums at times to which the teacher reacted with guilt rather than the anger which the same behavior might elicit from another child.
>
> The teacher brought out that she felt she could give Joey what he needed if she didn't have other children also demanding her attention. I recognized her frustration but questioned whether it was possible to give Joey all the affection he needed and pointed out that she really did have a responsibility to the other children too. This rather obvious remark evidently carried weight for the teacher returned to it at the end of the interview to say how much better she felt to have me recognize that she did have responsibilities to the whole class that "even with a Joey in the classroom" she had to meet.
>
> I wondered if there was some way to provide relief for the teacher so that she didn't reach the peak of exhaustion that necessitated taking time off. The principal spoke up and said that

really was her responsibility to be aware of how tired the teachers were becoming and that she needed to think of ways to relieve the burden. The principal and teacher moved into the area of the academic push currently going on in the school department and their own feelings of frustration when their youngsters didn't measure up. The teacher complained there was no place to report that she was giving Joey special attention to help him get ready to learn. I commented that sometimes one had to know what one's own goals could be realistically, and then work on them, insulating oneself from too much outside criticism. I also reminded them that Joey's problems had been developing for a long time and that the school's job was not and could not be to cure him of these—that this would be a job for a psychiatric clinic. . . . There was bitter condemnation of the mother so we had some discussion of what her problems might be; that forcing her and making her feel guilty would solve nothing. There seemed to be some carryover of this discussion when the assistant principal joined us. . . .

All adults connected with the school are fond of Joey. . . . One teacher, not his own, gave up part of her lunch hour to give him individual help in reading. I felt this could be helpful but that they needed to be aware of the manipulative aspects and make sure lines were firmly drawn so the boy would know the limits. The teacher returned to the subject of limits in the classroom, wanting to know what I meant by being firm. The principal discussed the need for each child to know what was really expected and being held to it. I pointed out this was different from being punished. The teacher commented this could be a learning process for the child.

The school social worker's report concludes: "The main thing accomplished was a relaxing of the school's demands on itself to help this child and the beginning of some kind of plan to handle him." The teacher became more relaxed about Joey and began to see her role as working with him within realistic limits that would not interfere too much with her major responsibility to the whole class. She also gave verbal recognition to the need for controls, both for Joey and for her maternal response to the child's great need for affection. The principal was helped to see that she needed to take more responsibility for relieving not only this teacher but others. In two instances in the conference she moved forward to assert her role in the school: in stating that it was her responsibility to be aware of how tired the teachers were and to do something about this, and again in reinforcing the social worker's statement that children needed to know what was expected of them and to be held to such expectations. What happened after the conference would depend upon the teacher and principal being able to proceed on the basis of their new understanding of Joey and their responsibilities in the situation.

Consultation can be one of the important and effective services of the school social worker. Although he may work with the school on the needs of a particular child, the results may benefit many other children because of the change in attitude of a teacher, as in the case of Joey, for example. Sometimes the activity of the social worker in the consultation process may be focused on evaluation of a specific situation for which help has been requested. Action may follow in modification of the school environment, or in referral to an outside community agency such as a psychiatric clinic, or both actions may occur together.

Responses to the questionnaire of the School Social Work Section, NASW, described above, showed that 90 percent of the 239 school social workers whose replies were analyzed considered that they engaged in some consultation. The responses revealed that a limited amount of time each week was given to this activity, and that the social workers, although they believed in the value of consultation, felt the need for help in understanding the consultation process and their role in it, and in developing criteria for selection of cases and areas to be serviced. Such help, they felt, would further administrative acceptance of consultation. They also noted that school personnel should have time allotted for conferences with the social worker. (Consultation is further discussed in Chapter 7.)

activities focusing on the general welfare of school children

The second kind of activities in which the school social worker engages in carrying out his function focuses on the general welfare of school children. These activities may take one of several forms: (1) participation in school administration, (2) educational programs for parents, in-service training of teachers and other school staff, and field instruction for students in schools of social work, (3) representation of the school in the community and representation of the community services in the school. These activities may not be concerned with the particular problems of particular children; but they are intended to improve the well-being of children in general, particularly school children.

participation in school administration

Participation in school administration has multiple expressions. The social worker is employed by the school system and should carry the same responsibilities and have the same privileges as teachers and other school employees. He participates in curriculum planning and in other committee work, he maintains case records, and he submits such statistical and other reports as may be requested or as he believes may be useful to the superintendent or other key administrators. He attends faculty meetings and PTA functions insofar as possible. When research projects are undertaken, he contributes in areas of his competence.

The place of school social work in the administrative structure of a school system may vary according to the geographical locality and the size of the school district. The larger the organization, the more likely it is to have the characteristics of a bureaucracy with both its strengths and its weaknesses. The social worker needs to understand and accept the fact that in a large school system there will be a distribution of functions, hierarchy, and professionalization. These elements are designed to insure reliability of behavior and conformity to established rules so that security and freedom within limits are possible. Three levels of personnel are characteristic of a bureaucracy: the top level of leadership, the rank and file personnel who carry on the main work of the organization, and a "body of functionaries" or sub-executives who carry out the policies and regulations of leadership and who supervise and direct the activities of the rank and file personnel.[9] When we apply this outline to the school, we find the superintendent and principals as representative of top leadership, the teachers as the rank and file of personnel, and a body of functionaries such as the curriculum supervisor, teacher supervisor, special education supervisor, and others who provide the sub-executive leadership.

The place of the specialists such as the social worker, psychologist, and others in the administrative structure often presents a problem. It has been solved by many school districts by creation of a bureau or department of special services with a supervisor or director who becomes a member of the sub-executive group. Sometimes such a bureau or department includes supervisory staff for each of the technical specialties. Here is a description of the operation of one program:

> The social service department is one of several special services (social service, special education, psychological service, research) in the Pupil Personnel Division. An assistant superintendent is in charge of the division. The director of the school social work program, a social worker, is part of the central office administrative staff and is responsible to the assistant superintendent for the administration, supervision, and development of this service.
> There are four district pupil personnel offices housing ten to

---

[9] Robert Dubin, *Human Relations in Administration* (Englewood Cliffs, N.J.: Prentice-Hall, Inc., 1951), p. 156.

twelve social workers, one or two psychologists, clerical staff, and a social service supervisor. Each worker is assigned to from one to four schools and maintains a regular schedule in each of these schools and their districts, as well as a regular schedule in the district office for case recording, supervisory conference, statistical reports, inter-agency conferences and similar duties.

The district supervisor is responsible for the administration of the district office, participates with the director in developing program, practice and policies of the social service division, and carries as well the function of supervisor.[10]

There are other arrangements within the administrative structure for placement of school social workers. In some school systems, the social worker is part of a child guidance service which offers psychiatric diagnosis and/or treatment to children in school. In other systems, the social worker may be in the attendance department and carry the legal enforcement of the attendance law.

Not all school social workers have supervision by members of their own profession. The Practice Committee of the School Social Work Section, NASW, concluded on the basis of its questionnaire inquiry that school social workers have less supervision than social workers in welfare agencies. About half of the 239 respondents whose replies were analyzed reported that they had supervision from a member of a school social work staff; and another 10 percent had supervision or used "consultation" from another source, most frequently on an individual, "as needed" basis, averaging two to four hours a month. Only 71 respondents out of the total of 239, however, felt that they had "too little supervision." [11] The committee suggests further study on whether the lack of supervision affects the quality of service to children and what influence it has on recruitment of workers.

Good school administration depends, of course, upon good administrative leadership in all three hierarchies of personnel and clear channels of communication throughout the system. Each staff member, however, can contribute to good administration by clear definition of his role-set, interpretation of his function to administrators and colleagues, and understanding the school as a social institution and his place in it in relation to all the other parts.

educational programs

The school social worker has opportunity to participate in various kinds of educational programs. Sometimes he is asked to help in

---

[10] Opal Boston, Supervisor, Social Service Branch, Indianapolis, Ind., Public Schools.

[11] *NASW News, op. cit.,* p. 18.

child study and other parent education groups. When the school has in-service training lectures and discussion groups, the social worker may be able to share some of his knowledge of behavior and how to work with groups; at the same time, he learns something of the problems and points of view of the teacher and other staff members.[12] When a school of social work is located in the same community as the school, the social worker may be permitted to include in his function the field instruction of one or more students placed in the school to learn the practice of school social work. Careful work with all three hierarchies of administration is required for acceptance of students in the school and for the social worker to be responsible for their assignments as representatives of the school. Advance planning and agreements between top administrators in both the school system and the school of social work must precede placement of students.

community representation

One of the original reasons for bringing the social worker into the school, it will be remembered, was to bridge the gap between the school and the home when a child was in trouble. As his services have expanded, he has been able to extend help to the child and his family by utilizing the social welfare resources of the community when the nature of the problem is outside the scope of the school's services. Often he is able to interpret the school and its frame of reference to the agencies so that they can work more effectively with all schools which refer children or families to them.

The social worker also acts as interpreter of the school in the community. He may be invited to speak before groups of various kinds, or he may be asked by the administrator to represent the school in community social welfare activities, such as co-ordinating or planning councils.

The school, too, needs to understand the opportunities and limitations in its own community for wholesome activities for children. Gaps in service, need for recreational outlets, lack of provision for supervision of children of working parents, neglect—these are all known to the school. The social worker has special responsibility for stimulating the school administration to make these needs and conditions known to appropriate planning bodies so that children's interests and protection can be furthered.

---

[12] For an account of how teachers and social workers co-operated in New York City to improve social services for school children, *see* Shirley Leonard, "Teachers and School Social Workers Learn from Each Other," in Grace Lee, ed., *Helping the Troubled School Child* (New York: National Association of Social Workers, 1959), pp. 420–429.

concluding comments

This overview of the way in which the school social worker carries out his function has distinguished two major kinds of activities: that which has as its focus a particular child and that which has as its focus the improvement of services for school children generally. The social worker in the school, it is evident, has a breadth of activity that is not found in most settings in which social workers are employed. While the child is the primary client, the social worker can help him most effectively by working simultaneously with school personnel, parents, and community resources. The skill required is different in working with each of these groups. This breadth of activity which demands knowledge of several methods, often used in combination, is a specific characteristic of school social work. It has important educational implications for social work at a time when trends in practice are in this direction.

ADAPTATIONS IN SOCIAL
WORK PRACTICE IN THE SCHOOL

6

On the basis of the foregoing de-
scriptions of the school as a field of practice for social work (Part I)
and of the functions and activities of the school social worker (Chapter 5), it is possible to formulate certain concepts that are specific
to this field of practice and that have significance for social work
education.[1] While the school social worker regards himself as
engaged primarily in casework practice, he draws on other methods
for selected knowledge and skills. An examination of his activities
reveals the importance of conscious use of knowledge of collaboration and consultation, administration, group work, and community
organization. Now that the schools of social work have agreed that
the curriculum at the master's level will not prepare for specialized
practice *per se,* it is essential that each field of practice contribute to
the basic curriculum.[2]

Harriett M. Bartlett has suggested that in the light of the present
stage of development of education and practice, the concept of
"generic-specific" needs redefinition. Practice should no longer be
considered only the "doing" but should also include conceptual
thinking. She states:

---

[1] This chapter is based in part on a paper by Elizabeth D. Keye, "Influence
of the School on Social Work Practice," (unpublished), on comments of consultants from the fields of psychiatry, psychology, anthropology, sociology, and
social group work, and records of the workshop discussion groups, presented at
the Conference on the Contribution of School Social Work to Social Work
Education, Highland Park, Illinois, August 2–8, 1959.

[2] Medical social workers, who have pioneered in the study of their practice,
have recently made a valuable contribution to both medical social work and
social work as a whole. *See* Harriett M. Bartlett, *Social Work Practice in the
Health Field* (New York: National Association of Social Workers, 1961).

The present idea that a field of practice is a constellation of essential social work factors, combined and used somewhat differently in each field, calls attention to the fact that there is conceptual thinking at the specific level. The adaptation of the constellation of factors which is social work to a particular field of practice requires a considerable degree of theoretical understanding and intellectual discipline, both in relation to the total field and the practice of the individual worker. . . . Thus a constellation of factors representing social work is being continually combined with another constellation of factors representing a particular area of human life and human need. In this process the wholes must be kept together.[3]

Because the school is a social institution of central and critical importance in a democratic society and because attendance at school in the United States is a universal experience, school social work is in a strategic position to help the profession of social work understand the meaning of this experience in our society. The practice of social work in such a setting offers many valuable insights into how to work with a wide range of types of children and parents and into the kinds of problems that they present to the school.

The School Social Work Section, NASW, in sponsoring the Highland Park conference, sought to factor out those concepts which have particular meaning and significance for school social work practice and for professional education. Those discussed below are illustrative of practice as at present carried on and give a glimpse of the possibilities in future developments in this field. Five significant aspects of practice are presented. Under each one, selected applicable concepts are discussed, followed by a statement of the specific knowledge, skill, and attitudes required for their execution.

some variables in casework practice

Direct work with children and parents has some variables from work with children and parents in the usual social agency. These concepts are applicable:

normality

The school social worker has the opportunity to see behavior as a continuum from the so-called normal child, with the usual adjustments that come with growing up, to the seriously disturbed child.

---

[3] "The Generic-Specific Concept in Social Work Education and Practice," in Alfred J. Kahn, ed., *Issues in American Social Work* (New York: Columbia University Press, 1959), pp. 186–187.

He is concerned with the dynamics of total adjustment of the child rather than with the dynamics of pathology. More than most social workers, he has direct contact with the child and is able to see demonstrated the child's capacity to become engaged in working on modification of his own behavior. The school social worker probably has more understanding of the latency period of development than other social workers. The literature has dealt mostly with the young child and the adolescent. (*See* Appendix A, Record 2, Normal "Growing Pains" of a Junior High School Boy, p. 191.)

parent-child relationships

The importance of the family and of the relationship of the child to his parents is well established. The school social worker sees a wider range of parent-child relationships than do most social workers because parents, like children, are seen on a continuum ranging from parents who are eager for their children to succeed in school and are anxious for help toward this end, to those who for emotional or cultural reasons may be resistant to any intervention by the school or the social worker. Parents also present a wide range of class, cultural, and economic statuses. Since the great majority of school children are living with one or both parents, child-school-parents is a constant factor. The focus of help to the parents is the child's problem in school; parents are helped to identify their part in the child's difficulties and to know what they can do about them. If a parent must have help on his own problems, he may be enabled to go to a community agency for treatment. If no resources exist in the community, the social worker must decide whether the situation for the child is so critical that he must go beyond his role and give emergency help to the parents. He would, of course, try at the same time to stimulate the school and the community to recognize the need for action to provide additional resources.

parent-school relationships

Since education is universal and compulsory in the United States, parents have feelings about school that come from memories of their childhood. These may be pleasant or unpleasant. Parents may reflect the respect for education that some segments of our society hold; or they may have stereotypes of teachers on whom they vent their feelings of hostility and frustration. At any rate, the social worker represents the school to the parents, with all of its requirements for attendance and for standards of achievement and behavior. Before he can gain their participation in working on the problems of their child he must interpret the school in realistic terms which they can begin to accept. He also needs to convey to parents his conviction that they have rights as well as duties, including their right to understand all the services the school can offer. (*See* Appendix A, Record 3, Brief Service, p. 201.)

case load selection

"Intake" for the social worker rests largely upon the judgment of educators. Selection of the children referred depends upon: (1) the seriousness of the child's problem for the teacher, (2) the teacher's understanding of the social worker's role and acceptance of the worker as a partner in realizing the school's goal of maximum development of each child, and (3) administrative policy with respect to the best use of the worker's time. Administrative policy determines whether the social worker should offer chiefly brief service for emergency problems or should give continued treatment service for serious problem cases, whether he should spend more time on consultation with staff than in direct work with children, whether he should make maximum use of referrals to community agencies, or what combination of these services should be undertaken. When the social worker is assigned to several schools, each one may have a different policy; moreover, the socioeconomic problems of each neighborhood may make different demands upon him.

Once his service is established and accepted within the school, he will be so surrounded by needful children and troubled staff that he will find it difficult to refuse a request for service or to escape the impact of unmet need. In general, case load selection seems to involve the principal, the teacher, and the social worker even when the referral comes from other school personnel, from children themselves, or from parents.

brief contact and evaluative services

The school social worker must seem immediately available to a wide range of coworkers and children. He has to meet many people briefly, between the ever present time pressures of the school day. He must utilize short contacts for quick evaluations and for the establishment of trusting relationships. Records of various kinds within the school are used to help him make judgments. The knowledge which other school personnel have about children is also a resource. But within the area of social functioning, the social worker is on his own; he must have the special knowledge which will enable him to put the parts together so that the whole child is perceived and interpreted to others.

decision-making

As the only social worker in one or more schools and usually working without any or only remote supervision, the school social worker has to make professional decisions independently and sometimes under pressure from the school for "action." These judgments and decisions are subject to scrutiny by the many persons concerned with the child and reflect, for better or for worse, on the worker. In this connection it was said at the conference, "Constant visibility triggers constant evaluation." Furthermore, the decision of the social worker is subject to acceptance or rejection by the principal with whom final decision rests.

Another aspect of decision-making relates to the client. The child is able to make choices only within the limits of his maturity. It was said, "Let the situation do the punishing," that is, anticipate the consequence with the child and offer him the opportunity to make a choice among alternatives. Keye states:

> The school social worker has something of particular value for the adolescent. He is able to offer a relationship with an adult of the same sex who is older but not related to him. The adolescent's dependency needs can be fulfilled in a way acceptable to him and there is freedom for expression of hostility. The goal of the social worker with the adolescent is to help him to grow, to support his non-conformance, his need to accept what must be accepted, to live and yet retain constructive rebellion.

Parents have a somewhat wider range of choices than do children but in the last analysis they must choose between working with the school in modifying the child's problems and accepting the final sanction of the school, suspension. Neglect in its various forms is often a baffling problem because community resources for dealing with parental neglect are usually very limited. If the school cannot influence change and is unable to ameliorate the child's behavior in school, it may have to choose between tolerance of the disturbing element, suspension of the child, or referral to the juvenile court. (*See* Appendix A, Record 4, Adolescent Boy Without Father in the Home, p. 207.)

knowledge, skill, and attitudes needed

In work with children and parents, the social worker must have certain kinds of knowledge, skills, and attitudes.[4] These include:

---

[4] Indebtedness is gratefully acknowledged to Elliott Studt for certain terminology and forms of expression as used in her excellent monograph, *Education for Social Workers in the Correctional Field* (New York: Council on Social Work Education, 1959).

Knowledge of:

Norms of behavior at different stages in the child's growth and development, as affected by chronological age, physical and intellectual capacity or endowment

Behavior of children and adults as it is affected by racial, cultural, and class values, and how these influence attitudes toward education

Educational and psychological measurements and how to utilize their findings

Learning theories held by educators and the implications for work with children and parents

Early symptoms of serious deviations from normal behavior and their significance

Institutionalized roles of teacher, principal, and others and their effects upon attitudes toward children and parents

Multiple causation and the various forms of behavior which may be manifestations of dysfunction.

Skill in:

Use of limits, of conveying consequences as well as choices open to child

Quickly establishing trusting relationships (with child and/or parent) and engaging and sustaining them in working on a problem identified by the school

Evaluation—accurate appraisal of situations and individuals, often under time pressures, and within the resources and facilities available

Understanding and modifying causes of stress—pressure upon the child, the teacher, the school, the parent

Sharing responsibility with others for evaluation, treatment, and termination of service

Identifying with the child's feelings rather than with the child against the school

Listening to teachers, hearing them (psychologically), utilizing their contributions for insight into a child's problems

Strengthening, creatively and co-operatively, the role of the teacher with the child

Selection of the form of treatment that will be most fruitful and efficient for the school to sponsor.

Attitudes of:

Acceptance of limits, for the child and for the worker himself, as these are defined by the school

Identification with the purpose of the school and its personnel

Flexibility and resiliency, even when the worker sees "the familiar in an unfamiliar form"

Awareness of his own feelings about education, school personnel, as affected by his life experiences

Readiness to merge his activity with that of others with whom he must share credit for accomplishment

Responsibility for defining and interpreting his role-set in the school.

use of authority: hazards and opportunities

The social worker must be able to understand authority, accept it, and assume responsibility for action which follows from such acceptance. Actually, social workers have considerable emotional reaction to their use of authority in work with others. This reaction stems from several causes: (1) incomplete working through of their dependency needs while students in the professional school, (2) certain social work concepts derived from Freudian psychology, such as the need for the worker to be non-judgmental and the client's right of self-determination, which have been only partially understood, (3) emphasis on "giving" in social work, with the result that limit-setting seems contradictory and produces conflict, and (4) failure of the social worker to perceive his role as encompassing more than the one-to-one relationship with a client.

Sources and kinds of authority need to be understood. Concepts would include these:

authority derived from law

The school operates as the legal sanctioning system for universal education and for compulsory attendance that is necessary if children are to receive such education. Special classes and facilities are also authorized by law. Boards of education, superintendents, and principals are the instrumentalities to which programs for carrying the law into effect are entrusted.

administrative authority

Administrative authority flows from legal sanctions and is based on them. Power is given to boards of education, superintendents, and their representatives to make policies, rules, and regulations for putting programs into effect. Since the school has responsibility for the education of *all* children and since it is geared to the teaching-learning of a preponderance of so-called normal children, it must make special rules and regulations for the minority of children who deviate in some way from the average. The child with behavior and personality problems may become so disturbed and dangerous to himself or others that the school must use its authority to exclude him. Taber reports that the policy in

Philadelphia is to delimit its responsibility for this type of child for whom all efforts have failed. He states:

> For many years the school system had not expelled a child because of his incorrigible behavior as provided under the School Code. The Case Review Committee (made up of the Superintendent of Schools, the Directors of the Divisions of Pupil Personnel and Counseling, Medical Services, Special Education, and a District Superintendent) initiated the first expulsion by submitting to the Superintendent of Schools a summary of the pupil's disruptive behavior and of the various steps we had taken to bring about an adjustment. In each instance, we notify the Juvenile Court of our action. If the child is not already with the Court, we petition the Court for supervision by the probation officer. The Committee has become increasingly convinced that the schools cannot be "all things to all people." We believe that we should accept our own limits as an educational institution and should recognize that some children have reached the point where they must become the responsibility of a highly specialized service.[5]

Here we find the school as a social institution using its authority to define the limits of its responsibility.

professional authority

Professional authority or the authority that inheres in function should be used responsibly and therapeutically. Enabling aspects of authority of this kind can be defined and can afford security to the worker if he has professional maturity and conviction about his function as a school social worker. He may sometimes have to use his professional authority to refuse inappropriate referrals and to channel them back to more appropriate services. He may have to use authority to set limits with a child. The social worker, conference members noted, seems to have more trouble with the use of professional authority than does the psychiatrist or psychologist, possibly because he has less conviction about his own competence than do the practitioners of these other professions; he often has less status. The inability of the social worker to come to grips with authority is reflected often in his avoidance of attendance enforcement or other activity involving legal procedures, although as a part of the school he may share this responsibility.

The school social worker, as a part of the school team, shares

---

[5] Robert C. Taber, "The Contribution of Social Work to the Social Planning Aspects of the School as a Social Institution," presented at the Conference on the Contribution of School Social Work to Social Work Education, Highland Park, Illinois, August 2–8, 1959, unpublished, p. 28.

responsibility for implementing policies, rules, and procedures. The limits these represent can be utilized to enhance the child's social functioning. A careful evaluation of the child's total situation, however, is needed in order to decide when and how to enforce limits. Authority, *per se,* is not bad. The child needs outside limits to help him find inner control. The authority of the school is different from that of the court, in that education is a universal experience, offered as an opportunity to all. While, in a sense, the child attends "involuntarily" he soon finds the rewards and satisfaction that come with learning. Most children accept referral to the social worker as a part of the school's services and find it a positive experience which peers sometimes want to share. In that case, the social worker has successfully found the voluntary in the involuntary. (*See* Appendix A, Record 5, Use of Authority, p. 225.)

authority of personality

Authority of personality, or leadership, is closely related to professional authority but is not necessarily synonymous with it. Members of all professions vary greatly in their ability to inspire confidence and trust in others. Personal characteristics, such as sincerity, integrity, freedom of libido, and command of professional function, are important; but, in addition, the quality of mind which can grasp a situation and see it whole commands the respect and attention of others.

School social workers need to be able to exert the kind of leadership that releases the energy of others but unites energies in carrying out services for children. The fact that one of the social worker's special contributions is in interrelating efforts of various specialists in behalf of the child makes it essential that he be accepted by colleagues. In Follett's words, "The leader guides the group and at the same time is himself guided by the group, is always a part of the group. No one can truly lead except from within. . . . The power of leadership is the power of integrating. . . . The person who influences me most is not he who does great deeds but he who makes me feel that I can do great deeds." [6] Social workers are accustomed to motivating individuals to "do great deeds" and in school social work they need to think of such a skill as applying to work with colleagues around the problems of particular children. As one of the representatives of the school, the social worker must work with the child and other authorities in his life (parents, principal, teacher, and other school personnel) in such a way that these authorities support one another in the child's behalf.

---

[6] Mary Parker Follett, *The New State* (New York: Longmans Green and Co., 1918), pp. 229–230.

authority of relationship

This kind of authority includes the relationship of an adult to a child, and the relationship of one profession to another profession with perhaps less prestige. When the child enters school he recognizes an adult other than his parents—the teacher—who has authority over him. To be sure, the teacher exercises a professional authority, but it includes regulation of conduct while at school and can be confusing if it is in conflict with conduct expectations at home.

The social worker has tended to rely on supervision of a member of his own profession and on consultation from a psychiatrist when he deals with certain kinds of problems. At the conference, the psychiatrist Dr. John R. Altmeyer urged that social workers "grow up" and "free themselves from nurturing disciplines." He believes their professional competence is sufficient for them to be able to practice with confidence in their own professional judgment and feel themselves on a par with other professions. Clarity of function and role-set, however, is essential if school social workers are to hold their own in the school's multidiscipline setting.

knowledge, skill, and attitudes needed

The understanding and use of authority in its various forms require that the education of the social worker should give him:

Knowledge of:

Legal framework through which society gives sanction to the school to provide universal and compulsory education

Laws which affect children such as child labor, guardianship and custody, compulsory school attendance

Administrative law of the school as expressed through policies, rules, regulations, procedures, programs

Sources and kinds of authority and their meaning and use differentially

Behavior that is expressed in trouble with authority

Influence of peer groups upon a child's feelings about authority.

Skill in:

Individualizing a specific school's use of authority in its various forms and effects upon children and staff

Helping children and others resolve negative feelings about authority

Using his own professional authority to set limits so as to further the child's growth

Differential use of authority, that is, knowing when and when not to offer choices (alternatives) and being prepared to accept the alternative selected

Mobilizing the various authorities in the child's life so that they support one another in his behalf

Understanding and accepting the authority implicit in his role and its relationship to other authorities.

Attitudes of:

Self-awareness of feelings which he has concerning authority and willingness to discipline such feelings

Confidence in his own profession and in his competence in its practice

Acceptance of his role in education; acceptance of limits this role places on him

Acceptance of responsibility for continuous and creative efforts with all other school personnel in achieving the purposes and goals of the school, and for his direct services to individual children and their parents

Respect for the authority of the school.

dynamics and problems in use of school structure

The complexities of the school social system (*see* Chapter 3) offer both opportunities and problems to the school social worker.[7] The fact that the social worker is an integral part of the school insures opportunity for helping the child work on a problem of which he is aware, his lack of success in some phase of school life. As Poole points out, "The school is a setting which, to the child, is very much his own and one in which he is very much on his own." [8] That this is so may complicate the task of the social worker. While he represents the purpose of the school, its authority and requirements, he must communicate at once to the child that his function is different from that of the teacher, that he will not be evaluating the child in the same terms but will give him individual attention to help him with the problem that is interfering with school adjustment. To make maximum use of the school structure in helping the child, the social worker needs a grasp of such concepts as these:

bureaucracy

Although the term "bureaucracy" sometimes carries a negative connotation in a popular sense, it has a useful meaning as defined

---

[7] For a good analysis of structure in relation to service, *see* Robert D. Vinter, "The Social Structure of Service," in Alfred J. Kahn, ed., *Issues in American Social Work, op. cit.*, pp. 242–269.

[8] Florence Poole, "An Analysis of the Characteristics of School Social Work," in Grace Lee, ed., *Helping the Troubled School Child* (New York: National Association of Social Workers, 1959), p. 49.

by the social scientist; *i.e.,* "a form of social organization for administering the affairs of a formal organization." The larger the organization, the greater the need for hierarchical relationships, distribution of functions according to technical qualifications, and formalized norms of behavior of personnel.[9]

The school as a social institution, regardless of size, is organized into a pyramidal type of authority and responsibility. At the top of the pyramid are the *school board* and the *superintendent* of the school district. They have broad powers and duties in planning and policy-making with respect to: (1) physical plant and supplies, (2) educational content of program from kindergarten through secondary school and sometimes junior college, (3) financial management including budget-making and forecasting, (4) personnel recruitment and placement, (5) special services, (6) public relations, and so forth.

As with any other part of the school program, the school board and particularly the school superintendent must take leadership in authorizing and supporting school social work as a special service to help the school achieve its educational objectives. The bureaucratic characteristics of school administration make it essential that the superintendent give social work service a "green light" if it is to be accepted by principals, teachers, and other school personnel as a legitimate part of the total program of the school. Conference members agreed that "structure must support function."

Principals of the individual schools in the district are immediately responsible to the top administration for carrying policies and programs into effect. The complex legal and interactional relationships of the school impose many pressures upon the principal. Since state reimbursement is based on attendance of children, the principal is expected to maintain good attendance records for his school. School staff are usually assigned to, rather than selected by, the principal. With the high mobility common in American society, the principal may be the only relatively permanent person in the school. This factor may make the movement of the social worker in, and out of, his school seem to be another fluid element.

Teachers are directly responsible to the principals of schools in the organizational hierarchy. They constitute the most important and largest body of personnel since they carry on the central activity of the school—teaching and learning.[10] The profession of education is vested in the teacher. Specialization, duties inherent in the position of teacher, career service are all aspects of bureaucratic administration. Yet great variation is found in attitudes of teachers toward administration. Some expect the principal to make all

---

[9] Robert Dubin, *Human Relations in Administration* (Englewood Cliffs, N.J.: Prentice-Hall, Inc., 1951), pp. 156–159.

decisions; others desire to participate in making decisions. If the principal is convinced of the importance of the service the social worker can render, the teachers will very likely become interested, so great is the pressure for conformity to administrative edict, so great is the power of the principal over personal advancement of the teacher.

Functional specialists constitute another part of the administrative hierarchy. These are the supervisors of curriculum, elementary education, secondary education, music and art, vocational education, guidance service, and so on. In their functioning, these staffs may be either consultants to administrators or operating departments handling auxiliary service, such as social work. At any rate, such supervisory staff become an integral part of the administrative bureaucracy. Their demands upon principals and teachers may be contradictory and confusing unless well defined.

The above outline of the meaning of bureaucracy as applied to the public school points up the importance of the school social worker seeing the total organization of which he is a part. Such understanding should enable him to act flexibly and intelligently in dealing with the rigidity and malfunctioning which may at times characterize school administration. When he proposes changes in curriculum or policy that would seem better to serve the needs of children, he will realize that decision about changes may often require approval of more than one level of administration. The conference workshops stressed the importance of social workers having knowledge of bureaucracy and power structure in the school system and in the community, so that they may understand how these factors affect both what goes on in the classroom and the way in which social service can operate to help alleviate stresses and strains in the school social system. The social worker at all times needs to know how to work through appropriate administrative channels so that lines of relationship are strengthened.

role perception and expectations

The school as a social system, as previously noted, is essentially bureaucratic; the universality of education demands a formal organization with hierarchical relationships. And such a structure requires institutional definition of roles; that is, of those things

---

[10] Latest available estimates from the U.S. Office of Education and the National Education Association are that a total of 1,462,002 elementary and high school teachers, superintendents of schools, principals, and supervisors are employed in the United States. Of this number, 93 percent (1,366,884) are teachers, less than 1 percent (13,008) are superintendents, and about 6 percent (82,110) are principals and supervisors. Education Supplement, *Saturday Review*, September 17, 1960, p. 71.

which staff members are expected to do in different contexts and relationships.[11]

Conflicts can arise when members of such an organization hold different perceptions of one another's role-sets. A role-set, it will be recalled, is an array of associated roles which accompanies a particular social status (*see* Chapter 3). In a large organization, conflicts of this kind may arise between members of the same profession as the social structure changes, or they may arise between members of two professions employed within the same organization when professional norms and values are not identical and not reciprocally understood. A brief discussion of these points should make clear the problem of role perception and expectations.

In a period of rapid change like the present, when educational goals and values are under scrutiny, it is inevitable that school board member, administrator, and teacher may each conceive his status and role-set to be different from those traditionally assigned to him. Increasing professionalization of education (*see* Chapter 4) may lead the teacher to question some of the extra-classroom duties expected of him. Professionalization may also be a factor in the growing criticism of local lay boards of education exercising control over educational practice as well as policy (*see* Chapter 3). Under these conditions, an individual may see himself as having a different status than that assigned to him and he may try to perform a role which is not expected of him; conflict and confusion result. Unclear delineation of roles within the school social system can be the cause of low morale and high turnover of staff. Leadership in all of the hierarchies of the organization is, therefore, essential if changes are to occur without undue disruption.

The social worker as one of the specialists in the school social system introduces another possible source of role conflict. He brings into the system the professional norms and values of another profession which are not always identical with those of education. A teacher, for example, is successful when children meet anticipated levels of educational achievement; the very presence of the social worker and his client, the child who fails to live up to educational expectations, may seem to represent failure of the school's program and of the teacher's efforts.

In any agency, the central core function (education, in the school) is most highly esteemed, and the farther a service is from the core function, the less esteem is accorded it. The social worker may be given a status that differs from his own perception of it; he

---

[11] An example of such an effort is the Los Angeles City School Districts' 3-year study of "guidance roles" of 12 positions, ranging from teacher and principal to guidance specialist and child welfare and attendance supervisor (school social worker).

may be expected to perform functions that, to him, are not in keeping with his professional role. If he tries to fit into behavioral expectations that have little relation to his professional competence, his professional identity is threatened. Under these conditions the social worker must have not only a clear perception of his role-set as a social worker, but he must also be able to communicate to school personnel the ways in which he can carry out social work functions in behalf of education. At the same time, he must have knowledge of the educators' conception of their statuses and roles and of the variations that may exist from school to school. He must understand that the school social system is a dynamic, changing network of relationships and that educators, like social workers, are only beginning to define, and distinguish between, related roles within the system.

A paper by Mary N. Taylor, entitled "Whose Child Is This?" vividly illustrates the social worker's conflict over role.[12] The dilemma of a young worker after two months in a school social work position is described. Some of the questions she ponders are, "Didn't casework principles really apply in a school?" "What made a school and an agency so different?" "Was there something to the Superintendent's concern that she had not had teacher's training and had not worked in schools—knew them only from her own successful student days and, of course, working with them during eight years of social work experience in agencies?" Reviewing the week past, she could recall some days that were good and some days that were bad:

> Bitterly Joan remembered the "worst" morning. Mr. Upton was the favorite principal in her four schools, until that morning. She'd walked into his office eagerly—only to be met by "Good morning, Joan. You'll find a referral on Bobby Hopkins in your box. He's such a friendly little boy we'd hoped we could keep him in school but I guess he's as feeble-minded as his brothers. Will you please get him over to the state school for evaluation right away." . . . Being told the diagnosis and ordered to carry out a pre-determined plan was bad enough but she nearly wept when Mr. Upton said, "And I'm sorry we had to exclude Joe while you were over at the clinic for that consultation yesterday. I know how hard you've been working with his mother to help her see that he needs to go to the clinic and I'd hoped we could keep him in kindergarten until she could understand the need, but he exploded all over the place yesterday—nearly strangled Sue, screamed until the whole class was on edge . . . and then kicked me black and blue when I took him home. He is such a huge

---

12 Unpublished. Miss Taylor is Associate Professor, School of Social Work, University of Michigan, Ann Arbor.

six-year-old that I'm sure it isn't good for him to be in the kindergarten class but he just can't sit still long enough to be in the first grade. I had to tell his mother we couldn't have him in school until we had a psychiatrist's statement that he was well enough for school."

The social worker continues to ask herself questions and to reflect upon her role:

What was the team here? Who was the captain? Who called the signals? Could she be a team member when the captain was an educator and knew less about dynamic psychology than she did? When he had less concern about children's emotional needs than she did? . . . Here, the program and staff were all primarily planned for scholastic and social achievement of "normal" children. "Her" children took more than their share of time and energy and understanding and most of them produced fewer of the rewards the community expected than most children. Certainly the perspective of the school staff was geared to more expectation of conformity and achievement and control of children than she knew in social agencies. Which was right? Suddenly, she knew that both were right in their own time and place. A society needed to train its children into conformity to its standards and goals and its public schools were established for this primary purpose. Laws require children to attend and to meet school requirements. Social agencies were established primarily to help those persons who were having special problems in handling or achieving society's expectations. So she represented one point of departure in a setting preoccupied with the other! She really couldn't expect the school to change its assignment— only to allow her enough room to make her contribution toward the school's goal—and, of course, that was really her goal, too.

The social worker's problem of finding his place in the school is additionally complicated for him when role conflicts exist within the educational system and when he is not able to define and interpret his role as the social worker-in-the-school. The workshops found great diversity among school social workers with regard to their own practice in the school and such questions were asked as "What are the core functions of the school social worker?" "What special competencies are required?" Unless the school social worker can answer these questions, it is obvious that he cannot function effectively in a social system as complex as the school in which members of another discipline, education, depend upon him to work with them toward their goals and expect him to interpret to them how this can be done. (Role expectations are discussed further in Chapter 7.)

formed groups and natural groups

The school structure can also be examined from the standpoint of groupings of children and personnel for educational purposes. While the basis is different from group formation found in social group work, the group in the classroom, arranged by age-grade, serves as a socializing experience for the child.

Recent research into the mental hygiene aspects of group learning gives evidence that teachers are becoming interested in "group dynamics" and in the use of class sociometry, grouping procedures, and means of using group guidance for the child who is isolated by his classmates. It is reported that schools of education are giving more attention to orienting students to personality dynamics and the relationship process in teaching.[13] In the meantime, social workers whose education now generally includes some understanding of group interaction and leader-group relationships can bring such knowledge to the school.

The social worker, when he first enters the school, is impressed by the organization of the entire personnel into groups, and by the time limits which the schedule imposes upon everyone. Here is a description from a group of school social workers:

A new worker is likely to be stunned by the throngs of children tramping through a school building and the throngs of school staff concerned with them. This is in real contrast to sitting down in a private office, where you see the individual alone. This being in physical closeness to the children, when they are in another person's hands, necessitates much self awareness on our part and constant effort to know what values to place first.

Learning what we are to do is a problem. The first day, the supervisor may introduce the new worker to the principal. He is likely to terminate the visit after politely expressing welcome by indicating a room in which you are to work. Then what? Everyone else is occupied with rooms full of children. How do you "catch" them to explain what you are there to do? They may resent your walking into their classroom. Just getting acquainted becomes a project, introducing yourself at lunch or at coffee while learning the folkways of each school. For example, an empty chair at a lunch table does not mean that *you* can sit there—it may be the regular place for the teacher who is on hall duty and will be coming in later.[14]

---

13 William G. Hollister, "Current Trends in Mental Health Programming in the Classroom," *Journal of Social Issues*, Vol. 15, No. 1 (January 1959), pp. 54–55.

14 Minutes of the Portland, Oregon, School Social Work Section, NASW, as reported by Mrs. Julia K. Hoffman, Chairman, July 1, 1960.

The groupings in the school are *natural* as well as formal. Children form friendship groups, sometimes gangs, to serve their peer group interests. Teachers, too, form subgroups and cliques which can support or hinder good administration. Much communication goes on in an organization through the "grapevine," or through gossip. While this is sometimes inaccurate, it gives release to pent-up emotions or serves to bind a group together. The social worker can learn a great deal about a particular school from listening to this kind of informal communication. He needs to be careful, however, not to become identified with any one clique in the school if he expects to work with all of the teachers.

time limits

The school is highly structured into units of time. These include the daily schedule of classes, the semester, the school year. The social worker can often use these time intervals to set goals, evaluate progress, plan ahead with school staff for "testing periods"; for example, summer vacation can be used to sustain progress thus far made. Conscious control of the use of time is essential.

Certain problems also arise from the school's organization. One is the difficulty the social worker has in finding allowance of time for interviews with children and staff. The child must be excused from his class in order to keep an appointment with the social worker. The elementary school teacher frequently has no free periods and must see the worker after the school day or interrupt her teaching to confer. A social worker may cause considerable resentment by walking unannounced into a classroom, the teacher's own province. This problem is described by a respondent to the School Social Work Section, NASW, questionnaire:

> It's the difficulty of finding time to consult. This is more a problem on the elementary level, rather than the secondary level where most teachers have a free period a day. On the elementary level, our teachers have no free periods other than those before and after school, coffee breaks and lunch periods. After school periods are usually crammed full of staff meetings, education association meetings, equivalent credit courses, workshops, extension courses, etc., until there is hardly a day in the week when there is not some after school mandatory meeting. Before school periods are usually spent with plan books, teaching materials, etc.

Unless administrative plans include allowance for school social work service within the time schedule so that children and teachers are not unduly interrupted in their work, it would seem that the administration has not really accepted this service as a part of the school program.

In concluding the discussion of the dynamics and problems in use of school structure, it should be pointed out that the four aspects presented—bureaucracy, role perception and expectations, natural and formed groups, and time limits—are only selected examples of how understanding of structure provides the social worker with a new dimension in practice. While the child continues to be the primary client in the school, all of the forces surrounding him need to be worked with to strengthen the social worker's activity in his behalf.

The conference noted that safeguards exist in school social work practice against the social worker's overemphasis upon a single approach to problem-solving, such as psychotherapy or environmental manipulation, or quick referral to an outside agency. Safeguards mentioned included the need for the social worker to collaborate with other school personnel in making use of available resources and sources of help within the school and community. The fact that social service is often time-limited makes it necessary for the social worker quickly to consider the child in his total environment. It was also noted that social work can be a force in participating in effecting changes in a social institution such as the school, since the worker is in first-hand contact with both school and community and is aware of the effects of rapid social change upon families and children, and also of the effects of the curriculum upon individual children.

knowledge, skill, and attitudes needed

To make constructive use of the structure of the school, the social worker needs:

Knowledge of:
Administration, its philosophy and procedures, in a bureaucracy; much useful knowledge about administration is available from social science, public administration, social psychology, as well as from social work literature

The school as a social institution and the types of institutional behavior which it embodies

School expectations of children and effects upon children

Realities and consequences of behavior as well as insight into the meaning of behavior

Constructive use of time limits

Limit setting as a means for furthering growth

Educational theories about curriculum building, discipline, promotion, retention, and so on

Planned change—how a social institution grows, develops, changes

Role of the social worker in a multidiscipline bureaucracy in relation to roles of other personnel

Groups and their place in social organizations for children and adults.

Skill in:

Establishing a relationship with children and others within time limits

Holding to the focus of the school in giving service

Interpretation of the social worker's role to children and school personnel

Problem-solving approach to groups and total school situation, as well as to individuals.

Attitudes of:

Self-awareness of feelings about schools, teachers, education

Emotional acceptance of, and identification with, the basic purpose and program of the host setting

Emotional acceptance of, and identification with, the social work role in that setting

Willingness to learn from, and work with, personnel whose contributions are different from those of the social worker

Emotional acceptance and creativity in use of such features of structure as both time and authority.

prevention as an activity
of the school social worker

Mental hygiene in the school has long been of great concern to all of the helping professions as well as to educators.[15]   The school has been seen as a most fruitful field for early detection and preventive treatment of incipient behavior disorders since all children attend school during formative years.

The school social worker can participate in several ways in activities that will promote mental health and mental hygiene. These include:

differential service to individuals

The "relatively normal" reactive problems of relatively normal children can often be handled so that the problem does not become extreme or internalized permanently.   The child and his parents or his teachers can be helped to find the dynamics of the disturbing symptoms and to work together on their alleviation or resolution.

---

[15] *Journal of Social Issues,* Vol. 15, No. 1 (1959) is devoted to the subject, "Mental Health in the Classroom." The contributions of various influences and writers to the present increased interest in mental health in the school are traced in pp. 1–5.

(*See* Appendix A, Record 6, Preventive Service to a Child in Kindergarten, p. 233.) The social worker needs to accept preventive intervention as a function quite as much as treatment of pathology.

The consultation process with teachers can be a means of helping the teacher in the application of mental health principles in the classroom, as well as a way to broaden his understanding of deviant behavior through co-operative effort on the problems of a specific child. What the teacher learns affects many children over a period of time. (Further discussion of consultation is presented in Chapter 7.)

differential service to groups

If the social worker sees the larger problem that lies behind each individual problem he works with, he will be aware of certain community situations. These may arise from population shifts such as from South to North with increase in racial contacts, families from rural areas adjusting to large urban centers, early marriages, changes in the labor market and their effects upon youth. The impact of social changes such as these is seen daily in the schools.

Group sessions with children centering on such common problems as school rules, vocational objectives, sex, movement from elementary to junior high—these and many other matters which are of concern to children and youth might be discussed so that fears and anxieties could be anticipated and difficulties dealt with. A development of considerable promise is group sessions with parents whose children have common problems.

The psychologist J. McV. Hunt reported at the conference that experiments and studies of work with parents and children together have been successful in reducing drop-out rates when the problem discussed was vocational objectives. He believed that "family group therapy" holds great promise for the future. He suggested that the increasing professionalization of social work had produced rigidity—as professionalization always tends to do—and that care should be taken that social work does not lose inventiveness, especially since social change produces new problems that need invention of new techniques.

referral

Improved referral process with community agencies was also seen as a means for checking behavior difficulties and providing better continuity in the services of the community and the school. In this sense, referral could be considered a preventive measure. The etiology of certain problems such as delinquency can be traced to neighborhoods known both to the school and to community agencies. The co-operative projects of the Neighborhood Youth Association in Los Angeles [16] and the Group Therapy Project for Delinquent Adolescents in Philadelphia [17] are only two of many school-community enterprises which are accomplishing more than either agency could accomplish alone. Often it is the school social service department which proposes the initiation of such a service.

knowledge, skill, and attitudes needed

If prevention is accepted as a function of the social worker, he will need knowledge, skill, and attitudes such as the following:

Knowledge of:
Crises in normal growth and development which may lead to ill health and how to handle them therapeutically
Psychology of the teacher and trends in teacher education as they bear on mental health principles
Group interaction and group discussion techniques
Research methods which are useful in assessing etiology of social problems observed as underlying children's school problems.

Skill in:
Working with children from divergent cultural backgrounds
Mobilizing teacher, principal, and others in preventive enterprises
Group organization and leadership
Community relations in behalf of school children
Working with the total school situation while working also with particular children
Use of referral process.

Attitudes of:
Willingness continuously to learn new developments in both social work and education
Sharing knowledge and skills with teacher but also taking from teacher some of her knowledge and skill in relation to the child in the classroom
Open-mindedness in finding new ways to serve child and school.

school-community relations

The school social worker is often the link between the school and the community for services to children and parents, for communi-

---

[16] Neighborhood Youth Association, "Changing the Behavior of Hostile, Delinquency-prone Adolescents" (Los Angeles: Neighborhood Youth Association, August 1960), mimeographed.
[17] Taber, *op. cit.*, pp. 24–26.

cating to other social agencies and professions the purposes, values, and goals of the school with its opportunities and its limits. He also brings back to the school information about the lacks in community services which the school, as a social force, might help the community to provide. While social work in all fields carries such responsibilities in greater or less degree, this function is especially significant in school social work because education is a basic social institution, everyone has had the experience of attending school, and the interests and welfare of normal children, as well as of those who suffer from some disadvantage, are safeguarded. All citizens have a stake in good education and good schools. (*See* Chapter 3.)

In giving his primary service, social casework, the school social worker has certain specifics of practice which are significant for all social workers.

evaluation of community resources

While the school social worker's service is limited to the child-in-school, the range of problems he meets covers the whole gamut of human dysfunction. In order for the child to have a chance at some measure of wholesome environment, the social worker must know his community resources in all of their provisions and lacks, and must use them as extensions of service of the school in behalf of the child. Such problems as financial assistance, marriage counseling, foster home placement require treatment which the school cannot undertake directly, but which can be obtained from public or private agencies in the community. The PTA is a strong resource in helping to work out programs for gaps in services.

The social worker needs to know how to make studies of agency programs, policies, and procedures and how to keep a live file of such information to be used as needed.

referral process

A high quality of casework knowledge and skill is required to make the transference of the parent and child from the school social worker, with whom they may have a relationship of trust, to an unknown social worker in a distant agency. The school is in the neighborhood, it is a respected institution of the community, and service from the school can be accepted, often without too much hesitation. Middle-class culture which places great value on independence, "respectability," and competition for success makes it difficult for a father or mother to admit inadequacy in some area of living and to take help. Similarly, it is difficult for middle-class parents to think of their child as needing psychiatric treatment which may be available only outside the school. (*See* Appendix A, Record 7, Referral to a Community Agency, p. 243.) When the child's difficulty involves some phase of sexuality, it creates feelings of guilt, since morality and sexual morality are often regarded as synonymous. Lower-class culture is more tolerant of sexual problems and of physical aggression; parents may seem "shiftless" and "lax" by middle-class standards. Minority groups constitute another clientele who require special understanding. The anthropologist Ruth Landes pointed out at the conference that matriarchal culture, which is characteristic of lower-class culture in industrialized societies, should be understood in its consequences for mothers and children. Since the largest proportion of teachers are from the middle- or lower-middle class (where striving for upward mobility is great), the conduct of a child and his parents may be severely judged.[18] The school social worker, therefore, works on two fronts in effecting a referral: one, the family constellation and the other, the teacher and school situation.

school-community agency collaboration

Administrative knowledge and skill, as well as casework skill, is required in building bridges of service between the school and the community. The social worker must often involve his department and/or school in written agreements. An interesting development in Portland, Oregon, illustrates how sound working agreements that have wide influence in the schools can be developed. Out of felt need for case conferences, the School Social Work Department and the Community Child Guidance Clinic extended their concerns to policies and conferences that reached beyond the needs of particular children. A report states:

> The Community Child Guidance Clinic, in developing a working relationship with the School Social Work Department, has placed emphasis on adequate referral information from the schools, as well as dynamically useful diagnostic information from the clinic to the schools. By mutual agreement, a referral form has been worked out so that the clinic has consistent collateral data for its use. In addition, there have been regular meetings for several years, on a bi-weekly basis, between the chief social worker of the clinic and the school social work staff. These meetings have served to evaluate more carefully the real emergencies in the face of a growing waiting list for the clinic, they have helped to establish priority of service, and to evaluate more adequately the usefulness of clinic referrals in certain cases.

---

[18] W. Lloyd Warner, *American Life, Dream and Reality* (Chicago: University of Chicago Press, 1953), Chapter IV, "The Family in a Class System," pp. 81–102.

This kind of working relationship was extended to include other parts of the school personnel.

As an outgrowth of conferences in individual cases, both clinic and school social workers felt the need to include all of the Department of Child Services (of which the Social Work Department is a part) within the school system. As a result, the director of child services, the school psychologist, the supervisor and assistant of the Social Work Department from the schools, and the clinic director, chief clinical psychologist, and chief social worker from the clinic meet at monthly intervals to discuss policies which could improve service to the individual child.

Among the outcomes of this administrative policy committee's deliberations are: (1) a "screening committee" made up of representatives from remedial psychological, medical, and social service staffs in the school which meets monthly to review problems in differential diagnosis, to determine optimal service to the child, and so on, and (2) research and experimental projects.

The report concludes:

The Social Work Department has been the medium of communication between school and clinic. Increasing use has been made of conferences which include not only the social service and clinic staff but also interested school personnel such as principal, classroom teacher, remedial teacher, nurse, and others. This device has served as a teaching vehicle to increase the insight of school personnel into behavior difficulties in all children.[19]

Taber reports a number of successful efforts in Philadelphia to mobilize community resources to make the school social services more effective than they would otherwise be.[20]

knowledge, skill, and attitudes needed

It seems evident that school-community relations require a high quality of social work practice. Desirable knowledge, skill, and attitudes include:

Knowledge of:
Community structure and organization, including the historical evolution of welfare service programs; effects of tradition as well as legal sanctions
Research methods by which community studies can be made

---

[19] Memorandum to the writer from Cora Bamford, Supervisor, School Social Work Department, Portland Public Schools, July 14, 1960.

[20] Taber, *op. cit.*, pp. 30–32.

Official and voluntary agency-relationships and agreements; structures and functions

Middle-class behavior and expectations of reactions to acceptance of service; reactions of teachers to lower-class behavior

Casework as a method of giving services to children and parents

Administrative procedures and how to develop working agreements with agencies most frequently needed to supplement school's services.

Skill in:

Community organization and administration

Interpretation and public relations

Public speaking

Holding to function while mobilizing supplemental services in the community

Developing collaborative relationships with community agencies, and knowing when to terminate activity on a particular case.

Attitudes of:

Responsibility for understanding and examining the program of the school and for contributing out of social work knowledge and experience to bring about change

Responsibility to understand the school as a part of the larger community in order to implement more effective interaction between the two for the welfare of children

Willingness to take legal action if that is the best way to help a child and his family

Willingness to share responsibility for the child with others.

concluding comments

The characteristics of school social work practice presented in this chapter have implications for social work education. The significance of these aspects of practice for social work education will be discussed in Part III (Chapters 8 and 9). Before undertaking this analysis, however, two more major activities—collaboration and consultation—must be discussed to round out the description of school social work practice. They are so important that the following chapter is devoted to them.

COLLABORATION AND CONSULTATION

7

Collaboration and consultation are activities that are inherent in the practice of all social work; they call for special kinds of professional skill that must be further developed.[1] In school social work practice, an understanding of certain relevant concepts—role expectations and role relations, and communication and confidentiality in client relationships—is especially important, since the school setting requires some adaptations in their use.

In varying degree, collaboration and consultation are a part of practice in all social welfare agencies, but they can be most clearly discerned and studied as professional processes in so-called secondary settings in which a number of disciplines are employed to give service to the clientele. Medical and psychiatric social workers, for example, who practice primarily in hospitals, clinics, and other medical settings, were the first groups, perhaps, to analyze the social work component in total patient care and the relation of the contribution of social workers to those of physicians, psychiatrists, psychologists, and other medical staff members. Only relatively recently, however, has the literature about collaboration progressed

---

[1] This chapter is based, in large part, on a paper by Eleanor Loeb, "Some Concepts for Interdisciplinary Practice," presented at the Conference on the Contribution of School Social Work to Social Work Education, Highland Park, Illinois, August 2–8, 1959, and published in abbreviated form in *Social Work*, Vol. 5, No. 4 (October 1960), pp. 83–90. The quotations in this chapter are from the full paper, rather than from the shorter published version. The author has also drawn on the conference workshop discussions, comments of consultants in sociology, psychiatry, psychology, anthropology, and social group work, and other sources.

from description to analysis of the process.[2]   Consultation as a process is also receiving increasing attention from social work educators and practitioners.

As school social workers have recognized the extent to which their service is dependent upon collaborative and consultative activities with teachers, principals, and other school personnel, they have felt the need for more knowledge of, and skill in, the use of these processes.   Accordingly, the program for the conference included a paper by Eleanor Loeb which describes some of the concepts that emerged from efforts of Loeb and colleague Ursula Lewis to teach students in a school of social work how to work in a multidiscipline setting, in this instance a psychiatric hospital.   So provocative and relevant to social work education were the findings that it seems worthwhile to discuss the concepts developed in the context of interdisciplinary practice in the school setting.

collaboration

Collaboration is the process of interaction that takes place when two or more persons work together on the solution of a problem and share responsibility for the results.   Therefore, to work closely and effectively in an interdisciplinary setting, members of all the professions involved must have recognized expertness in their respective fields and be able to distinguish their role expectations, one from another, in terms that are mutually acceptable.   When this kind of understanding prevails, participants can define their role relations and each one can behave appropriately.   This statement by Loeb helps to make clear the meaning of collaboration:

> Collaboration in interdisciplinary practice involves a division of the total task by reason of the authority of knowledge and expertness in specialized areas assigned to various participant roles. . . . The collaborative relation, then, is an interaction characterized by division of labor, equal responsibility for each of the role partners in performance of his share of the group task, equal administrative authority, and differentiation of authority on the basis of expertness.   Group task goals are binding on all the collaborators.

---

[2] Loeb notes: "Early writings were chiefly descriptive. . . . Other contemporary writings described the climate or social and emotional milieu prerequisite for successful team operation. A few of the latter articles were beginning to identify attitudes destructive of team work. . . . Most frequently mentioned of these attitudes were competitiveness, hostility, and attitudes about authority." *See* Maurice Connery, "The Climate of Effective Teamwork," *Journal of Psychiatric Social Work*, Vol. 22, No. 2 (April 1953), and Arthur Leader, "Some Problems in Collaboration with Psychiatric Residents," *Journal of Psychiatric Social Work*, Vol. 24, No. 4 (September 1955).

As a starting point with the students, Loeb and Lewis used a record of a series of social worker-psychiatric resident conferences, recorded by an experienced social worker over a two-year period. During this time, three psychiatric residents were on rotation. With the first one, the social worker looked to the resident for instructions about what should be done in working toward discharge plans for a paranoid patient. The resident responded with rather explicit directions. The social worker found it difficult, however, to evoke any involvement from the next two residents. Loeb states:

> The reaction of the class to the recorded material was very different from what Miss Lewis and I were beginning to see, namely, that the social worker had thought of the psychiatrist as teacher or supervisor, had worked happily with the first man, who had responded in those terms. With the second resident, we saw an insecure worker, faced with a changed situation and a need to adapt to that, defensively maneuvering to control the situation and dictate the team's future work with the patient. Next, we saw the worker entering into his third interdisciplinary doctor-worker relationship by carrying over some of the hostility evoked by the last experience. . . . The class completely identified with the position taken by the worker. . . . When Miss Lewis and I asked "What do you expect of a psychiatric resident?" a student flared up "Well, he's a doctor, isn't he?" Another student answered thoughtfully, "Yes, but he's not yet really a psychiatrist. He's just learning. He's in a student role just like us." That is how a student backed us into the concepts of status, role, and role expectation: what does one expect of a doctor? of a medical learner? of a teacher? of a social worker?

Loeb describes the gradual unfolding of student understanding of the hospital as a social system, of the use of concepts of status, role, and role expectations, and of some of the derivative insights. From this material, workshop discussions, and other sources, the following concepts which have meaning for the collaborative process are summarized.

role relations

The long-term objectives of group task goals can usually be identified and agreed upon without difficulty: the teacher and the social worker, for example, both aim to help the child to learn and grow. This goal is one that develops out of the purpose and values of the school. An important characteristic of the collaborative process, however, is that the various participants engage not only in activities in interaction with one another but also work by themselves in operations that are aimed at furthering the group goals. The *role* of each is different. To make progress toward the goal, each participant must understand what the other is doing.

Loeb quotes Merton and others in defining role as "a complex set of anticipated behaviors," and "a pattern of attitudes and actions," [3] and states that role has a transactional dimension in that "any item of behavior must always be placed in some self-other context." She concludes:

> Role concept, then, conceives of the behavior and attitude of a role performer as interaction with another role performer, a role partner. The implication for interdisciplinary practice is obvious since such practice is essentially nothing more than interaction between or among different disciplines.

Furthermore, role behavior and attitudes are learned behavior and attitudes within the framework of each profession's status or position within a social system.

The group work consultant at the conference, Florence Ray, raised the question of the extent to which participants in interdisciplinary practice engaged in "group process" thinking in working toward group task goals. If there is conscious effort to interrelate or integrate thinking, movement toward goals will be more rapid because all will be moving in the same direction while each participant will be performing his unique part. This process of interaction includes these elements:

1. Group morale is high when all members of a group subscribe to a goal, need each other for achievement of the goal, and feel some movement toward the goal;

2. Each individual on the team has a status or position in the social system, determined in part by his defined status in the structure of the organization, his power in decision-making, his personal qualities and cultural background, his role as perceived by himself and others;

3. The location of responsibility for leadership must be known and accepted. The social worker has social functioning as his special province and must take initiative for that aspect of the team activity, regardless of the discipline at the top of the hierarchy. To do this, he must respect the contribution of other members of the team, must understand realistically the approach of the other disciplines, and must be able to work with them toward solution of the problem. At the same time he must not give up his values or self expectations, otherwise his contribution to the team will be lost.

---

[3] Robert K. Merton, *Social Theory and Social Structure* (Glencoe, Illinois: The Free Press, 1957), and Theodore R. Sarbin, "Role Theory," in Gardner Lindzey, ed., *Handbook of Social Psychology* (Cambridge, Mass.: Addison-Wesley Publishing Co., 1954).

Unless the social worker has clarity about his role as a social worker and as a team member and unless he has strong identification with his own profession, he may find it difficult to hold his own with others who represent the core operation of the organization. This is true especially if the school social worker, for example, has relatively low status in the hierarchy. Attitudes essential for good interdisciplinary practice include clarity about and emotional acceptance of: (1) the basic purpose of the host setting, (2) the place of social work in that setting, (3) the goal being sought by the collaborative team, (4) the function and role of other members of the collaborative team, and (5) the concept of shared responsibility.

The fact that status and role in the school are highly structured affects the collaborative process. In the individual school, authority is vested in the principal and the extent to which he shares it varies with his democratic or authoritarian philosophy. The status of the school social worker is not yet clearly defined and he must usually begin by building a working relationship between himself and other members of the staff. While eventually his role-set in the school needs to be understood and put into written form by the administration, the school social worker must first create in the minds of colleagues an image of his profession's competencies through demonstration and interpretation. This means that he must have skill in involving principal and teachers in his contribution to helping the child in school.

The individual school as a social system has the potentials for strengths and weaknesses found in any social system. With the principal as head, rivalries may develop among groups of teachers or between professions. If the school social worker is accepted by the principal, he works closely with the principal and may eventually be given a certain amount of authority to act on his own. This may lead to jealousy on the part of other personnel. A group of school social workers have described their relationship to teachers in this way:

We must be aware of what the teacher thinks of our having the ear of the principal. She may be fearful that we are judging her, personally or professionally, or that we will repeat her confidences to someone else. We must manifest understanding and sympathy concerning the many problems, demands, and short-comings as well as appreciation of the strengths and interests in each classroom, the gym, cafeteria, etc.

Individual differences are as characteristic of teachers as of anyone else. They vary in their backgrounds, interests, experience, strengths and weaknesses just as one school varies from another even within the same school system. The school social worker must be flexible, must clarify his own function for himself and the school staff. Success is in proportion to how the demands of each particular individualized situation are met.

The teachers and staff must make their own plans and decisions. The social worker can encourage, support, guide and bring out aspects of the problems, make recommendations, but frequently he does not make the decisions. This is kept in mind in determining whether a teacher should make a referral, whether the school social worker should accept it, what is to be done, evaluation of progress, and when to discontinue service.[4]

Obviously, the social worker has a number of role relations with teachers and others in the school. Appropriate professional behavior for these should be learned as part of professional education. Loeb comments:

Their [the students'] behavioral processes existed within and were in interaction with a network of defined and undefined, structured and unstructured, formal and informal relationships that constituted the social system of their agencies, whether hospital, court, clinic, or school. Recognition that they were a dynamic part of an interactional system constituted a base for all subsequent learning. At the same time, this concept was not one that students could absorb in one piece. Rather, it was incorporated bit by bit as students examined each interactional process and identified their responsibilities, rights, and obligations in each in the light of three sets of interdependent criteria: the values and expectations of their own profession, the values and expectations of other personnel, and the values, expectations, and structural provisions for interaction between them and within the agency as social system.

It seems evident that the student placed for field instruction in a multidiscipline setting must be mature and experienced. While he is learning skill in individual diagnosis and interviewing, he has to extend his understanding and struggle for skill in working with all others who have a share in the client's welfare. As Loeb says, "We were asking students to give up a professional ethnocentricity . . . to share before they had the security of knowledge and skills in their own profession that would enable sharing."

role expectations

Role relations are dependent, in great measure, upon each member of the team having accurate expectations of his own role and those

---

[4] Minutes of the Portland, Oregon, School Social Work Section, NASW, as reported by Mrs. Julia K. Hoffman, Chairman, July 1, 1960.

of others. Loeb found that as students discussed what they expected of a doctor, they came to realize that most of their expectations were socially and culturally determined, that is, students had been influenced by personal experiences and observations. In general, however, the status "doctor" carried authority, high social standing, and prestige. Loeb states:

> In time, the students came to see that they were displacing expectations consonant with one role in the set for doctor on to other roles in the set. They were attributing the authority, prestige, and standing associated with doctor as leader in community, doctor as therapist and healer, doctor as member of the upper-middle class, doctor as administrator, to roles of student-doctor and collaborator in collaborative interaction with themselves. They were thus illustrating a characteristic of role, namely, that the total role-set or network of roles is interrelated and that qualities and attributes of one role thus become associated with other roles by a sort of haloing process. As a consequence, role expectations become distorted.

Distortion in role expectations can be of the self-role or of the role partner, but both are usually involved because of the reciprocal relations of self-and-other-expectations. In working with doctors, the social worker is in danger of conceiving of his role as subordinate to that of a superior, the doctor.

If we examine the role expectations of social workers in relation to educators, a somewhat different set of expectations emerges. While contacts with doctors as children or as adults occur in most people's lives because of crisis (illness), contacts with teachers, principals, and other school personnel are a universal and normal experience. Furthermore, contact with many different educators over the years may leave mixed impressions. Loeb found it was more difficult to draw from the social work students their expectations of teachers than of doctors. Social workers and teachers, like members of other professional groups, are likely to carry stereotypes of one another's professions. Since the two professions are usually rated as having middling prestige when occupations are ranked, it is not surprising that neither commands the high respect of the other. In a study of the prestige rating for 90 occupations, for example, physician received a score of 93 while public school teacher was rated 78 and "welfare worker" was rated 70.[5] Both teachers and social workers complain of the lack of public recognition and their professional

---

[5] Harold L. Wilensky and Charles N. Lebeaux, *Industrial Society and Social Welfare* (New York: Russell Sage Foundation, 1958), p. 310. The figures quoted are from a study made in 1947, but the authors quote two other more limited studies made in 1953 which corroborate the middling prestige of social work.

organizations are concerned with the problem. This marginal status of social work and education may lead to a sense of rivalry between social worker and teacher in the school. (*See* Chapter 4).

In order to enter into a collaborative relationship, social worker and teacher each need to have a set of organized expectations of self-roles and statuses, and expectations of the roles and statuses of the other person. Loeb found that the most common stumbling block for social work students was their misunderstanding of authority and power attributes which they wrongly ascribed to themselves and their role partners. Basic concepts here are that authority and power reside in the office and not in the person, that distortion of role expectations occurs when the network of roles or total role-set is not understood. Qualities and assets of one role may become associated with other roles by a sort of haloing process, as in the case of the resident psychiatrist whose authority and power was equated with that of full-fledged doctor for whom high social standing and prestige had been haloed.

In an effort to help students understand the authority associated with roles, Loeb undertook an analysis of the sources and degrees of authority and influence.[6] These include, among others, the concepts of authority which were discussed in Chapter 6—authority derived from law, administrative authority, professional authority, authority of personality, and authority of relationship. Loeb's comments on these add insight, *e.g.*, with respect to authority derived from law and the authority the agency derives from it. She states that authority from these two sources give the social worker in interdisciplinary practice a minimum of difficulty "provided the worker has clear knowledge of the prescribed authority patternings. This becomes largely a matter of formulation and communication." With respect to professional authority, she notes, "Expertise bestows the right to give orders and make decisions but confines that right and further limits the authority to the roles in which that knowledge is agreed to have pertinence, the areas of special competence. . . ." When there is ambiguity about areas of competence, however, serious distortions of role expectations may occur.

To these sources of authority, Loeb adds *status in the hierarchy;* *e.g.*, the teacher who is head of a department will have greater authority than the person lower in the hierarchy. Closely related to this status is the prestige and ranking which is accorded to certain

---

[6] Authority has been defined as "the power to make decisions which guide the actions of another. . . . It involves behaviors on the part of both superior and subordinate." *See* Herbert A. Simon, *Administrative Behavior* (New York: Macmillan Company, 1947), p. 125. *See also* Talcott Parsons, "Motivation of Economic Activities," in Robert Dubin, *Human Relations in Administration* (Englewood Cliffs, N.J.: Prentice-Hall, Inc., 1951), p. 30.

positions, thus reflecting the social values of the group. Another determinant of authority, of special interest to school social workers, is the "distance from the core operation of a task group or social system." In Loeb's words:

Authority can originate from the degree to which a role is involved in the central task. In a school, education constitutes the central task, and teachers of all the disciplines are the most closely involved in that task. . . . Regardless of degree of competence in their own fields of operation, social workers are generally at a considerable remove from the core tasks of the school and the hospital. Social work in settings in which social work itself is not the core task offers many gratifications. It rarely, if ever, offers the gratification of responsibility for work which is considered most important in that institution. This is a reality with which workers have to come to terms before they can successfully meet role expectations in such settings.

Influence over others, not sufficiently institutionalized to be called "authority," can be found in the prestige, fame, or reputation of a role partner. Moreover, the subjective needs of the social worker may endow a role partner with power and authority out of his own "insecurity and powerlessness," for instance, when the social worker looks to the psychiatrist for direction. Still another kind of influence is that of seniority in time within the agency, when the newcomer tends to regard everyone with whom he interacts as more powerful and knowledgeable than he, beyond the realities of the situation. Loeb concludes:

Mapping out authority patterns . . . helped students locate themselves in their professional relations with other disciplines. It forced them to involve themselves at an ego level in their learning and role performance with their professional and non-professional partners. It also set them off on the trail of agency structure in terms of administrative provisions for interdisciplinary work and reinforced learning from their classes in administration. Their purposeful attention to their own activities with role partners from other disciplines gave vital meaning to the intertwining of formal and informal communications and interaction channels. Not the least incidental accrual was the obligation of students to become alive to the content, educational requirements, task goals, values, and role expectations of their role partners.

communication

From the foregoing discussion, it is evident that the collaborative process is greatly dependent upon the ability of the participants to understand the meaning of what each is saying, to understand one another's language. Organized effort depends not only upon the use of words but also upon the referents which the person speaking has in mind when he uses certain words. Personal observation provides an illustration. At a state committee meeting of educators and of a group composed of social workers, PTA representatives, and a psychiatrist, the subject under discussion was mental hygiene in the schools. The educators were resistant to the group's proposal that the schools take advantage of the consultation service available through the state department of mental hygiene, until a PTA representative spoke of the "school in the community," of the need for the school to relate itself to community resources. At once there was a positive response from the educators—the trigger phrase, "school in the community," was part of their professional vocabulary.

Too often in interdisciplinary practice, professional language is a barrier to communication. The same words may have different connotations to the members of different disciplines. It becomes necessary, therefore, for all members of the team to have a working comprehension of the common language of the institution; *e.g.,* in the school, the meaning of "cumulative record," "home room," "discipline," "ability grouping of children," and other terms. Team members also need to listen and learn the meaning of one another's technical language to the extent that it has bearing on group goals and tasks. Otherwise, professional terminology and mannerisms may serve to isolate team members from one another.

Workshop discussions brought out a number of helpful ideas about communication in the school. The school social worker must have skill in interpreting his role-set and its relation to those of other staff members. In doing this, he may find that behavior can be a more effective means of communication than speech; that is, he demonstrates through help to a child what his role is and what he does. In the early stages of his work, it was said, he must be able to listen with understanding to what he is told by the teacher and others, and to do relatively little "telling." The less knowledge the school has of the social worker's function, the more important it is that what he says be stated in specific, concrete terms; as understanding grows, he can use more abstract language. The school social worker must at all times strive to be aware of his own emotional attitudes which may affect his formal and informal communication with school personnel. He needs also to keep in mind that personality relationships frequently enter into a situation and may lead to irrational behavior. In the beginning, school personnel may "try out" the social worker's feelings toward children and teachers; some may fear invasion of their roles, others may be fascinated by, and eager to work with, emotional problems even though they have limited preparation.

The effectiveness of communication is, of course, influenced by the personal acceptability of the person making the approach, and his status in the hierarchy. The lower his status, the less likely are his recommendations to carry weight. When the status of the school social worker is low, therefore, he must carefully build a relationship which will bring respect for his contribution and thus raise his status. He may need to go more than halfway in his generosity in recognizing the contribution of others to the solution of a child's problem, but he must never lose sight of what his goals and values are, as they contribute to the group task. Otherwise his contribution is lost. Over-collaboration can be as detrimental as inflexibility.

A case record offers an example of a conference between a teacher and a social worker and illustrates some of the problems in communication and how to work with them.

I had talked with Miss M., Jane's (13 years old, 8B) home-room teacher, about her cumulative record; she offered to stop in my office later today.

When she came into the office, she at once drew up the chair and asked what was the problem with Jane and had she been referred and what have we been helping her with. She seemed much more on the defensive than she had been this morning. Before I could answer she asked if our information was confidential and if she should not ask about it. I said that I felt the more we could talk with her and the other teachers, the more helpful we could be to the children.

I said that Jane had been referred last year by the vice-principal because of frequent absences for rather slight illnesses. We had tried to help with this. Miss M. said rather skeptically that Jane's attendance had improved this year. "Do you think your interviews caused that?" I said that it would be pretty hard for us to prove that we had been the cause of Jane's improved attendance but that was the focus of our work with her. Miss M. asked just what help we had given. Did we arrange for medical care or just what "concrete" help can we say we had given her. I said that was a difficult question to answer because we did not give concrete help. I then explained to her how we saw the death of Jane's father and brother both occurring early last year as affecting Jane's school attendance.

After some further discussion of the causes of the deaths and the mother's wish not to talk with Jane about it, the record continues:

Miss M. said that what the social worker does then is "psychological." I said that it was in a way.

I had lost sight of the fact that Miss M. is a gym teacher and in correlating Jane's fears and illnesses to school adjustment, I brought out that Jane seemed to catch cold every time she went swimming. Miss M. at once rejected this and said that many girls exaggerated in this way because they did not like the set to be

taken out of their hair by going in swimming. She said that many
of them will not or cannot get bathing caps or gym suits. She is
furious with some of the parents and she intends to visit some
of the homes as soon as possible just so the parents will have to
tell her personally that they do not intend to get the children
caps or suits.

I said it must be hard for the girls not to have these things like
everyone else. Miss M. agreed and said they feel different and
quite out of place. She thinks it is not right. She said that she
had been meaning to visit the homes for quite some time. I said
that if she found from her visits that there was some way we could
help with the children's problems, we would be glad to do so.
Miss M. assured me this had nothing to do with attendance. I
said that we are here to help with any problem that is interfering
with the child's school work or his getting along in school and
not just attendance. She was surprised and asked if we could
get the children caps and gym suits. I said we could not do so
ourselves but sometimes we can let parents know what agencies
they can turn to for financial help if that is the difficulty. Miss M.
said that is often the cause since many of the parents in this
district are poor. Also, she said that they do not see the value
in getting the gym suits but of course they could not be blamed
if there were more important things that had to come out of
the budget first. Also, she said the children do not save their
spending money for swimming caps and she felt they could not
be blamed for this either, because when other children get ice
cream, they want it too.

After further discussion about Jane's situation:

Miss M. went on to say there were many other children who were
greater problems than Jane. I asked if she felt there was some
way we could help with any of these children. She asked what I
meant, saying she thought that only the home room teacher
referred the child—or the vice-principal. I said that any teacher
who noticed the difficulty a child was having could refer him to
us. However, the referrals did go through the vice-principal. I
asked if she had some referral blanks. She thought they were
only for attendance reports. I showed her where she could write
in the other kinds of problems. She added that she actually could
refer her "whole home room class" as they were all "dull normals"
and have many difficulties in school. I said that we would be glad
to consider helping any child whom she felt was having more
than the average amount of difficulty. I said that we cannot say
we can solve the problems right away but by working with the
teachers, we could attempt to help the child with the difficulties
he was having in getting along in school.

The period was up and as Miss M. left she said she certainly would refer other children "if you can help them as much as you helped Jane." We agreed, however, that sometimes a call or letter from the teacher is all that is needed to straighten out some situations.

This interview shows the lack of communication in the school social system. The teacher lacks information and her attitudes show apprehension about the unknown. She does not understand the social worker's function and has to test the social worker's response, first through readiness to defend herself and then to retreat if the activities of this unknown person are "confidential" and not to be shared with her. Finally, she challenges the social worker to say just what help she has given Jane. As the social worker shares information about Jane with her, the explanation leads her to say that what the social worker does is "psychological," still a somewhat vague activity. When the social worker accidentally threatens her status by connecting Jane's cold with swimming for which the teacher is responsible, she again becomes attacking, this time of parents, and asserts she will visit the homes, something she is aware that the social worker does. The social worker continues patiently and objectively to interpret the behavior of parents and children and the teacher relaxes and reveals her own sympathy for them. As the social worker offers help with the problem, the discussion reveals that the teacher has thought that the social worker helped only children who were truants from school; furthermore, she did not understand the method of referral.

The social worker had obviously not taken his share of responsibility for communication. At the beginning of the school year he had not routinely established contact with Miss M. to let her know of his previous work with Jane. If he had done so, Miss M. might have been enabled to become a partner in helping Jane much earlier in the year. The social worker showed skill, however, in clarifying and holding to his function while emphasizing the importance of the teacher's role even to the point of concluding that some problems could best be solved by the teacher without the intervention of the social worker.

Communication within a social system like the school is both horizontal and vertical. The social worker must be able to operate skillfully in both directions.

confidentiality

A significant aspect of school social work is the sharing of information with school personnel. The social worker is often in a close and trusting relationship with child and one or both parents, and sometimes with community agencies which have known the family. The school is uniquely the child's own world and his relationships within it—to teachers, other children, and staff members—need to be recognized and safeguarded as he reveals them to the social worker. Perennial questions are, to what extent is information to be shared with teacher, principal, and other school staff members, and how can this best be done? The child's cumulative school record is available to all who may have occasion to work with him. It has value especially in case the child transfers to another school, when he begins a new school year, or when a case is transferred from one social worker to another. How can the social worker contribute to this record and add to its usefulness, and at the same time protect the confidential aspects of client relationships?

Confidentiality in use of information is a part of the casework process and is inherent in the social worker's preparation for practice. Safeguarding what is sometimes referred to as "privileged communication" between social worker and client is taken for granted among social workers with professional training. The Code of Ethics of the National Association of Social Workers includes these pledges:

I respect the privacy of the people I serve.

I use in a responsible manner the information gained in professional relationships.

What problems arise, then, in interdisciplinary settings where members of the team have different frames of reference about behavior and its meaning, where teacher-training has not included emphasis on protection of confidential information as does the training of lawyers, physicians, social workers?

Workshop discussion dealt with these questions to some extent. There was general agreement that teacher and social worker must establish a sense of mutual respect and confidence if the child is to be helped; sharing of information is of utmost importance. The social worker should be guided in sharing information by what contribution it makes in helping the person, especially the teacher, to perform his role better in the child's behalf. Moreover, the social worker should try to transmit his frame of reference concerning confidentiality to the other members of the school staff so that they come to understand the effects of use and misuse of information. Sometimes the teacher or principal may need to know details of a family's interpersonal relationships that affect the child's behavior. Some confidences, however, as the fact that a child was born out of wedlock although the mother is now married, would not be shared when such information does not affect the child's school performance.

School Social Work Practice, the proceedings of the Lake Forest Workshop held in 1956, contains this balanced statement on the subject of sharing information:

The school social worker and teacher should plan together for the kinds of responsibility each will take in trying to help the child with his difficulty. . . .

The school social worker, because of her special competence and skill, is able to help the teacher toward a better understanding of a child's behavior, problems, and needs. It must be recognized as equally important, however, that the teacher will know best how to meet the needs of the child in the classroom situation because of her special competence. . . . The continuing contacts between school social worker and teacher permit them to share, day by day, facts and feelings about the child and his reactions to his school experiences, both in the classroom and with the school social worker. It is important for the teacher to receive the proper interpretation of the school social worker's work with the child so that she can understand the nature and objectives of this relationship. . . .

In this collaborative work with the teacher there are other kinds of information that need to be shared in addition to what is gained directly from working with and observing the child. The school social worker may have acquired facts and impressions from the parents, from home visits, and from contacts with other agencies and resources. The question of confidentiality often arises about sharing certain kinds of information with the teacher whether obtained from the child, his parents, or other sources. The school social worker shares with the teacher the information that will help the child; the fact that it must be shared is handled appropriately with the child, his parents, or other sources. Because so much of the work is of a confidential nature, school social workers, like other social workers, sometimes feel that they have a monopoly on confidentiality and do not realize that teachers and schools, too, have a responsibility to respect and protect confidentiality. It should hardly be necessary to add that sharing of pertinent, personal facts must be on the professional basis which the nature of the service and the setting demand and should never fall into the realm of gossip.[7]

How best to share information with others in the school system is another part of the problem of confidentiality. The school is not a social welfare agency in the usual sense and its records differ in purpose and form from those of a welfare agency. Verbal reports and brief memoranda are used extensively in work with teachers and others. Some type of written report which can be incorporated into the child's cumulative record seems desirable. The form and content of records, however, do not seem to be standardized. A

---

[7] Virginia Quattlebaum, ed., *School Social Work Practice, Proceedings of the Lake Forest Workshop* (New York: National Association of Social Workers, 1958), pp. 14–15.

sample of nine school social work services revealed that four school systems recorded on an average of once on each case, at the time of closing or of transferring the case to another worker, or on referral to another resource; two systems recorded chronologically and regularly on each case; three others recorded following intake and at one other time, either at closing or referral.[8] Consensus seems to be that verbal reports should be given regularly to the teacher and other school personnel during case activity, and that a summary-type of recording useful as a permanent record for the school's purpose should become a part of the child's record. The social worker of necessity, however, keeps working records of each situation for his own use.

In brief, sharing of information with colleagues must always be guided by professional judgment. What is to be shared must be evaluated from the standpoint of relevance to the client's interest at a particular time, and to the use which the role partner can make of the information to enhance his part of the group task. Since the school is not a treatment agency but uses the treatment services of nurse, physician, psychologist, and social worker to help children learn and develop physically and emotionally, it needs selected information that will further its objectives.[9]

Collaboration is central to school social work practice. To understand the collaborative process, the school social worker must understand the meaning and implications of role relations, and role expectations of himself and of his role partners. His knowledge and use of such aids as skillful communication, sharing of information while observing the confidential relationship between himself, children, parents, teachers, and others, are part of the process.

consultation

Consultation is a part of practice that is becoming distinguished from other activities, such as collaboration and supervision.[10] It is of interest in many professional fields.[11] Hamovitch and Green define consultation in this way:

---

[8] "Recording Problems in the School Setting," Panel Discussion, Seattle Public School Social Workers, 1959. (Typescript.)

[9] For a good statement of working relationships *see* Dollie R. Walker, "Use of the Knowledge of the Casework Process in Collaboration with School Personnel," *Social Work*, Vol. 3, No. 3 (July 1958), pp. 97–103.

[10] Grateful acknowledgment is made to M. B. Hamovitch and Rose Green of the faculty of the School of Social Work, University of Southern California, who generously gave "consultation" on this chapter out of their background of seminar and institute teaching on consultation.

[11] *See*, for example, "Consulting with Groups and Organizations," *Journal of Social Issues*, Vol. 15, No. 2 (1959), entire issue. The following areas are listed as in need of further research: "(1) The determiners and effects of *entry*

Consultation is a way of giving advice and counsel to a person on a specific problem in a defined area—advice and counsel which this person is free to accept or reject. Its purpose is to add to and enhance the knowledge and understanding of the particular area on the part of the person seeking the help in order to solve a problem. The consultant does not have ongoing responsibility for the client being consulted about, or for the evaluation of the work of the consultee, or for the development of the program being discussed.[12]

It is evident that consultation differs from collaboration in these ways: (1) the consultant has *expertise* or special knowledge that is desired as help in the solution of a problem, (2) he is not within the task group responsible for ultimate performance in solving the problem, (3) his participation is temporary, that is, it has a point of entry and a point of termination, (4) he may be a member of the staff of the organization or he may be invited in from "outside" for one or more sessions with the consultee, (5) his advice or counsel is not binding on the consultee—his responsibility ends when he has given it and the consultee can make such use of it as seems appropriate, (6) the consultee may be an individual or a group of people.

Medical and psychiatric social workers have for some time been drawn into team relationships with psychiatrists and other physicians as consultants on the social component of a patient's situation. They work with medical staff but not directly with patients. Dr. Gerald Caplan of the Harvard School of Public Health has undertaken research on "mental health consultation" with social workers, psychiatrists, and psychologists as consultants, and teachers, nurses, and child-care workers as consultees. Social psychologists, sociologists, and others in the behavioral sciences have done research on the consultation process with groups, organizations, and communities on problems of social interaction.

Consultation in school social work, as already noted (*see* Chapter 5), is a promising aspect of the social worker's activity. The flood of children in the schools in the 1960's and the shortage of personnel

---

into, attachment to, and withdrawal from social systems, (2) The nature and meaning of *dependency* and counter-dependency, and their correlates, (3) The effects of various kinds of *feedback* upon social systems, (4) The nature of the processes of behavior *change* and resistance to change, (5) The *communication of theory* and experience with a minimum of interpersonal and defensive resistance, (6) The process of role perception, *role allocation,* and role change," p. 3. *See also* Lorene A. Stringer, "Consultation: Some Expectations, Principles, and Skills," *Social Work,* Vol. 6, No. 3 (July 1961), pp. 85–90.

12 M. B. Hamovitch and Rose Green, Institute on Consultation (Sacramento: California State Department of Social Welfare, March-April 1961). (Unpublished.)

are leading educators to consider ways of teaching children with the personnel available, through such aids as teaching machines, audiovisual material, team teaching, and other devices. The social worker, similarly, needs to consider how to extend his services under the same conditions of increased numbers of children and limited staff. Consultation to the teacher to help him work with children who have problems in the classroom would seem to offer possibilities for extension of the school social worker's services. (*See* Appendix A, Record 8, Consultation to a Teacher, p. 249.)

Careful evaluation of a situation must be made before consultation is sought by the teacher or given by the social worker. What criteria might be guides in selection of cases for consultation? Experience suggests a few:

1. When readiness of the teacher to share a problem and to utilize what the social worker has to offer is evident;

2. When the nature of the problem or the adequacy of the teacher indicates that the problem can be lessened or removed through the teacher's efforts;

3. When the child's problem is severe and referral to an outside resource is to be made but time will be required to effectuate such a plan, the social worker may be able to give the teacher support and understanding of the dynamics of the child's behavior so that the teacher can tolerate the situation until the child improves under treatment. The case of Joey (pp. 94–95) is an example of such a problem.

Consultation as a helping process needs further delineation but certain of its outlines are clear. It differs from supervision in that consultation leaves the consultee free to use whatever part of the help given seems to him useful while supervision implies agreement upon how to proceed. When the consultant, for instance, the school social worker, is a part of the social system, there needs to be well understood differences between his activity as a consultant and as a collaborator so that carry-over of one role to another does not confuse the relationship. Hamovitch and Green conclude:

> Where good working relationships are established, however, and the "potential consultant" is seen as a helping, flexible, reasonable person in matters where choices are limited, he may be called in also to provide consultation on matters where his expertness can be helpful, and the consultee can feel comfortable about rejecting the suggestion if he is so inclined.[13]

An essential characteristic of consultation is its limited goal—the aim is not to teach in the large but to bring knowledge and learning to bear on a specific situation for the purpose of helping the consultee solve a problem that is of immediate concern.

---

[13] *Ibid.*

School social workers are often called in when crises arise. A child's behavior may be so disrupting to the school and may harass the teacher or principal to such a point that the school social worker is asked to help in resolving the irritating situation. As a consultant, the social worker accepts at face value the reason for which he is asked to help. As Caplan puts it, he does not make "his own contradictory ideas explicit," but he does define his function so that he has freedom to focus discussion. Under conditions of tension, the consultant should be supporting but not reassuring; he should accept both school staff and school social system in a non-judgmental way.[14] The aim of the consultant is always to build on the strengths of the consultee's role-functioning so that the latter becomes able to perform independently and adequately. The consultant undertakes to give the consultee new awareness and insight into the psychological and environmental needs of a child and into professional techniques for meeting these needs, thus enabling the teacher to deal with the problem. If use of community resources is the problem, the social worker is able to provide specialized knowledge that will enable the administration to make decisions and to take action.

Consultation in most school districts is not a standardized procedure. The school social worker may, in effect, give a teacher consultation when the latter wishes to talk over a child's problem several times but does not make a referral. As noted in *School Social Work Practice:*

> It must be recognized that much of what school social workers label as consultation is not identified as such by teachers. Although some teachers are at a stage in the use of the service to define the help they want, many requests for consultation come to the school social worker as comments, inviting exploration, expressing concern over a specific incident, or in the form of questions concerning the cumulative effect of disturbed behavior of an individual child or group of children.[15]

As teacher education comes to include, more generally than at present, further training in the development and use of a professional self, the teacher will gain a clearer delineation of his role. Such clarification of the professional role of the teacher with problem children should identify limits of his function, the collaborative aspects of it, and the advancement of his teaching role through consultation with the school social worker. The social worker, at the same time, needs to define and make more formal his consultant

---

[14] Gerald Caplan, *Mental Health Aspects of Social Work in Public Health,* based on the Proceedings of an Institute Given by the School of Social Welfare, University of California, Berkeley, June 6–8, 1955, p. 150.

[15] Quattlebaum, *op. cit.,* p. 16.

role in the school, for himself as well as for his role partners. And as he can demonstrate and interpret his profession's competencies, he establishes the base and climate for using the school social worker as a consultant.

Part 3

Implications for

Social Work Education

On the basis of the analysis presented in the foregoing chapters, a summary of what school social work practice has to offer social work education is now possible.[1] Throughout, references have been made to the significance of certain aspects of practice for social work education. What synthesis, of value for all social workers, can now be made of the emphases, the variations in practice, the adaptations in use of common elements of social work content that distinguish the field of school social work practice? What can school social work practice contribute to the curriculum of the professional school?

The thirteen-volume *Social Work Curriculum Study*, published in 1959 by the Council on Social Work Education, would seem to offer a frame of reference for relating school social work practice to professional education. In Volume I, *Objectives of the Social Work Curriculum of the Future,* the major questions selected for study are explained.[2] One of these questions concerns the organization of the curriculum and provides an approach for a discussion of school social work practice and social work education. The areas described are the scientific-philosophical and the methods components of the curriculum. The other questions, which relate to the selection of desirable educational objectives and their appropriate distribution over the undergraduate-graduate continuum, would seem to be primarily the concern of educators.

---

[1] Part III (Chapters 8 and 9) are based in part on two papers—"Social Work Education Today" by Mildred Sikkema and "Implications for Curriculum Building Suggested by the Four Conference Papers" by Ruth Smalley—presented at the Conference on the Contribution of School Social Work to Social Work Education, Highland Park, Illinois, August 2–8, 1959, and on conference workshop discussions.

[2] Werner W. Boehm, *Objectives of the Social Work Curriculum of the Future* (Social Work Curriculum Study, Vol. I; New York: Council on Social Work Education, 1959).

An overview of the educational implications of school social work practice reveals that the following general statements hold true for both the scientific-philosophical component and the methods component of the curriculum:

The preparation of school social workers is rooted in the basic preparation of all social workers.

The constellation of knowledge, value, purpose, sanction, and method that characterizes social work is the foundation for practice in any field. School social work begins with this foundation, but its practice requires an extension of preparation in certain directions.

The breadth of practice required in school social work demands the kind of breadth of professional education that is forecast for the future.

The basic activities of the school social worker (*see* Chapter 5) show that the worker needs to be able to practice highly qualitative casework while, at the same time, he has understanding of the dynamics of groups, communities, and social systems, and of how to work with them. This is in accordance with an emerging trend described by Sikkema: ". . . the social work role in any practitioner position increasingly requires familiarity with, and ability to use, group and administrative processes, casework principles, community organization skills, and so on."

The application of certain social science concepts to school social work practice illustrates their value in the education of all social workers.

The concept of what constitutes behavior in its many manifestations needs to be broadened from concentration on individual behavior to consideration of group and community behavior. There is increasing need for social work to add insights from the social sciences to those it has already gained from psychiatry, social psychology, biology, and other fields. For example, school social work illustrates the importance of understanding the school as a social institution (*see* Chapter 3) with all that that implies in knowledge of organization as a social system, and such concepts as status, role, authority, groupings, and value conflicts.

School social work is practiced in a social institution, the school, which provides historical perspective on growth and change.

Social work, as part of its inheritance, is concerned with social reform, which today is designated as "planned social change." Renewed interest in this aspect of the social work function is leading to studies of how to use new scientific knowledge in furthering planned social change. As pointed out in Chapter 2, social work as an influential force in our society has an obligation to help the public school achieve its goal of self-fulfillment of every child. This task means constant evaluation and assessment of public education and of the changes taking place in it.

THE SCIENTIFIC-PHILOSOPHICAL

COMPONENT OF THE CURRICULUM

8

In this chapter, the scientific-philo-
sophical component of the curriculum is presented as two components, as a matter of convenience, although it is evident that they
are intertwined and are essentially a unit. Cognitive learning
is not enough; it must be infused with the meaning that comes
from feeling and deep conviction about the use to be made of it.
Social work practice makes its contribution to professional education when it constantly brings a fresh supply of experience to bear
on theory, and thereby tests it and adds to it.

the scientific component

The scientific component of the curriculum is intended to give the
student an understanding of the "determinants of social functioning." It covers understanding of the individual, the group, and
the community (sociocultural factors). Boehm proposes that the
meaning or use of this understanding should be organized, for
application in professional activities, into curriculum sequences of
human growth and behavior, social welfare policies and services, and
social work values and ethics.[1]

The field of school social work has a contribution to make in all
of these areas. In order to discuss its contribution to the scientific
component of the curriculum, a series of statements are offered under the headings: knowledge about the individual, knowledge about

---

[1] Werner W. Boehm, *Objectives of the Social Work Curriculum of the Future*
(Social Work Curriculum Study, Vol. I; New York: Council on Social Work
Education, 1959), pp. 79–82.

the individual and the group, and knowledge about the individual and the community (sociocultural factors).

knowledge about the individual

School social work provides an opportunity for students to learn about the concept of normality. A wide range of behavior is represented as on a continuum. Latency, about which less is known than some other stages of maturation, can be understood through observation in the school.

The *Social Work Curriculum Study* volume on human growth and behavior points out the lack of sufficient content on the latency period in courses, and notes that such content would supply "an understanding of a phase when life experiences especially contribute to the person's development in the social realm and to his competence in interpersonal reaction." [2]

The child from about six years of age to puberty is not in as spectacular a stage of development, perhaps, as in the earlier years of childhood or in the years of adolescence, but this is a period of great significance in the development of personality. Dependence upon the parents is displaced to some extent by attention to other people, peers, and adults, such as teachers. The child's social horizon is widening, he is experiencing self-reliance and enterprise. One authority observes:

The importance of this period for mental hygiene is liable to be neglected. . . . It seems to be normally a time when elementary processes are organized . . . for making habitual the alphabets of learning, of health, and of morals; a time when objective thinking gradually takes the place of the autistic thinking of the earlier period; especially a time when the background and essential elements of the wholesome personality that form the basis of the individual's sanity are acquired. [3]

Erikson points out that latency is a period when the child begins to learn "to win recognition by producing things"; he is in the stage of being "a worker and potential provider." He needs opportunity to have a worthwhile task to do and freedom to do it in his own way. The danger in frustration of these impulses is that he may develop a sense of inadequacy and inferiority; he may try to destroy things instead of constructing them. Erikson concludes, "Many a child's development is disrupted when family

[2] Ruth M. Butler, *An Orientation to Knowledge of Human Growth and Behavior in Social Work Education* (Social Work Curriculum Study, Vol. VI; New York: Council on Social Work Education, 1959), p. 41.

[3] William H. Burnham, *The Wholesome Personality* (New York: D. Appleton and Co., 1932), pp. 39–40.

life may not have prepared him for school life, or when school life may fail to sustain the promises of earlier stages." [4]

The interaction and interrelationship of endowment and environmental forces, and their effects upon the child's growth and behavior are clearly evident in the school situation.

As the school social worker is well aware, "Endowed capacities of an unusually rich nature give no assurance by themselves that they will enable the person to realize his full potential for social functioning; conversely, a person with serious limitations of endowment may, with environmental reinforcement, reach an unexpectedly effective level of social functioning." [5] (*See* Appendix A, Record 2, Normal "Growing Pains" of a Junior High School Boy, p. 191, and Record 4, Adolescent Boy Without Father in the Home, p. 207.)

The span from kindergarten through high school enables the school social worker to observe and understand the whole child in all aspects and stages of his growth and development—physical, intellectual, emotional, cultural, and spiritual.

Social work education has tended to emphasize some of these aspects, notably the physical and emotional, more than others. School social workers also daily see the significance of environmental forces and can affirm Butler's three principles:

1. "Environmental forces are of greatest influence when the person is most plastic and changing most rapidly." She notes, for example, that the disruption of interpersonal relationships in the immediate family is especially significant to the adolescent when the youth is experiencing rapid physical and emotional changes.

2. "Environmental forces must satisfy the needs of the person with a balance between their protective functions and their challenge and stimulation to his further development." School social workers are continuously aware of the effect of parents' expectations upon a child's school performance, either stimulating his ability and readiness to learn or blocking him when expectations exceed his capacity.

3. "Environmental forces increase in number and complexity throughout the life cycle, simultaneously increasing the variety and unfamiliarity of the person's experiences, and altering the significance to him of his experience in the past." The school is one of the environmental forces that lead the child from one stage of maturation to another and helps him to assume appropriate responsibilities. The school social worker deals with the children who have been unable to make progress satisfactorily in some aspect of social and emotional growth and development. [6]

---

[4] Erik H. Erikson, *Childhood and Society* (New York: W. W. Norton and Co., 1950), pp. 226–227.

[5] Butler, *op. cit.*, p. 32.

[6] *Ibid.*, pp. 44–45.

The school contributes to the child's learning about social role and social control as it helps him move from one set of expectations to another. The school social worker aids in this development.

Workshop discussion brought out some of the ways in which the school helps the child in his social growth: (1) he learns about some of the authorities which impinge upon individuals in our society and how he can relate to them, (2) he is helped to learn progressive physical and emotional self-control, (3) the school teaches much about the importance of time in our culture, (4) the school affords many opportunities for co-operation and leadership and the child learns to distinguish acceptable kind of conduct from unacceptable. The significance of the use of limits in furthering the child's development has been noted (*see* Chapter 6).

knowledge about the individual and the group

The groupings of children and personnel in the school structure provide many opportunities for understanding the importance of membership in social groups.

The family is a primary group that has earliest and most lasting effect upon the development of the child's personality. The school social worker has opportunity to observe a wide range of family constellations on a continuum from positive to negative in influence, and he develops a concept of normality which covers a wide range of behavior. Cultural differences and their effect upon family relationships can be known first hand.

Peer groups are also of great importance and can help or hinder the socialization aim of the school. (*See* Chapters 3 and 6.) The school provides rich illustrative experience about the place of groups in the social development of the personality. Workshop discussion elucidated these points. Students of all ages learn from, and teach, one another. Values are learned from peers more easily than from adults at certain stages of maturation. Opportunity is offered for study of group behavior and for analysis of which kinds of behavior are tied to psychosocial development and which are culturally determined or influenced. The statement was made that the normal range of behavior through which the child searches for his identity in his interaction with others can be discerned more clearly in the school than anywhere else in American culture. The child neglected and rejected by his parents may find acceptance from his peers and/or faculty at school and utilize their help in adapting to stress.

A gap in professional education is evident when one examines the many group relationships which the school social worker must maintain with students, teachers, committees, and so on, and the limited extent to which school social workers are at present prepared for such responsibilities.

Throughout this study reference has been made to the importance of school social workers having a knowledge of the group
process and ability to work with groups. Increasingly, schools of
social work are including in the curriculum instruction about the
dynamics of group interaction and its meaning for social work
practice; nevertheless, the survey conducted by the School Social
Work Section, NASW, indicated the extent to which practitioners
felt the gap in preparation in this area (*see* Chapter 5). It is hoped
that the professional schools will give attention to the needs of the
social worker for knowledge of the scientific component of group
interaction and group process.

knowledge about the individual and the community

*The school as a central social institution provides many facets for
learning about the community around it and about the larger
society of which it is a part. The interaction between school and
community can enhance or retard social functioning of individuals.*
    Illustrations of contrasting communities in Chapter 3 show
how applicable to the individual and the group are some of the concepts of behavior already discussed. "Endowment" of a community can be thought of as relating to family stratification, class, economic need, mobility of a community surrounding a school. The
school is an "environmental force," but interaction between the
kind of communtiy and the school determines the educational
product in that community. Organized groups, such as the PTA
and the school board, are other interactional forces. Because the
school is a universal experience in the United States, the study of
its "behavior" in its sociocultural context is very helpful in understanding other social institutions.
    *The school illustrates many social science concepts which give
meaning to the individual, group, and community in their interrelationship.*
    Such concepts as social system, sub-groups, social role, role con-
flicts, and social stress are applicable to a social institution (*see* Chapter 3). They give insight into the interaction between the individual, group, and organized social system and lay the foundation
for understanding their applicability in casework, administration,
collaboration, and other processes.
    *The school social worker understands the total web of social
welfare services in the community as resources for helping enhance
the social functioning of the child in school. When needed resources are lacking, he endeavors to bring about change to provide
them and also tries to improve the integration of services.*
    Social welfare services in all their ramifications are a form of en-
vironmental force that can enhance or block the growth and devel-

opment of the individual or the group. The community described in Chapter 3, which had no playground facilities although a majority of the mothers of school children were employed outside the home, is an example of a lack of a service needed for the protection and social development of children. Just as the person needs to be seen as a whole, so do community problems, resources, and policies need to be seen in their total interrelationship.

the philosophical component

A person's understanding of the values he holds and their integration into the values of his profession is a mark of a truly professional person. Furthermore, one criterion for a profession is a code of ethics which is a guide in the use of values in practice. School social workers must daily demonstrate their identification with their own profession as they relate their own values to those of another profession.

All social workers need to understand the meaning of public education, its goals, the contradictions in its values, and trends in its development. Such learning can be transferred to the study of other institutions.

Of all social institutions, the school, next to the family, probably has the greatest influence on the child. All social workers have some contact with children in school and with school personnel. From personal experience, they may halo the school or may stereotype its deficiencies. It is essential, therefore, that students in schools of social work become informed about the school as a social institution and understand present trends in education as a profession (*see* Chapter 4). School social work makes real the meaning of public education, including the value-conflicts in goals. Smalley puts it this way: "It is the philosophy, values, objectives of social welfare programs and such important social institutions as the public school which need to be stressed rather than a catalogue of facts about them, although facts are important as illustrations."

The school social worker must have an especially strong integration of his personal and professional values, and a positive identification with his own profession because he often needs to work alone in relating social work to another profession.

Some of the demands and pressures upon the school social worker as he operates within the school structure (*see* Chapter 6) show clearly the need for professional integrity and maturity. While he shares with teachers and other school personnel the same *ultimate* values (concepts of what ought to be or should be), he must have a command of *instrumental* values (the means by which ultimate values can be achieved). As noted in Chapter 2, the social worker and the teacher have common ultimate goals derived from the humanitarian-democratic foundations of our culture, but their ways of working are related to separate functions and they develop quite different instrumental values. Since all social workers need awareness of what distinguishes the lay from the professional person, the teaching of values and ethics should permeate the curriculum, including the administration of the school of social work. Direct instruction is also essential to further integration. School social work can provide many illustrations to help illuminate teaching, such as the use of values in the helping relationship, the inevitability of value-conflicts and their significance as a part of societal growth and change, and, finally, the appreciation of different professional value systems all based, perhaps, on the same ultimate values but each developing its own instrumental values.

THE METHODS COMPONENT

OF THE CURRICULUM

9

Discussion of the contribution of school social work practice to the methods component of the social work curriculum is complicated by the unsettled terminology in social work and by the uneven movement of education and practice in their acceptance of certain emerging concepts.[1] Initial progress in finding a frame of reference for curriculum planning was made by the schools of social work, and subsequent efforts have been directed steadily toward integration of knowledge and concepts. Since the formation of NASW, the single national professional membership association, such efforts by practitioners have been consolidated under NASW's Commission on Social Work Practice, and significant formulations are appearing. As Bartlett notes, improved communication and collaboration between educators and practitioners are needed to strengthen the profession.[2] At present, however, certain differences in conceptualization and terminology are apparent.

current concepts on methods

The Curriculum Policy Statement of the Council on Social Work Education, adopted in 1952, emphasizes the generic content of the two-year curriculum for the master's degree. One of the three areas of learning prescribed is "social work practice" which encompasses

---

[1] For a penetrating analysis of the relation between education and practice, and their contributions to social work theory, see Harriett M. Bartlett, "Responsibilities of Social Work Practitioners and Educators Toward Building a Strong Profession," *Social Service Review*, Vol. 34, No. 4 (December 1960), pp. 379–393.

[2] *Ibid.*

instruction in the "professional methods," namely, casework, group work, community organization, administration, and research. These methods are described as having common as well as distinguishing characteristics. Students are expected to develop skill in the use of one method (usually casework or group work) and to become familiar with the use of the other methods. In 1959, a further step toward integration of the curriculum was taken when the Council on Social Work Education discontinued accreditation of specialized sequences, for example, medical and psychiatric social work, school social work, group work. It now bases accreditation on the quality of the total two-year curriculum for the master's degree.

The *Social Work Curriculum Study,* made for the Council on Social Work Education, affirmed the importance of the integrated curriculum and proposed that it be considered to have two major components, the scientific-philosophical component (discussed in Chapter 8) and the methods component. Boehm held that the methods—casework, group work, and community organization, and also administration and research—constitute the methods component of the curriculum, and that the purpose of this component is to help the student "to develop the requisite skills whereby the social worker helps individuals, groups, and communities to attain mutually established goals for enhancing the social functioning of people through institutional provision of services and resources." [3]

The question whether the various methods may in themselves constitute a "social work method" has been raised from time to time by educators and practitioners. In 1955 the author wrote:

It may be that eventually the present specializations and designations of methods will disappear in favor of a *social work method* in which new forms of specialization will emerge that will be based on broader foundation than any one of the methods has developed to date. Need for movement in this direction is found in the multi-faceted approach demanded in public assistance and in certain other areas of practice such as rehabilitation, corrections, geriatrics, and protective services. [4]

Boehm, however, rejects the idea of one method. He states:

To arrive at the conclusion that there is a single method of social work, the problems of concern to each method would have to be generalized on a high level of abstraction as problems in social functioning. No opportunity would remain of arriving induc-

---

[3] Werner W. Boehm, *Objectives of the Social Work Curriculum of the Future* (Social Work Curriculum Study, Vol. I; New York: Council on Social Work Education, 1959), p. 130.

[4] Arlien Johnson, "Development of Basic Methods of Social Work Practice and Education," *Social Work Journal,* Vol. 36, No. 3 (July 1955), p. 111.

tively at a classification of knowledge or a specification of skills needed for effective problem-solving at the level of actual giving of service.[5]

It is of interest, therefore, to find that practitioners are discovering the unitary nature of practice as they undertake to formulate a working definition. The NASW Commission on Social Work Practice began by examining empirically a wide range of instances of practice in a variety of fields. This analysis led to the concept of practice as a constellation of components—value, purpose, sanction, knowledge, and method—which are always present with particular content and configuration as *social work*. From this base or foundation as a center of gravity, so to speak, it then becomes possible to examine the variations in emphases and the interrelationship of these factors in different fields of practice.

With respect to method, the *Working Definition* as formulated in 1956 states: "The social work method is the responsible, conscious, disciplined use of self in a relationship with an individual or group." Method is defined as "an orderly systematic mode of procedure" encompassing casework, group work, and community organization and making use of techniques or regularized or patterned responses. Administration, teaching, research, it is suggested (and, the writer would add, possibly collaboration and consultation), might be considered as supplementary to, or facilitating, the methods used in direct social work practice. The 1956 *Working Definition* states, however: "The individual social worker always makes his own creative contribution in the application of social work method to any setting or activity." [6] The commission uses method in the singular but recognizes that social work method includes all of the knowledge and techniques usually described as "methods."

Deliberations of the Commission on Social Work Practice have shown a trend toward further refinement of this concept of practice with less emphasis on method and more effort directed toward isolation of the core activity of practice. Bartlett states:

The concept of *method* has customarily been used in a broad sense and without precise definition in social work. Examination of practice suggests that ordered sequence of actions (in the sense of systematic modes of procedure) is perhaps less characteristic of social work practice than highly flexible action responsive to a wide variety of situations. A new approach, that of professional intervention to bring about change through a variety of tech-

---

[5] Boehm, *op. cit.*, pp. 134–135.

[6] "Working Definition of Social Work Practice," conveniently cited in Harriett M. Bartlett, "Toward Clarification and Improvement of Social Work Practice," *Social Work*, Vol. 3, No. 2 (April 1958), pp. 7–8.

niques, is being explored as possibly more useful and relevant than the customary concept of method.[7]

"Professional intervention" would be guided, of course, by the value assumptions, knowledge, and techniques of social work as such intervention is directed to specified purposes under appropriate sanctions.

This brief statement about current concepts on method is made to explain the frame of reference for the presentation of the material in this chapter. While the study of school social work has focused on practice, the findings should be useful to educators. For this reason, Boehm's classification of the methods component as one part of the curriculum has been adopted, but with some modification, in an effort to put the findings into a form familiar to social work educators. The use of this classification also gives opportunity to illustrate how the study of school social work corroborates the concept of practice as a constellation of components common to all fields of practice, with variations in emphasis and use in specific fields.

The findings of the study of school social work as they relate to the methods component of the curriculum are discussed under three headings: (1) contribution to direct service processes, (2) contribution to processes supplementary to direct service, and (3) field instruction. (In discussing field instruction, it is obviously necessary to consider the total curriculum, rather than only the methods component.) The term "process" is used instead of "method" because it has a more generalized meaning and also because it is freer of the connotations which attach to the term "methods" through usage.

What is meant by the term "process"? A *primary process* may be defined as a progressive transaction between the social worker and the entity—individual, group, or community—to which professional service is given.[8] The progressive transaction has been said to consist of a series of problem-solving operations carried on within a meaningful relationship.[9] A *secondary process* would be a progressive transaction between the social worker and colleagues who are involved together in the operation of primary processes (for example, collaboration or consultation) or are working together on the improvement or analysis of primary processes (for example, research).

---

[7] Harriett M. Bartlett, *Analyzing Social Work Practice by Fields* (New York: National Association of Social Workers, 1961), p. 24.

[8] "Community" is an indefinite term. As used here it signifies a secondary group of people or one in which the members come together to solve a problem or problems for the benefit of the social welfare community, not for themselves personally.

[9] Helen H. Perlman, *Social Casework: A Problem-solving Process* (Chicago: University of Chicago Press, 1957), p. 5.

The "meaningful relationship" in secondary processes would be with fellow social workers or with members of other professions or occupations, when they are all part of an organized structure, that is, an agency or institution. (Administration, which is, in effect, the facilitating of the over-all relationships among those engaged in a common enterprise, might also be conceived of as a secondary process.) To sum up, the secondary processes support and implement the services given directly to clients or groups.

contribution to direct service processes

The foundation for social work practice is laid in the scientific-philosophical part of the curriculum; here *knowing* or knowledge is emphasized. But the test of knowledge is in its use or in *doing*. The study of school social work has provided many specifics of practice with children and families and has shown the possibilities in work with groups of children and of parents, and with community groups. Generalizations are offered to summarize some of the contributions of school social work practice to the development of direct service processes.

School social workers have more direct contact with children than social workers in most of the other fields of practice; they develop skill in forming professional relationships with children.

While the foundation courses in human growth and behavior provide knowledge about children from the prenatal period through adolescence, first-hand contact with children requires selected use of what is known. Special skill is needed to communicate with, and relate to, children and to free them to take help with their problems. Smalley states:

> Students whose field placements are in school social work have an unexcelled opportunity for "experiencing" children and their own reactions to them, to say nothing of experiencing teachers, principals, and members of other professional disciplines. This is all part of their daily experience which then comes into class within the form appropriate to each particular sequence or curriculum area. . . . [Special skill] is the necessity not for observing a normal child, if one could be located . . . but of having to offer service to one squirming, rebellious 8-year-old child, fresh from a fight on the playground (one of many which have eventuated in his referral) which asks the school social worker student from the first day of school to see and experience a child in distress, to discover what wells up in himself at being expected to offer school social work help and motivates him to use all the knowledge he can acquire to do what he must do.

All social workers might profitably have more direct contact with children to increase understanding and skill in work with them. *(See Appendix A, Record 1, Typical Example of School Social Work Service; Record 2, Normal Growing Pains of a Junior High School Boy; Record 3, Brief Service; Record 4, Adolescent Boy Without Father in the Home; Record 5, Use of Authority; Record 6, Preventive Service to a Child in Kindergarten; Record 7, Referral to a Community Agency, p. 177 ff.)*

School social workers develop understanding of the parental role as it affects the child's functioning in school, and they are often able to modify parental attitudes and behavior.

Although the school social worker has contact with parents who present a wide range of behavior, who come from many social classes and backgrounds, and who have various types of problems, his focus is on one aspect of the parents' behavior, the parental role as it affects the child in school. The school social worker develops depth of understanding and skill in work with parents. Since parent-child relationships are of such psychological significance in a child's growth and development, the school social worker can contribute to general social work knowledge in this area through sharing experience and generalizing from it.

School social workers acquire special knowledge of parental roles in general and are able to work with families as on a continuum from so-called normal parents to those who present disturbed family relationships.

Just as the school social worker has the opportunity to observe and work with children as on a continuum from normal behavioral problems of growing up to highly disturbed behavioral symptoms, so also does he have the opportunity to understand and work with a wide range of parental attitudes and behavior. These are sometimes linked to class, cultural, or economic statuses but they may also be related to the interaction within a specific family group. Understanding of the dynamics within the so-called normal family aids in understanding family life in general and can be helpful in working with families who present disturbed relationships.

The school social worker develops skill in brief contact evaluation; he must be able to communicate his evaluation promptly to school personnel.

The school social worker must be able quickly to relate to the child who is disturbed or disturbing; he must also relate quickly to the teacher or other school personnel concerned about the child. In utilizing school records he must be able to evaluate readily their usefulness as they bear on the child's present situation. He may have to relate to the parent or parents immediately; and he must be able to be guided by all of these findings as he proceeds. Some of the values and expectations of the school may not be the same as some of his (*see* Chapter 6) and this discrepancy has to be reconciled for the benefit of the child within the limits of the school's structure. All these factors call for deep perceptiveness and ability to sort out the dynamics of the problem. While he works with the problem, he interprets it to his collaborators in the school. The fast tempo of the school requires that the social worker sharpen his evaluative skill. Sometimes he cannot wait until he has had several interviews, as is possible in a welfare agency, before he makes a plan. In view of the great demands upon social welfare agencies for service, perhaps the school social worker can offer experience in brief contact and time-limited evaluation that will help other fields of practice.

Treatment offered by the school social worker is often preventive of further breakdown in social functioning.

The opportunity to help children and parents with problems that, if neglected, might lead to more serious disorders of one kind or another is a preventive aspect of school social work.

The school social worker develops special competency in the use of the referral process.

Referral of a family to an agency outside the school for help demands skill in transferring a family's trust from the school, a known and generally accepted source of help, to a community agency, unknown and often outside the neighborhood. Such a referral demands of the social worker that he be able to transfer to the agency his understanding of the family situation in such a way that service can be continued without interruption. Skillful use of the referral process enables a family to accept help from an agency other than the school, and at the same time enables a community agency to maintain the positive relationship with the family for which the school social worker has laid the foundation. Referral does not mean abandonment of the child and his family by the school; it means that the social worker continues to try to help the child in his school adjustment. He must now distinguish clearly his activity as it relates to the child in school from activity in the family situation which may be inducing the child's problems. He works with the child on the school situation until it is alleviated. (*See* Appendix A, Record 7, Referral to a Community Agency, p. 243.)

The use of authority as a dynamic in service relationships is a part of the school social worker's skill.

Authority of one kind or another is a characteristic of all social life. The school social worker must be able to distinguish the various kinds of authority to which he is subject and the kinds which he can use with clients when they are derived from his position as a representative of the school, his expertise as a social worker, and his role as an adult (*see* Chapter 6). The skillful use of authority in the casework relationship aids growth; *e.g.,* the child needs limits within which to develop independence and self-reliance. School social work offers many illustrations of the positive use of authority as a part of the helping process.

School social work has much to offer the school about group formation, group cohesion, interaction, and the mutuality of influence of individual-group and group-individual behavior.

Throughout this study, reference has been made to the importance of the school social worker having knowledge and skill in work with groups. Opportunities abound in the school to use a helping relationship with groups of children, teachers, parents, and family groups. At present, this aspect of school social work has been developed only to a limited extent. Social work education should take note of the importance of this aspect of practice and further integrate learning about groups in the curriculum; the school setting might be utilized for observation and instruction.

Community problems and the provision of resources to meet them differ widely from one school neighborhood to another; hence, the school social worker must be able to individualize the community much as he does the individual.

The problems which children have in school are often closely related to external environmental factors, as well as to psychological factors. Applying the concept of interaction of endowment and environmental forces (*see* p. 27) to the study of the community will help the student in field placement understand the meaning of society and culture and will reveal the variation that can be expected in norms of behavior in different sociocultural segments of society. The concept of individualization of work with a community is made real to the student.

The importance of the school social worker having knowledge and skill in the community organization process has already been stressed (*see* Chapters 5 and 6). Although his chief activity is social casework, his activity in the community in behalf of the school increases his effectiveness in helping children.

Some aspects of the community organization process can be observed and experienced in school social work.

Because the focus of school social work is on helping the child in school, the student in school social work placement has a more specific approach in community organization assignments than is possible in a more generalized welfare placement. He can learn about, and to a limited extent participate in, evaluation of resources in his school district, the referral process, and school-community-agency projects. This will help him to realize the breadth of knowledge and skill required in school social work practice and should illuminate relevant professional courses. The school offers opportunity for understanding how the social worker can be an agent of social change to the extent that he commands a working knowledge of institutional behavior and its relation to community behavior, and to the extent that he can use his knowledge in relating school and community for the development of services for parents and children.

contribution to processes
supplementary to direct service

Supplementary or secondary processes are those which implement, facilitate, and improve services offered directly to clients or groups served. In school social work, as noted above, important secondary processes include collaboration, consultation, administration, and research. These activities are carried on in relation to, or with, colleagues; they support and aid the social worker in giving effective service to children.

School social work is practiced in an interdisciplinary setting which provides rich opportunities for learning how to relate the social work function to that of another profession, education.

In any interdisciplinary setting, the central task or core function is the most highly esteemed; the farther a specialized service like social work is from the core function, the less esteem is likely to be accorded it. The school, therefore, is an excellent place for the social work student to learn how to participate in group goals while learning to differentiate his own part of the operation. He learns why and how to identify strongly with social work while, at the same time, he is learning how to extend his understanding of what other professions represented in the setting do as their parts of the group task.

Collaboration with teachers, principals, psychologists, and others is at the heart of the school social worker's activity and requires him to have a grasp of the meaning of role perception and of expectations of self and others.

In order to enter into a collaborative relationship, the social worker and the teacher each needs to have a set of organized expectations of self-roles and statuses and an understanding of the other person's roles and statuses. The social worker may first have to create an image of his profession's competence through demonstration and interpretation before he can put a definition of his role-set into written form for administrative approval.

All social workers are becoming increasingly aware of the importance of collaboration as a part of their work. School social work provides an exceptional opportunity for studying and learning about collaboration as a process.

167

Social Work Education

Communication with team members or role partners is both horizontal and vertical in the school setting; confidentiality is an aspect of communication that requires professional judgment.

The collaborative process requires ability to communicate with persons whose referents with respect to the meaning of certain words and concepts are not the same as those of the social worker. The school social worker must learn to express himself so that his role partners can understand him; he also needs to learn to listen and to try to understand what members of other professions in the team are saying. All team members must have a working comprehension of the common language of the school and of education. The hierarchical organization of the school requires that the social worker communicate upward to the principal and, at the same time, horizontally with the teacher as a co-worker.

School social work can help students develop understanding and skill in the use of communication and confidentiality which are inherent aspects of all social work practice.

Consultation is a means of extending the social worker's services in the school and at the same time of helping school personnel become better able to help the child with problems.

Consultation, which differs from collaboration in that it carries no binding responsibility for group task performance, is increasingly a function of the school social worker, and is a way of extending his services at a time when school enrollment is booming. School social workers need to define and to make more formal their consultant role in the school, for themselves as well as for their role partners. As this role is better established, school social work will provide the student with good examples of this part of practice.

The school social worker to a greater extent than the social worker in the usual welfare agency must have a firm grasp of the principles of administration that every staff member should have; he must have skill in performing the administrative aspects of his function.

The school as a social institution is usually a large organization, with well-defined hierarchies and many role-sets among the personnel (*see* Chapter 3). The social work student who has knowledge of such concepts as bureaucracy, social roles, authority, and social system which he is learning in the scientific-philosophical component of the curriculum will find these illustrated in the school setting. He should be able to understand the place of school social work in the administrative hierarchy and to be able to learn how to utilize structure in giving service.

Policy making in the large and in the school itself is another area that provides school social work students with an understanding of the administrative process in all its ramifications.

As previously pointed out (*see* Chapter 5), the school social worker participates in administration through such activities as membership on curriculum and other committees, and through endeavoring to contribute appropriately to changes in policy which would be advantageous for the child's learning and social adjustment. Use of, and participation in, the administrative process is one of the requisites of school social work.

Acceptance of the authority implicit in administration and ability to follow channels of authority and communication are especially important in school social work.

The school social worker is disciplined to act within the limits of his function in an organization in which education rather than social work is the central task. He must share with principals and teachers decisions about such critical matters as intake, selection of case load, termination of service. He must be constantly aware that his role is supplementary to that of the core task personnel and at the same time he must help them utilize his service as an enlargement of their own. This requires skill in grasping administrative structure and in communication within that structure.

The school social worker usually does not have the kind of supervision or consultation from a social worker that the social worker in the welfare agency has as part of the administrative organization of the agency. Hence, he must be able to work independently.

The school social worker may be the only one of his profession in the schools to which he is assigned. He has no one at hand with whom to share his confusions. The extent to which supervision is provided by social workers in the school hierarchy differs from school district to school district. As noted in Chapter 5, the inquiry by the School Social Work Section, NASW, revealed that only about one-half of those responding to a questionnaire reported that they had supervision from a social worker who was a member of the school staff. Even when a school social service department is part of the school administrative structure, the individual school social worker must sort out his function as a specialist and his function as a school staff member. This dilemma is well described by a group of school social workers:

> In some respects school social work resembles independent practice more than work in an agency. We are not physically surrounded by the walls of an agency, and lack support of other social workers. We are unprotected in our decisions. . . .
>
> These things make it hard for a new staff person to learn the structure within which we operate. Flexibility is essential, but can be confusing too. We are part of a social work department and do have guiding policies. Much supervisory help is needed to clarify these policies as well as school policies, which are not necessarily in complete agreement. Supervision is needed for continued growth in understanding and in the use of casework dy-

namics. A school social worker must be able to work more independently than in an agency but supervision is needed to maintain uniformity of standards. At the same time, allowance must be made for each worker to do different things in different schools due to different expectations of teachers, principals, etc. A new worker is especially in need of supervisory help to learn the framework within which he must operate.[10]

The independence with which the school social worker must practice highlights the importance of the student having a sound background in administrative theory to reinforce other aspects of his practice.

Many areas of school social work would benefit from research; social work students might profitably contribute through individual or group research projects.

The Curriculum Policy Statement of the Council on Social Work Education, which is accepted by all accredited schools of social work, includes research as one of the prescribed content areas for course sequences. Sikkema states:

All students meet specific research requirements which consist of classroom instruction in research method and completion of a research project or thesis. . . . It is the impression of Council [on Social Work Education] Consultants that research is permeating the curriculum in new ways and that a research attitude and a sense of need for research is increasingly evident among all faculty members.

The following list of possible studies has been suggested by this study of school social work:

1. Time-limited aspects of casework
2. Short-term contacts: focus, purpose, possible use in social adjustment
3. Analysis of case records to illustrate such problems and processes as:
   a. Referral process in families of different social classes
   b. Analysis of elements of skill in relating to and communicating with children
   c. "Growing up" problems in the latency period
   d. Use of authority as a dynamic in treatment
4. The school as a sub-culture in a particular neighborhood
5. The school as a social system: a specific school
6. The role-set of the school social worker
7. The use of group work knowledge and skill in school social work

---

[10] Minutes of the Portland, Oregon, School Social Work Section, NASW, as reported by Mrs. Julia K. Hoffman, Chairman, July 1, 1960.

8. School-community relations in two neighborhoods of contrasting socioeconomic composition.

This list is suggestive only. Some of these topics would be too difficult for the master's degree candidate but might be suitable for research by faculty or advanced degree students. It is hoped that educators in schools of social work may find other ideas for research in this study of school social work practice.

field instruction

Field instruction, or student learning through practice under a competent social work instructor in an agency, is the cement that holds all of professional education together. Here the student is helped to integrate his learning in the scientific-philosophical and the methods components of the curriculum; he begins to understand how the direct service processes are supported and facilitated by the supplementary processes. As Perlman puts it, "Integration, the coalescence of knowledge and experience, is never a static, achieved goal. It is a continuously 'being-achieved' process, an on-going raveling and knitting together of what the student is learning, theoretically and experientially, about using himself as well (that is, as skillfully) as he can in the service of the client." [11]

Workshop discussions brought out some pertinent and meaningful evaluations of the use, management, and place of field work in professional education. It was said that field work forms the "muscles of the profession" in that it represents a synthesis of the total curriculum, in application.

Field work in an interdisciplinary setting like the school presents certain difficulties that require careful consideration and planning. As pointed out in Chapter 7, the student must maintain role relations and meet role expectations of other professions before he has a firm grasp of his own professional identity and skill. Here the field instructor may need to protect the student from too much involvement in carrying the social work role in interdisciplinary tasks until he is well-oriented to the school and to the meaning of the collaborative process. Guided observation might be an intermediate step in preparation. Here also, through careful planning, use can be made of a "multiple disciplined teaching staff"; that is, the principal, teachers, and others can be involved in the teaching of the collaborative process. It was said that the imaginative and creative use of this concept would not only provide a broadening of student learning but would also add to the strength of understanding between team members.

---

11 "The Social Casework Method in Social Work Education," *Social Service Review*, Vol. 33, No. 4 (December 1959), p. 427.

The management of field work placements in the public schools requires sound planning. A keystone in such planning is agreement between the school board and superintendent of schools, on the one side, and the university and its school of social work, on the other, that training of students in school social work is an acceptable responsibility for the school to undertake. Although the schools have long participated with schools of education in the training of teachers and educators are generally favorable to the educational objectives of colleges and universities for providing personnel, the schools are accustomed to some kind of payment or form of reimbursement when they provide practice teaching for students. Commitment to preparation of social workers would be less probable, in most communities, than to preparation of teachers; hence, considerable advance planning over a period of time may be necessary to build a foundation for placement of social work students in the schools, especially when time of already overburdened school social workers must be allotted to student instruction.[12] More information on the variety of arrangements which might be possible is needed.

Another aspect of field work management is the selection of schools for student placements in which principal and teachers have already had satisfactory working relationships with school social workers and role-sets have been defined. As in any field placement, selection of field instructors in school social work should be those who are highly skilled practitioners and who have capacity for field teaching.

In conclusion, a statement by Smalley would seem to sum up the relation of field instruction to the rest of the curriculum:

> The principles of social work practice taught will be the same for every field of practice considered. Yet the purpose of the specific agency or social institution, always affect, in significant ways, the *use* of general principles. . . . Teaching from school social work case material offers unusual opportunity to work on the giving of casework help in situations when it is sought and when it is not sought or even desired, on direct work with children of all ages, with parents as parents, on the relating of one's own skill and purpose to the purpose of personnel within a larger and different whole. . . . I attach great significance, as must be apparent, to the intimate relationship between class and field teaching for the enriching and vitalizing of every content area, and for giving dimensions and theoretical base and wider social purpose to what is taught in the field.

---

[12] For this reason, in some communities field instructors have been provided by the schools of social work through appointment of school social workers as full-time members of the faculties while serving as school social workers of the public schools. Funds from the National Institute of Mental Health are sometimes available for this purpose.

school social work
and professional education

A statement of the specific contribution which school social work can make to professional education has been presented in Chapters 8 and 9. The emphases and adaptations in the practice of social work which it represents can, it is hoped, enrich the main body of knowledge and theory. At this time, when the child population of the United States has been increasing, the strengthening of all measures that protect and enhance the welfare of children is of vital importance to the nation. Social work is one of these measures. It can help to prevent social dysfunction and can restore impaired capacity; and school social work in so doing will aid the school in achieving its goal of development of the maximum capacity of every child.

If, in certain aspects of practice, the reach of school social workers would seem to exceed their grasp—as in utilization of opportunities for work with groups and for consultation—it should be remembered that "a man is known by the aspirations he keeps." The same could be said of an organized professional group like the School Social Work Section, NASW, which has devotedly and steadfastly sought to clarify and improve its practice, thus adding to the vitality of the profession of which it is a part.

Appendix A

Records Illustrating School
Social Work Practice

RECORD 1

TYPICAL EXAMPLE OF SCHOOL SOCIAL WORK SERVICE

**Direct work with a child utilizing resources
within the school, the family, and the community**

MICHAEL HARRIS.....10 years old, 5A grade

Family members: Mother and stepfather, Mr. and Mrs. Brown. Siblings: Lorraine Harris, 14, 8A grade; Dorothy Harris, 11, 5A grade; Martha Harris, 9, 4B grade; Daisy Brown, 4; Mabel Brown, 1.

School personnel: Miss Hess, principal, Mr. Davis, teacher, Mr. Todd, attendance officer, Miss Loeke, school nurse, and school social worker.

Reason for referral: Absence from school; disorderly behavior, home conditions. Mother requested help of the school social worker.

September 30, 1959

First interview with mother. Mrs. Brown brought Michael directly to my office. Michael knew me and understood my role in the school because of several brief contacts I had had with him last year. Mrs. Brown was also known to me, since her present husband and other members of the Brown family had been pupils in our school many years ago.

Mrs. Brown is a tall heavy-set young woman, pleasant and soft-spoken, the mother of six children, four of whom (Michael included) are not by her present husband. Michael is a stocky little boy, outwardly angelic but capable of causing plenty of trouble in school and at home. I knew that his school record shows that his work can be fairly good when he puts forth effort. Most 4th grade scores were at grade level or only slightly below. He had not repeated any grade.

Mrs. Brown smiled and asked if she could talk with me for a little while. She had a problem and wondered if I could help. The attendance worker suggested that she see me. I asked her to tell me about her problem and said I would be glad to help if I could. Without further encouragement she began at once to tell me what was on her mind.

Mrs. Brown confessed that even though this was three weeks after the opening of school, none of her children had attended yet because she was keeping them home. She stated this as a simple matter of fact, without defiance or resentment, and went on to say that she had only brought Michael in (the others were still home) because his teacher had reported his absence and the attendance officer had already been at the home. I asked why the children had not yet started the new term. Were they sick? Mrs. Brown answered "No" and seemed a little hesitant about going on. I said that whatever her reason was for keeping them home, it must be a pretty good one. This started her off again. She said that she thought it was good enough but didn't know how I would feel about it. Well, I encouraged her, did she want to try telling me? She blurted out, "What's the use of sending children to school when they don't get enough to eat? How can anyone learn on an empty stomach?" Without waiting for any comment, she went on to explain that her husband did not make enough to take care of a family of eight. Besides he wasn't at all interested in the four children who were not his and was very mean to them. He gave her very little of what he did make —she didn't know what he did with the rest—and it simply was not enough to feed, let alone clothe, them properly. When she saw me glance at Michael, she hastened to say that what he was wearing (he looked very presentable) had been given to her by friends.

I agreed that feeding and clothing six children these days when everything was so high was indeed a problem, but how did she expect to solve it by keeping the children home from school? How did she feel that would help? She said that during the summer she had applied to several agencies for assistance and had hoped that something would come through before school time. (Previous to this they had gotten along fine because her mother had helped a lot, but since her mother had passed away she just couldn't "make out" on what Mr. B gave her.) I asked if she had heard from any of the agencies. She said "Yes" but they had all turned her down, saying that what she got from her husband, while not too much, could be made to do. Mrs. Brown told me all this in an even, quiet tone of voice without bitterness or anger, just insisting again that her children did not get enough to eat and it was not fair to send them to school and expect them to learn.

I said that she was right about the importance of enough food, of course, especially at breakfast time, and I could understand her feelings about not being able to provide this for her children. On the other hand, the school has laws which require them to be in school, as she well knows, and if she did not send them she would only be making matters worse for them and herself. She said that she knew I was right because the attendance worker had told her the same thing. If she didn't return the children to school it might even mean court and what would she gain by that. That's why she had brought Michael in, but she had wanted to talk to me first. I said that I was glad she could see that prolonged absence would not help the situation and asked what she was going to do now. She said she guessed Michael might as well go to his room now if it was all right since it was already two o'clock. I said I would send a note to his teacher and then explain more fully when I had a chance to talk with him.

I asked Mrs. Brown what she intended doing about the other children who were still home. She said she would send them to school the next morning. She seemed relieved to have settled this much at least. Actually, she admitted, she knew it was wrong to keep the "kids" at home but guessed she thought she could force some action that way. Then she looked at me and said, "But it still doesn't settle the food problem, and I don't know where to turn." I said I didn't blame her for being concerned and now that the attendance part of the problem was out of the way, maybe we could see if anything could be done about the other. I went on to explain that in our school we had no funds for assistance or any means of even supplying the children with lunches, but perhaps I might be able to refer her elsewhere. I would let her know.

Mrs. Brown was very grateful for the time I had given her, then said she would like to ask my help in one more matter before she left. Would I keep an eye on Michael now that he is back in school? If he followed true to form, I surely would hear from his teacher. All of his teachers had trouble with him and there was no reason to believe that he had changed. His teachers always had to send for her regarding his behavior. He even steals and then lies about it. I said that I thought it only fair to give Michael a chance to get started in his new classroom first. Maybe things wouldn't turn out so bad after all, but if he needed and wanted my help, I would be glad to see him. Mrs. Brown said she hoped I was right. She thanked me again, and left.

October 2, 1959

Mr. Todd, attendance officer, called. He asked if the Harris children had reported. The information he shared was the same as that given me by Mrs. Brown. (The children were all in school.)

Conference with teacher. I gave Michael's teacher the facts concerning his delayed return to school and advised that his attendance be carefully noted and reported to the attendance officer in the event of absence. We also talked about his mother's concern over his previous school record of behavior and her feeling that he had not changed. Mr. Davis said that of course it was impossible to tell definitely yet, but that he could see even now in just two days that the boy was an "itch." He would keep me informed.

October 5, 1959
A note to Mrs. Brown. Note sent to Mrs. Brown referring her to two possible sources of temporary assistance, Surplus Foods and Needlework Guild, with a few words of instructions on procedures.

October 9, 1959
Michael referred by teacher who said that Michael had been acting up all week. Several things were missing from children's desks. Michael was suspected but denied any knowledge of anything. He spoke very glibly and smoothly and at length, but was the innocent victim. Mr. Davis now felt that the mother's fears about Michael's behavior were justified. Besides, Mr. Davis said, being a new teacher, he had more problems than he could handle and would be grateful If I would help with this one. I said I would arrange to see Michael the following week.

October 13, 1959
Conference with principal, Miss Hess, to discuss work with Michael.
Interview with Michael. Michael came to my office promptly at the time previously arranged for in a note to his teacher. He remained standing in the doorway until I greeted him and asked him to come sit beside my desk. This he did without a word. He appeared fearful and unhappy, sat with his hands in his lap, and looked straight ahead. When I asked if he knew why he had come, he said "Yes" rather abruptly and no more. I waited, but Michael just continued to sit in the same position, very still, ill at ease, with a rather "stony" expression on his face. I said that it seemed to me that he might not want to be here at all, that maybe he wasn't in the mood to talk with me today and hadn't wanted to come. To this he replied, without looking at me, that he didn't care, it was all right with him. After another brief silence, I commented on how nice he looked. I particularly liked his red shirt, since red was my favorite color. He glanced at me quickly out of the corner of his eye, looked down at his shirt, hesitated, then told me that a neighbor had given it to him in return for some work he had done for her. She was an old lady who had trouble getting around, so sometimes he went to her house after school and helped with the housework. Once in a while she gave him money, but this time she gave him a shirt. He liked the shirt but would rather have money

so that he could buy things himself. It was nice to have your own money especially at recess time. He hardly ever had any to buy things with like the other "kids" did and sometimes when he was hungry he wished he could buy some pretzels or cookies. Michael told me all this in a rush without once moving his eyes from the point on which he had focused them. When I agreed that it was indeed hard to stand by and watch the other children spend their pennies on so many goodies when he had none, he turned his head slightly in my direction. I said that maybe being angry about not having as much as the other children is what made him misbehave. He said "could be, but that's not the only thing." I waited. When he said no more, I asked him if he wanted to talk about the other things that were bothering him, but he said he'd better get back to his room now. He still had plenty of work to do to try to "catch up" on account of being absent the first three weeks of school. I said that making up work was always hard. It took up lots of extra time and I guessed he would be glad when he was all caught up. He said, "You ain't kiddin'," and looked up at me for the first time.

When I suggested that he could come back another time to talk about his problems if he wanted to, he seemed pleased but only shrugged his shoulders, hesitated, and said, "OK—I guess so—when?" We decided on the following Tuesday, same time. Michael continued to sit, then blurted out, "I know I get into a lot of trouble, but what makes me real mad is I always get blamed for everything even when it's not my fault. No matter what happens the teacher jumps on me. Sometimes I can't even breathe." I said I could see how this could make him very angry and we could talk about it next time since our time was up for now. This time he got up quickly, said "All right" and, reminding himself and me about the extra work he had to do, left my office seemingly more relaxed than when he had come in.

October 16, 1959

Michael rushed in at morning recess time. He had been in a fight. Some kid hit him first, he hit him back, then managed to get away so that he could come in to get me because the other boy said he wasn't finished with him yet. I explained that this was not part of my job, that I could not go out into the yard to talk to the other boy, but suggested, instead, that he speak to the teacher on yard duty who could then, if necessary, get the principal's help. I reminded him about our regular appointment and although he said he'd come, I got the impression that he was angry at me for not refereeing his battle.

October 19, 1959

Conference with teacher. Mr. Davis told me that after my first conference with Michael the previous week, there had been a slight improvement in his conduct for the rest of the week until the fighting incident Friday morning. The remainder of that day and especially all of this morning Michael was a "real mess." He seemed determined to misbehave to the point where teaching the class with him in it was almost impossible. He related several instances of what Michael had done: writing on his desk with chalk, calling out, walking around the room, hitting a child with a coat hanger in the dressing room, sticking a child's paper to his desk with scotch tape, etc. He then asked if he couldn't please send him to me for the rest of the afternoon. He couldn't stand him any longer. He'd had all he could take for one day. Since Mr. Davis is a new teacher, I reviewed my function with him again. I agreed that it must be very difficult for him to give his attention properly to the class with Michael disrupting it so much of the time, but explained that it was not up to me to "get rid of" Michael for him. I suggested that he speak to the principal about this. She could and probably would relieve him of Michael, at least temporarily. He thanked me and said he would.

October 20, 1959
Interview with Michael. Michael was 10 minutes late for his appointment. He looked sullen and on the defensive. With a "poker face" expression, he sat down and waited for me to begin. I said he must be real busy—still catching up on his work—since he was late coming down. He didn't answer. I commented that he seemed very angry today and wondered if part of his feeling could be against me for not helping him out of the fight last week. At this he gave vent to many negative feelings, about some of the "kids," about the teacher who was always picking on him and had sent him to the office yesterday afternoon, about the principal who had given him a lecture and said he'd be suspended if he didn't behave, and last but not least about me for refusing to help him in the fight. That's why he was late for his appointment. He had left his room on time but wandered around the halls making up his mind whether or not to see me. What good was it? I was supposed to be a "friend" who helped kids in trouble, but it didn't look that way to him. Finally he decided to come anyway. It was better than going back to his room where his teacher would only "start in on him again." I let Michael talk without interruption. He spoke resentfully. His facial expression did not change. When he stopped for breath and I said that it must seem to him that everybody is against him, he said, "They are, even you."

I said I could understand why he felt this way but went on to explain my role again. I tried to show Michael that there were some things that only a principal could do best and stopping fights was one of them. My job was to help him with his behavior problem so that he would get along better with his teacher and classmates and so learn better, too. But I could do this only if he himself wanted to do something about it. It was not up to me to make him do anything. I could not tell him what to do, or scold him, or punish him. If he wanted to continue coming to me for awhile, we could talk things through so that maybe he could make up his mind if he really wanted to change. Michael looked at me a little doubtfully, then said, "That's easier said than done." I replied that he was probably right. It might not be too easy, but was it worth a try? Or did he want to go along doing the same things which would only lead to more trouble such as suspension and then maybe even worse. It was up to him. He was thoughtful a moment before he said he would like to try to behave better and would keep on coming if I wanted him to. I said it wasn't what I wanted; what did he want? It depended on him and he would have to decide all by himself.

He asked if he could think about it a minute more and when I nodded he got up and walked away from my desk. After leafing through a magazine on the table, he came back to me and said, "OK, I've decided I'll try. It's not bad coming here to talk to you. At least you don't pick on me. Besides, there is something else I want to tell you, about how things are at home, that I guess nobody else would bother to listen to. When can I come again?" We arranged a schedule of four conferences. Michael thought that should be enough "for a good start anyway," because when he made up his mind about something he was pretty sure he could do it. Trouble up to now is that he never made up his mind. The conference ended on a happier note. Michael seemed to feel challenged and left my office in a much better frame of mind.

October 27, 1959

Interview with Michael. Michael came to my office on time. He greeted me with, "Hello—guess what? My extra work is all finished. I don't have to lose recess or stay after school anymore." When I replied that this must be a big relief to him, he actually smiled a little (first time) and said "You bet!" I asked how things had been going in the classroom since I last saw him. He said, "Not too bad, not too good" then quickly reminded me that we were to talk about his home problem today. For the rest of this interview Michael did just that, with very little help from me. He spoke of his stepfather's being mean to him. He wasn't allowed to watch television or play outdoors with other children. He hit him a lot, too. When I wondered if that might not be because he spent too much time on other things and not enough on his school work he said, "No, because he was that way during the summer too." He leaned over my desk and pointed to one of his front teeth showing me where a piece was chipped off the bottom. He said it happened when he was taking a bath one night, after first having refused to do so. His stepfather came upstairs and "banged him one over the head." He fell against the tub and broke his tooth. Michael asked if I thought it could be fixed. I said I didn't know and thought it was such a shame because his teeth looked so fine and strong otherwise and this one was right in front.

He sat back in his chair, looked at me rather helplessly, and said, "What's the use of not doing something. You only get into trouble, then wind up doing it anyway." I agreed that this was usually so. We discussed it a little further and talked about how this applied in school. Michael was able to see that while it was often fun (for a while) to misbehave and make the teacher "mad" he was always punished for it in the end, and that was no fun. He sighed and said, "You can't win." I said it depended on what he wanted to "win" for himself, a better relationship with his family at home, with his classmates and teacher at school, or the consequences—trouble, punishment, or even a broken tooth. At this he touched his tooth, looked at me, and said derisively, "Are you kiddin?" then asked if the nurse would know if it could be fixed. I said she might and suggested that he ask his teacher's permission to see her. I added that I would be glad to know what she thought about it. With a smile Michael said, "Gee, I hope so. I'll tell you what Miss Locke says next time I see you," and left my office.

October 28, 1959

Michael stuck his head in my door (recess time) and asked if he could see me for just a minute. He was coming from the nurse's office and felt pretty good about what she told him, so he wanted to tell me now instead of waiting until next week.

November 2, 1959

Interview with mother. Mrs. Brown apologized for not coming in sooner to thank me for referring her to Surplus Foods. She had followed my advice and applied. She was hoping the additional food allotment would help conditions at home, but right now she wanted to talk about Michael's school problem. He wasn't saying much at home (he did tell her about his visits with me) and she had heard nothing from his teacher. This was report day. If Michael brought home a bad one again, he would surely "get it" from Mr. Brown. He would probably beat him because there were hardly any "privileges" left to take away as punishment. I explained that Michael's report might not be too good at best because of his extended absence at the beginning of the term. It had been hard for him to make up the work which he finally did only a few days ago.

I wondered if beatings and taking away of privileges were the answer or could it be that Michael took too many privileges in school because he had too few at home. Mrs. Brown was really surprised at this and said it had never dawned on her to look at it that way. We discussed the fact that there could be time for a little of everything, school work, television, play, and even helping with chores. She said she would talk it over with her husband and see if they couldn't plan some way to arrange this. Then, in an apologetic sort of way she said, "The reason my husband is so mean to Michael is that he gets on his nerves something awful." She thought she could try to be a little more patient too. It was hard, though, with all that had to be done. I said that it certainly was, but it could be that if Michael got a little more pleasant attention at home he would not feel the need to attract so much attention to himself in school. She shook her head and said again that this was certainly a brand new idea to her, but she would try it. Mrs. Brown asked if she could see Michael's teacher. I suggested that she stop in the office so that the principal could arrange it for her. She thanked me and asked that I keep in touch with her concerning Michael's progress.

November 4, 1959

Michael did not keep his appointment.

Note from Michael's teacher. Mr. Davis wrote that Michael had just asked to see me even though he had refused to keep his regular appointment that morning. I sent back word that I would be free to see him at 3:15.

Interview with Michael. (3:15 P.M.) Michael came in looking quite upset, but determined. He "marched" right over to me, sat down, and slammed a fifty-cent piece down on my desk. I looked at it and at him questioningly and waited. He was very tense and when, after a few minutes, he burst into an explanation, it was as though he had been holding his breath before letting go. This was the fifty cents he had taken from the desk of a girl who sits near him in his room. He saw her put it there and managed to "hang back" when the teacher took the class to the head of the stairs at morning recess. He was afraid to spend it during recess for fear someone would see him because everyone knew he hardly ever had any money, especially so much. So he decided to hold on to it until after school. Then he could spend it when the kids weren't around. So he left it in his desk under a pile of books. When 11:30 came he didn't want to see me. He was afraid he would tell me about it when we got to talking and he didn't want to. He was a little ashamed because he had told me that he was pretty sure he could make things better for himself. And they were getting better too—until now. He didn't know why he took the money. This wasn't the first time. He sometimes took money and other things that didn't belong to him, but he didn't know what made him do it. Michael was juggling a little game in his hand all the while telling me this. Then he looked up and said, "I never before told you, but that's what I do sometimes, I steal, but I don't know why." He looked at me as though waiting for me to tell him.

I said I wondered if it could be because he didn't have as much as the other children and this was his way of getting it. He thought a minute then said he guessed this might be a reason. When I asked how he felt after taking something that didn't belong to him, he said that was the funny part of it. He wasn't happy because he always got scared. First it felt good for a little while because he had something he wanted. Then he began to worry about being caught because he knew it was wrong and would get him into real big trouble some day if he didn't stop. This I agreed with, and we went on to talk about the fear of being caught and its possible consequences as against any temporary benefits. Michael said he didn't know if it was really worth it because he felt very funny when the class came back to the room in the afternoon and Brenda reported her half dollar was missing and the teacher began asking all kinds of questions. The money was now in his pocket and he thought everybody was looking at him. He was sure the teacher really did look at him, so he opened his desk and pretended to be looking for something. That's when he decided to tell me all about it. He was afraid to tell Mr. Davis, so a little while later when the class was busy copying homework he went up to Mr. Davis and asked him if he could come down to my office. Mr. Davis said he would get in touch with me and let him know later. He was glad when the teacher told him I would see him. All the way down he kept "thinking and talking to himself."

Michael took a deep breath and, pointing to the half-dollar on my desk, said, "So there's the money. I don't want it anymore. I'm sorry I took it." I said this must really have been a hard struggle for him and I admired his courage in reaching this decision. It was a big step in the right direction. What did he want me to do with the money? He asked if I would give it back because he was ashamed. He didn't think he'd have the nerve. I said I would if he really wanted me to since it had been hard enough for him to get all this off his chest. However, it was too late now (3:40) so we would have to wait until morning. Michael said that was OK with him but I would have to keep the money till then because he didn't trust himself that much. I agreed. When he left he said he felt better already and would see me tomorrow.

November 5, 1959

Michael came in at 8:45 before going to his room. I was surprised and said I hadn't expected to see him so early. There
hadn't been time yet for me to see his teacher. He said, "That's
good. That's why I came now. I've been thinking some more and
decided I might as well give the money back myself. But I'll only
give it to Mr. Davis not Brenda. He can give it to her. I figure
I'll get punished, but he can't kill me so I'll take a chance." I
smiled and remarked that he was being very brave and that I could
positively guarantee that he wouldn't be killed! Anyone with his
courage deserved another chance and he probably would get it. I
gave Michael the money. With a rather sickly grin, he took it
and left.

I called Mr. Davis and gave him a quick briefing on what had
happened the previous day and now.

November 10, 1959

Interview with Michael. Michael was on time. He came in
smiling, seated himself and started with, "I went to church on
Sunday." This unexpected opening took me by surprise. After
a minute I said, "Do you go every Sunday?" He replied that he
didn't always go but he did this time—then stopped. When he
didn't go on (I was beginning to surmise what this was all about),
I wondered if he had some special reason for going this Sunday.
Hesitantly and sounding almost embarrassed he told me that he had
prayed that he wouldn't steal any more. I smiled at him and said
that he was really trying so hard to do something about it. That
was the important thing. It would probably take time—maybe a
long time—and even if it wouldn't be too easy, he now seemed to
think it was worth the effort. He nodded his head in agreement
and said he sure did want to keep on trying and hoped he could do
it. He had also confided in his mother and she had promised to
help by giving him a few pennies whenever she could possibly
spare them. Then maybe he wouldn't be tempted so much to take
from others. I agreed that this, too, might help him and we went
on to talk about his school work. Michael mentioned many ways
he thought he could improve. He had already started to be a little
better before the stealing business. Now he would see if he could
keep it up. Our time was not quite up, but Michael seemed eager
to get back as though ready to prove this to himself. He said he'd
see me next week—with good news, he hoped.

November 16, 1959

Conference with teacher. Mr. Davis wanted to know what I was
doing to Michael. I laughed and said I wasn't doing anything to
him but rather *with* him and that actually Michael was doing most
of it himself. Mr. Davis said whatever it was, it seemed to be

working. Michael was improving. Not that you could say he was really good by any means, but so much better by comparison with how he had been. I was happy to hear this and hoped it would continue but had some doubts. The important thing was that he seemed determined to try, but it would be wiser not to expect too much, too soon. "Well," said Mr. Davis, "for Michael to stay in his seat all day and not get into any trouble for three days is enough for me for now. Why, he even passed his spelling test on Friday." I agreed that these were promising signs, and I was glad to know that Mr. Davis was finding Michael less difficult.

November 17, 1959

Interview with Michael. Michael walked in almost jauntily. I remarked that he seemed to feel pretty good today. He smiled rather sheepishly and stuck a paper in my face. It was Friday's spelling test. Sixteen words right out of twenty! This was really good. No wonder he was acting so pleased, I said. He confessed that this was the first test he passed this term. Now he was on his way and it wasn't a bad feeling. I mentioned that his teacher had told me about the improvement and how glad he was too. Then I reminded Michael that this was the last of the four conferences we had arranged for, just about a month ago. Did he remember saying then that he thought four would be enough? How did he feel about it now? He looked at me somewhat in alarm and shook his head vigorously from side to side. When he spoke, he was very emphatic. How could he stop now when he was only just beginning to improve? He didn't know if he could even keep it up, especially all by himself. Wasn't I allowed to help him anymore? He was visibly relieved when I assured him that I could and would until he felt better able to continue on his own. We both agreed that it was too soon for that and I, for one, felt he was making the right choice in asking for further help. I was pretty sure his teacher would feel the same way.

We then talked about how many more times he was to come. He said "Three?" with a question in his voice, then looked at me and said quickly "You don't think it will be enough, do you?" I said I didn't know. It would depend on him, but there was no reason why we couldn't make it three for now and then see how he felt about it when the time came. This satisfied him. He got up to go, but not before first reaching for his spelling paper with the remark, "Maybe I'll bring you some more of these next time I come." I remarked that he had good reason to be pleased with this one. It could be the first of a collection of such papers. He said rather skeptically, "I don't know, maybe. I'll have to study hard, but if I did it once I guess maybe I can do it again." With a "See you next Tuesday" and waving the hand holding the paper, he left my office.

November 20, 1959

Conference with principal. I brought Miss Hess up to date on my interviews with Michael and his teacher. She was pleased with his progress and said she had judged things were better from the fact that Michael had not been on the office bench for several weeks—an unheard of length of time for him. Nor was Mr. Davis complaining as much. Miss Hess had not known about the incident of the money. She considered Michael's decision to return it a very significant step forward and was glad. I was to continue seeing him. She felt that it was helping him a great deal and asked that I have another conference with her at the end of this new three-week working period with him.

RECORD 2

NORMAL "GROWING PAINS" OF A
JUNIOR HIGH SCHOOL BOY

Direct work with a boy and his mother in a situation in which the boy's school problems reflect some typical adolescent problems heightened by stress in family relationships

---

PHILLIP PARKER......12 years old, 7B grade

Family members: Parents: Mr. and Mrs. Parker.
                             Siblings: None.

School personnel: Miss Daniel, principal, Miss Jefferson, home-room teacher, first semester, Mr. Bach, home-room teacher, second semester, two other classroom teachers, school social worker.

Reason for referral: Unruly behavior; not working up to intellectual capacity. Referred by the principal.

October 9, 1958

                       Conference with principal. Miss Daniel referred Phillip to the social worker because of his behavior. He had always been somewhat difficult to handle but had not been referred to social service before because she and the teachers thought his behavior was something they could handle. She explained that he was a likeable boy with better than average intelligence. His behavior was not "mean" but he made himself "a nuisance." He would push, poke, laugh, talk out, and in other ways create a disturbance.

    Yesterday, Miss Daniel took Phillip out of his music class when she saw him poking another boy. He came back to the school at 4:15 hoping to find Miss Daniel there; as it happened she was in her office. She described Phillip as being really upset. When he came to her, he had been crying. It seemed that when he went home, he "bared his soul to his mother and she whipped him." He said that everything was his fault. He was all wrong. Miss Daniel thought he was actually asking for more punishment. Plans were made for his mother to come to school the next morning. When Miss Daniel talked with her, she learned that the parents were having problems with Phillip at home and that the mother wanted help. Miss Daniel discussed the services of the social worker with the mother and told her that she would ask that the social worker consider Phillip an "emergency" and talk with him just as soon as possible. The social worker would call the mother for an appointment.

October 9, 1958

Conference with teacher. Miss Jefferson, Phillip's homeroom teacher, said that he was doing average work. He was not working up to his intellectual ability. He had difficulty keeping his mind on his work and caused trouble in the classroom by talking with the other children and bothering them. She said that she felt sorry for Phillip and wondered if she could have been more helpful to him. She understood that his father was not well because of a stomach ulcer.

Later. Miss Jefferson explained my services to Phillip and introduced him to me.

October 9, 1958

Interview with Phillip. Phillip is a good looking boy and gives the impression of being healthy and strong. He seemed a little anxious at first about talking with me but showed considerable poise. By the end of the interview he seemed quite comfortable.

At first, Phillip expressed contrition. He said that everything that had happened was his fault, that he had to get himself straightened out on some things. He wanted me to know that he intended to get himself straightened out and that everything would be all right. I said that if he really wanted to get "straightened out" he probably could; that sometimes even when we wanted to do something, however, we had trouble managing it. Phillip began to relax and gradually began talking about his problems. He said that his father had a stomach ulcer and this worried his mother; most of the time his mother was "nervous." Sometimes he got the feeling that everyone was against him. His mother explained things to him and he knew that she was right because what she said made sense but sometimes he didn't feel the way she did about things. Phillip said he knew he had it better than either his father or his mother had it when they were young. Knowing all these things doesn't keep him from getting depressed sometimes.

He said that when he got to feeling "real low" he would talk to his dog and sometimes he even talked to himself. Phillip seemed to feel that talking to himself was pretty bad; he suggested that I keep this information confidential. He often wished that he had a brother. He had a number of friends and he thought the fellows liked him but sometimes he wasn't even sure of this.

Phillip said that his parents were not "tough" when it came to making grades. Last year he thought he got three As and one C and the rest Bs. They seemed to be satisfied with his card. They wouldn't put up, however, with his having trouble at school. Phillip has had an evening paper route for about three years. He said that he enjoyed having a paper route and he particularly liked to have this money of his own.

At the end of the interview, Phillip said that he could see why the school provides someone for "kids" to talk with. He thought this was better than talking to himself. He showed a sense of humor when he said this. We decided that he and I would have an appointment at one o'clock each Thursday for a while. I told Phillip that I would later talk with his mother when I knew him and his problems well enough to be helpful to him and his mother. I let him know that I would not be quoting him when talking with his teacher or with his parents.

October 9, 1958

Telephone call to mother. After this first interview with Phillip, I called his mother and made an appointment for November 6. I told her that Phillip and I would be talking together each week until that time. She expressed appreciation for the time given to Phillip.

October 16, 1958

Interview with Phillip. During the second interview, Phillip told me he found it very hard to do things when he was told to do them by his mother. He said that he didn't know what was wrong, but that was the way he felt about it. He thought that he really didn't want to treat his mother in that way. He often felt sorry for her because he knew that she worried about his dad. He then said, "I worry about my dad, too." He explained that his dad had a stomach ulcer because his boss was so impossible.

Phillip told about a particular incident in order for me to understand what happened between him and his mother. The day before, he had misplaced his coat at school; after basketball practice he could not find it. He had to hurry home to his papers. He decided that he could get along without his coat until the next day, and he felt sure he would be able to find it at school then. He thought that one of his teachers might have put it somewhere. When he got home, his mother asked about his coat and he told her what had happened. His mother then got mad, and this made Phillip mad because she didn't have any confidence in him. He left the house to deliver his papers feeling very angry but by the time he returned from his paper route, he was no longer mad and he guessed his mother had gotten over it too. He then located his coat at school the next day. When his mother got mad, he didn't say anything and she didn't "say much, but it was the way she looked." When Phillip's dad got home from work, Phillip told him that he had made his mother mad and maybe she was still mad. Phillip explained that it wasn't good for him to tell his father this kind of thing because he and his mother were not supposed to worry his father at home. Phillip thought that taking care of his coat was his business.

Phillip said he didn't like for his mother to be looking after him all the time. She treated him as if he were much younger. She was always wanting to do things for him, such as tying his tie. He thought that she didn't really want him to grow up. She would say such things as "Where is my little boy?" He thought that telling her that he could do certain things for himself would only hurt her feelings. Phillip felt that he could really take responsibility and that his mother could depend on him and trust him. As he continued to give this some thought, he acknowledged that he might "pull a boner" sometimes, but he thought that if things went wrong, he could get them straightened out. As we continued to talk about this, Phillip found that he wasn't entirely sure what he wanted his mother to do for him and what he wanted to do for himself. We talked about the fact that when boys and girls grow up, things change and that changes are hard for both the parents and the children. As time was up, we agreed that we would talk further about this another time.

October 30, 1958

Third interview with Phillip, two weeks later. We discussed my talking with his mother the next week before I would see him. He needed reassurance again that I would not be quoting him. I told him that his mother would be talking with me about some of the things that seemed most important to her. He said, "If you let her know that I don't want her to do things for me, she'll probably start blubbering." Phillip has been getting along better in school during the past two weeks, and when he realized that his mother would be learning when she came to school that he had been handling some of his problems at school, he seemed relieved. Phillip then said, "I like to do things for my mother. I took her out to dinner the other night because my dad can never take her out because he can't eat restaurant food. We had a real pleasant time."

November 6, 1958

Interview with mother at school. The mother appears to be in her thirties. She was carefully groomed with tinted auburn hair. She has a full face and a square jaw which tends to give her a rather stern expression. I found her to be intelligent, thoughtful, and to have a sense of humor.

The mother started the interview by telling me that there had really been no problems with Phillip until the past year. She didn't know why he seemed to like to aggravate her. To illustrate what Phillip would do, she told me of what happened the past Saturday morning. They had a strict rule that Phillip was to use the back door so that he wouldn't be walking over the living room rug which was light in color. Because he couldn't seem to remember to come around to the back door, the mother had locked the front door Saturday morning. When Phillip came home and found it locked, he went around to the back door, through the house, and unlocked the front door. He then went out again and the mother locked the front door. He soon returned, tried the front door and on finding it locked, went to the back door and through the house to unlock the front door again. After he was gone the second time, the mother again locked the front door. The door was locked by the mother and unlocked by Phillip twenty-five times between breakfast and lunch time. When the father came home, the mother told him what had been happening. The father then told Phillip that he was to come in the back door and there was to be no more trouble about it. Phillip said nothing by way of reply to his father and since that time has been using the back door. Another example of his attitude was the bad manners he showed when he and his mother went to a neighbor's for lunch. Phillip slumped over on the table and the mother told him that if he couldn't straighten up, he could go home. The mother felt that Phillip was only trying to embarrass her.

Phillip had told his parents the evening before his mother was to talk with the social worker, "Miss Hayes told me exactly what's wrong with me. She said that I need to take more responsibility for myself." The father then said, "Well, how many years have we been telling you that very thing." The father then reviewed some of the things they had tried to get Phillip to do. (These words which Phillip put in the social worker's mouth seemed to be his effort to let the parents know that he could do more things for himself.)

The mother told of Phillip's failure to take care of his room and do the few things which were expected of him around the house. It was always very difficult to get him to bed and to get him up in the morning. She said that he had come to school today upset because his mother had not taken his good pants to the cleaners, and he was going to have to wear them to the dancing class party the coming Friday. The mother had told him that she could not take the pants to the cleaners because she did not have the car that week. She told him that he should have thought about having his pants cleaned earlier. She then told me that she would, of course, get his pants ready for him. She would clean them up herself and press them good, but she hadn't told him that she intended to do this. She planned to clean and press them and hang them in his closet so that he would be surprised when the time came. I asked the mother if she would ordinarily take care of seeing that his clothes were sent to the cleaners, and she said that she did this for him. I asked her why she didn't want to give Phillip the satisfaction of knowing that his pants would be ready for the dancing party. She looked a little surprised at the question but seemed to get the point. She referred back to the trouble she and Phillip had Saturday morning about his coming in the front door. She wondered what she should do when he treated her that way. She thought, as she looked back on the whole affair, that she had handled it very badly and that the whole thing was ridiculous. We discussed the possibility that Philip did actually forget when he came in the front door and that if this were true, she might have suggested that he lock the door himself as that would act as a reminder. The mother spoke of Phillip's rebelling against her, and I suggested that sometimes she felt rebellious too. She smiled and said, "That's true."

I asked the mother to tell me about some of the good times that she and Phillip and the father had together. She related a school incident which had made the parents realize that Phillip needed some sex instruction. He had used the word "whore" at school and did not know what the word meant. When he was corrected at school, he came home and told his mother exactly what he had said. When the father came home, the three of them sat down and talked about sex and the relationship between a man and his wife. The mother recalled this as being one of the most satisfactory times that the three of them had ever had together. She felt that she and the father had really handled Phillip's problem very well. When he told her about the word that he had used at school and said that he had learned it from another high school boy, she knew immediately that he didn't know what the word meant.

Phillip had had a wiener roast on the Monday night before. The mother thought that she had handled this well. He had first planned to have the party on Saturday evening but it was raining and she and the father and Phillip decided together that it should be called off until Monday evening. They allowed Phillip to decide whether he would invite both boys and girls, or just boys. Phillip finally decided to invite just his boy friends. They had also encouraged Phillip to go on a hayride which his group at church was having.

The mother and I talked about the emotional conflict in a boy of Phillip's age because he wants to be big and independent but is at the same time a little afraid of growing up. We discussed the need for them to tolerate some of his rebellion against authority. In this part of the discussion, I said that most parents had some mixed feelings about seeing a child this age change from a small child to a young man or young woman. I said, "It's hard for grown-ups to realize that children feel older and are a little afraid of getting older." The mother related her own feelings as a child. She said that she always rebelled against her father's authority and had made up her mind that she would never tell her child to do something without explaining why. She felt that she and the father had always been very careful to explain to Phillip exactly why they expected him to do certain things. We talked about some of the times that we, as adults, need to stand by and let a child learn from his own experience. At other times, the child lets us know that he needs reassurance and support. The mother told about Phillip, not long ago, taking something to bed with him that he had had as a small child.

The mother also told me about the father's illness, saying that she and Phillip had talked together many times about the importance of their not worrying the father with their problems and of making home life pleasant for him. I tried to help the mother to see that a child could not always have things under control. He was not an adult, and we could not expect him always to behave as a well adjusted adult. The possibility that Phillip would feel guilty if he made things unpleasant for the father was discussed. I tried to help her understand that this kind of guilt would not be good for Phillip.

At the end of the interview, I told the mother that we felt that Phillip was doing a good job of working on problems which he had at school, and we believed that he was getting along all right.

Interview with Phillip (later). Soon after Phillip and I settled down to talk, he said, "You know, I feel the same way that I did the first day when I came to talk with you, that is, before we got acquainted." He explained his feeling as being jittery and uneasy. He said he didn't know why he felt this way. I suggested he was a little anxious about his mother coming to talk with me in the morning. He immediately said that this was not true and then said, "Well, maybe it is a little." Phillip and I devoted this interview to talking about his father's illness and what his mother had said about the effort that both he and she had made toward keeping things happy at home because this would be best for his father. I tried to help Phillip to understand that this is the kind of thing that we try to do and want to do, but we are not always successful in keeping our feelings under control. We talked about anger and love being very closely related, and we also talked about the fact that his father would want to know about his problems. Phillip and I decided that we would talk further about this in our next interview.

Conference with classroom teachers. After seeing Phillip and his mother, I talked with two of Phillip's teachers. They said that he was getting along pretty well in school. There had been some difficulty about his talking too much to his neighbors, but he had been consciously working on this. I told the teachers something of Phillip's problems because of his father's poor health.

November 20, 1958 to February 12, 1959

Summary of five conferences with homeroom teachers. During this period, five conferences were held with Miss Jefferson and Mr. Bach, homeroom teachers. Phillip was moved to Mr. Bach's homeroom at the beginning of the second semester. During the last half of the first semester and the beginning of the second semester, Phillip had made definite progress in using his time at school. His work improved, and his grades at the end of the first semester were tangible evidence of better use of his time and ability. There have been some days when he seemed quite irresponsible and immature. His teachers have tried to be firm but patient on these days and have reported to the social worker that Phillip seemed to come to school in the morning "feeling stirred up." When Phillip has been corrected, he has expressed disgust with himself.

Shortly before Christmas Phillip was involved in a classroom skirmish which ended in one of the girls breaking her arm. Phillip took the girl's pencil off her desk. She went to Phillip's desk for the pencil and while she was gone, another boy pulled her chair out of place. She sat on the floor, breaking her arm in the fall. This affair was very disturbing to Phillip. He felt that he was to blame. His teacher reported that he was very upset. The girl and her parents regarded the whole affair as an accident and did not blame either of the boys.

November 20, 1958 to January 15, 1959

Summary of four interviews with Phillip. During this period, Phillip has talked about his resentment when his mother tries to make him do things. These periods of resentment have been followed by guilt because he has not co-operated with his mother.

He and his mother have often had trouble because she has tried to get him up in the morning. One morning he resisted and "accidentally scratched her hand." He and his mother had also had considerable trouble about his cleaning his room. This was his responsibility, and he thought it reasonable that he take such responsibility, but he thought he should have some say about when he did the cleaning. At the December 4 interview, Phillip decided that he would ask his mother to call him at seven in the morning and give him fifteen minutes to get up. He explained that he wanted her to call him if he went back to sleep, but he liked to have a while to wake up without being reminded by her. He also decided that he would ask his mother to give him until Saturday noon to clean his room each week. He could understand why she wanted the room cleaned for the weekend. He wasn't sure whether he would clean it on Friday evening or Saturday morning, but he didn't want to be reminded by his mother. In a later interview he told me that he had worked out these two plans with his mother and that he was having no difficulty about getting up in the morning or getting his room cleaned. He said that he and his mother were having less difficulty since they were following the plan he suggested. He expressed surprise that his mother had been so willing to co-operate with him. Having said this, he almost immediately decided that maybe he hadn't been fair to her.

February 5, 1959 and February 12, 1959

Interviews with Phillip. In each interview, Phillip talked about his father's health and whether he would make his father worse if he discussed his own problems with him. I have tried to help Phillip understand that ignoring problems does not help anyone. He has made definite progress in his ability to see that coming to a better understanding of his problems and doing something about them is the best way to relieve tension. He has applied this to his father's problems, and has talked about his father as a tense person who worries about everything. Phillip agreed when I suggested that his father would want to know about Phillip's difficulties at school and what Phillip was trying to do about them. Later, Phillip said, "I talked with my father about a lot of things and I feel a lot better." He and his father had talked about the mother not wanting Phillip to do things away from home and to be independent. Phillip said "My dad and I understand each other." He continued, "It wouldn't be right for me to tell my mother I am older than she thinks. She will realize that pretty soon, maybe before the end of this year." He talked about his parents being his bosses. He thought that they should see to it that he did the things that were right for a boy of his age to do. Phillip had told his father about the girl at school breaking her arm and how this happened. He said that both of his parents felt that the accident was regrettable, but told him that there was no reason for him to worry about it. Phillip had also talked with his father about having dates with his friend, Mabel, who is a high school freshman.

In the two interviews, Phillip and I looked forward to discontinuing our interviews. We reviewed some of the things that had been accomplished at school. He was making better grades and having less difficulty in the classroom. He felt that he was in better control of himself and not talking to other boys and girls as he used to do, although he sometimes forgot. He was on the basketball team and looking forward to being a four-letter man in high school. He explained, "That will be my best way of getting through college." He had taken over a Star paper route, having saved enough money to pay for it. He thought that the best thing that had happened was learning how to talk with his mother and his father about some of the things that worried him. Phillip said that Mr. Bach was being more helpful to him as a homeroom teacher than Miss Jefferson had been. He then laughed and said that he guessed Miss Jefferson had had more to put up with than Mr. Bach had. He felt that since he was able to discuss his feelings and to talk about them with his mother and father, he could concentrate better on his school work.

Phillip and I agreed that we would discontinue regular interviews but that he should feel free to get in touch with me on any Thursday that he felt that he had problems and wanted to talk them over with me.

February 20, 1959

Case closed. Phillip's school work and behavior improved.

RECORD 3

BRIEF SERVICE

Help to a child, primarily through work with the father to modify his negative attitude toward the school and work with the teacher to further her understanding of the child

DAVE CUTTS	7 years old, 2nd grade.
Family members:	Parents: Mrs. Cutts, housewife, and Mr. Cutts, Army Sergeant. Siblings: Harry, 18 months old.
School personnel:	Mr. Taber, principal, Mrs. Wood, teacher, school social worker.
Reason for referral:	Aggressive behavior, refusal to conform to school rules. Referred by teacher.

November 23, 1955

Conference with teacher. Mrs. Wood, Dave's teacher, requested help from social service because of her concern over the child's repeated failure to conform to school rules. He throws rocks, uses fists freely, and does not get along well on the playground. In the school room he is sly, tries to hurt other boys by tripping them, twisting arms, poking, and otherwise misbehaving. Mrs. Wood had attempted to handle the problem by depriving Dave of play periods and by sending him to the principal's office, but she does not feel that these measures have helped. At one time she saw Dave's mother and discussed some of these problems.

In discussing this problem with Mrs. Wood, I recognized how upsetting Dave's behavior must be to her in her class, and she agreed and admitted that she felt very angry with Dave. I suggested that Dave must be very unhappy since children feel more comfortable and happy when they get along with their teacher and with their fellow pupils and I thought it would take us some time to explore together what was bothering Dave. It was agreed that I would see Dave and his parents and keep in touch with Mrs. Wood.

Interview with Dave. In my office, Dave played with the clown quite viciously but apparently was still afraid that his feelings would not be acceptable. When he found that he was accepted, however, he put the clown away and asked to play with the checkers—which we did. During this game he told me that his father plays with him but that his mother is too busy; he expressed negative feelings about his young brother, aged one and one-half years.

November 30, 1955

Interview with Mrs. Cutts. Dave's mother told me that Harry, Dave's brother, did bother Dave somewhat. He interfered with his toys and now and again Dave hit the baby over the head with something he might be playing with. Most of the time she felt they played fairly well. She went on to say that one of the problems was that Dave did not have children of his age to play with, but played with younger children. Where they had lived last year, Moses Lake, there had been many children, because it was an Army station, and Dave had become quite rough while he was there. I wondered if Dave's behavior now might be related to the fact that he is a newcomer in the school and perhaps his way of initiating relationships with other children is to be more aggressive. This might cause the children to reject him. He might feel discriminated against in the household because of the attention his mother and father pay to the younger child. It is possible that Dave is reacting to his younger brother, Harry, who might be getting more attention in the family because of his age. It was agreed that we would continue to explore this and arrangements were made for Mr. Cutts to call me regarding an appointment in order that we might help Dave as much as possible.

November 30, 1955 to December 22, 1955

Conferences with teacher. Periodic conferences were held with Mrs. Wood during this period. She felt that Dave was still exhibiting the same behavior—using his fists freely and acting in what she felt was a rather sneaky way. At one conference she told me that Dave had been acting up with the ball in the play yard and she had forbidden him to use the ball for a week, but the very next day she had seen him playing with it and he had denied it. She had sent him to the principal's office, where he was to sit until the principal could see him.

December 22, 1955

Interview with father. I saw Mr. Cutts by appointment. He is a very tall man and very aggressive. He is a sergeant in the Air Force at Forest. He was very angry that the teacher had made complaints about Dave, and had had a telephone conversation with the principal about this. According to Mr. Cutts, he told the principal that his job was to teach his child, and his job as a parent was to see that he behaved at home. I recognized how angry he was about something and wasn't quite sure what, and he told me that he felt that Dave was being picked upon at school, and I wondered what made him think that. He floundered around at this and I helped him by mentioning that he probably did have feelings about Dave being criticized for his free use of his fists. He told me at great length that he had had to fight his way to and from school until he was in the fourth grade, at which time his father had taught him to fight sufficiently well so that he wasn't molested any more, and that this was his idea of bringing up Dave. He was also very angry because his wife reported that Mrs. Wood had told her that Dave was the worst boy she had taught. I recognized that this indicated rather strong feeling on the teacher's part. I pointed out that teachers were human beings just as we are. I was sure he often got angry with the thirty-five men whom he said were under his control on airplane maintenance and possibly felt very angry with them at times. I was sure, I said, that the teacher was just as human in this respect as he was. The significant thing was that Mrs. Wood wanted help from him as a parent and from his wife as a parent in order to help with this problem; I had been called in on the same basis.

His general feeling was that nobody was going to pick on his boy. In order to do this they would have to go through him and he felt that he was big enough and strong enough to defend himself and his son. I wondered whether he really thought that the group of adults who were responsible for Dave while he was at school were deliberately trying to destroy Dave, since to me picking on a child constantly in a way that Mr. Cutts was suggesting was an attempt to really destroy a child psychologically. I agreed with him that if he felt this then he certainly should remove the boy from school as soon as he could, since I certainly wouldn't want my child subjected to such treatment. At the same time, I told Mr. Cutts, I felt this was far from the truth; actually it was our concern for Dave that he get the most out of his school experience and learn to socialize with other children that was causing us to pool our resources and to call on the parents to share with us how we could best help Dave develop into a mature adult.

Mr. Cutts became a bit less aggressive and pointed out that he wasn't criticizing the schools and that his experiences in schools, especially the Air Force, was very good and he had been able to progress as a result of the training he had received in the Air Force schools. I wondered whether he thought that he would have gotten as much out of the Air Force schools as he had if he had been engaged aggressively with the other students in the class and suspicious of his teachers' motives toward him. He thought that he had gotten along very well in school and had enjoyed his experience. I told him that this is what we wanted for Dave; yet at this point Dave must feel very hostile in his school setting, otherwise he wouldn't behave the way he is behaving. Mr. Cutts thought there were other children to blame and that they were probably picking on Dave. I felt that this might be so, but we had not seen any indication of it. While we could be wrong, I felt, from what he told me of his own experiences and what he had been teaching Dave, that it was very possible that Dave was merely identifying with him and his experiences many years ago. I pointed out that the school system had changed radically in the last twenty or twenty-five years, just as the Air Force had, and our educational purpose was to help each child to become a good citizen and learn to use himself to his fullest capacity. Mr. Cutts embarked upon a discussion of the importance of the service, that we should be ready for aggressive behavior on the part of other nations; I agreed that these were valuable concepts from a national point of view but that, hopefully, a child's relationship with his school and with his fellow students should be a much more amicable one based on much more trust than was possible at this time in international relationships. It was only when we could identify with each other in our country and trust each other that we could present a united front to the outside aggression.

I helped Mr. Cutts to look at the needs of Dave as a child and at the fact that it was not fair to Dave to impose on him aggressive behavior which was bound to get him into all sorts of trouble. Perhaps later, when he was older and had first learned how to be friendly with other children, he could learn self-defense as a means of protecting himself instead of as an aggressive weapon at a time when he was too young to use it wisely. I compared the discipline of the army with that of the school and pointed out that one was developed for the purpose of helping adults to work as a team; whereas, the school was dealing with young pliant children who had to be taught ways of behavior and self-control. We parted thoroughly good friends and Mr. Cutts told me he had been ten years in the permanent Air Force and would be retiring in four years. He said that Dave had been in various schools, both in this country and abroad. I pointed out to him that this was rather difficult for a child because it meant that he was uprooted from time to time and really never got to know the children in his group well. This was something that would have to be taken into consideration and he could be very helpful to his son if he tried to understand what the boy felt, and helped him express a lot of his feelings which might be anger toward adults because of what he might feel has been done to him. We all know how we hate to leave our friends; how much more cruel this is for a little boy who got to like other little boys and then was taken away from them when his parents were transferred from one station to another, and to him this was his parents' decision because they were God Almighty in his eyes.

It was agreed that Mr. Cutts and I would have a further conference sometime this spring to see how Dave was getting along. I was to call his wife about this.

Conference with teacher. I later talked with Mrs. Wood and gave her the gist of what had taken place between Mr. Cutts and me. At this point she was able to say that she did have very strong feelings about lying and she recognized how her moral concepts had made her feel harsh with Dave. I pointed out that lying, to a child Dave's age, could be a defensive mechanism, rather than a moral failure. I also felt that it might be helpful if she had deprived him of playing with the ball for just one day, since it was difficult for a child Dave's age and maybe with Dave's personality makeup to sustain such obedience for a longer period, and perhaps this would be sufficient to help him realize that he had to conform to discipline of the school. Mrs. Wood related very well to this discussion. She thought that she would try out what I suggested, agreeing with me that we did not know whether or not we would be successful. If we tried to understand the child and to know something about what motivated him, it could give us a different idea of what was involved and make us less judgmental. She recognized that she had been imposing her standards on Dave and that it would be more helpful to him if she tried to understand his standards and helped him achieve the standards of the group.

March 12, 1956

Summary. I did not see Dave again because I felt that more could be accomplished in his behalf through work with his parents and his teacher. His father had ended our one interview on a very positive note. I consulted with Mrs. Wood, Dave's teacher, periodically. She reported that after the Christmas Holidays Dave had behaved like quite a different boy and was getting into no further trouble. She had been able to tell the parents this when she saw them at a PTA meeting.

Conference with principal. Mr. Taber, the principal, said that Dave had commented to him that he was no longer being sent to the principal's office. Dave remarked that he had changed his ways.

Telephone call to mother. When I called Mrs. Cutts, as I had promised her husband I would, she said that Mrs. Wood had told her what a change there was in Dave and that she saw it herself around the house, too. She felt that one reason for his change in behavior was the fact that they no longer let him look at TV nearly as much as they had before; rather, they utilized some of this time to do things with him, especially with his father. They felt gratified that Dave's behavior had improved. They intended to continue doing things with him.

Case closed. Child no longer a problem to the teacher.

RECORD 4

ADOLESCENT BOY WITHOUT FATHER IN THE HOME

Direct work with an adolescent boy and his mother; the father had deserted the family and the boy had no male figure with whom to identify

---

JAMES MASON.........13 years old, 7B

Family members: Mrs. Mason, mother, employed as a medical secretary. Siblings: Helen, 18, telephone operator.

School personnel: Mrs. Davis, principal, Miss Wagner, teacher, Miss Andrio, teacher, homeroom teacher (woman), shop class teacher (man), school social worker.

Reason for referral: Absence from school, sullen attitude, no friends; not working up to intellectual capacity. Referred by principal.

November 15, 1959

                       Conference with principal. Mrs. Davis, principal, referred James because he had not been in school for ten days and his whereabouts were unknown. He had missed over thirty days of school during the current semester. Three periods of absence had been excused because of illness. Mrs. Davis said that he usually remains away from school for two or three days at a time and is then returned by his mother who says that she is "helpless" and unable to make her son go to school. She works as an office secretary and needs to leave home for work before it is time for James to leave for school. He promises her that he will go, dresses for school and pretends to be going. She is never aware that he has not been in school until she is called by the attendance office. She has tried punishment of various kinds but recognizes that this had had little effect. The mother expressed a wish that the school be more active in "forcing my son to attend."

Examination of school cumulative record. The record shows that James is a physically well developed boy, 13 years and 3 months of age. He has an I.Q. of 128 (Stanford Binet). In spite of his frequent absence from school he has made average grades and has been regularly promoted. He is in 7B. He has had a poor attendance record over a five-year period.

The teacher's evaluation reports describe James as being: "cooperative, somewhat sullen at times, preoccupied during class period, appears restless and indifferent, fails to work up to his capacity, seems to resent other pupils."

There is no record of James ever having been in any serious trouble. This past year he had been sent to the principal's office for having created a situation of disturbance in his homeroom, when his teacher had been talking about the Easter Season and had made mention of "God." James interrupted the teacher by saying, "I don't believe there is a God." Other children in the room became badly upset and vented their feelings against James. He, in turn, became sullen and defensive. The teacher had been frightened by the disturbance and took James to the office, as a solution to the classroom situation. He had refused to discuss the matter with the principal and spent the rest of the day in the office. Following this incident, he was absent for a three-day period. The mother returned him to school, saying that he had been ill with a stomach upset. For some time afterwards, the other children seemed to be indifferent to James and he was unusually sullen. The mother was "horrified" when she was told what her son had said in class. She said that he had certainly not gotten this idea at home, and she just doesn't know where he gets "all his crazy ideas."

One other instance of misbehavior in school occurred when James was in the fifth grade and destroyed his report card. He gave no explanation as to why he did this, admitted to doing it and said he would do it again, at the end of the semester. Neither his teacher nor his mother could understand his action, since his recorded grades had been reasonably good ones.

November 17, 1959

Interview with mother at home. An appointment was made with Mrs. Mason for an evening home call. The Masons live in a downstairs flat in an old building in fairly good repair. The flat has only one bedroom, which is shared by Mrs. Mason and her daughter. James sleeps on a cot in one corner of the living room. He has a closet of his own in which all his possessions are kept. The flat is reasonably well furnished, though the family does not own a television, radio, phonograph, or piano. One gets the feeling that there is little in the home that would interest a teenager.

Mrs. Mason had been expecting me and was obviously very anxious over my coming. At first we felt ill-at-ease with one another and had some difficulty making conversation. It was evident that she assumed I had come in the capacity of a policeman and I felt it important to clear my role with her. She then expressed a belief that I probably couldn't be of much help to James, since what he needed was "strict authority." She launched into a long discussion about how difficult it had been for her to try to raise him without a "man in the house." She explained that the father had left the family when James was only three years old and she had had full responsibility for earning the living and giving care to both her children. I agreed that this had been a big responsibility for her alone and said that she had done very well to raise her children, and keep them with her until now. She cried and said it had been "too great a struggle." The daughter had never been any trouble and James had been a "good boy" until he was around eleven or twelve years old; since then he has been a "constant source of worry and concern." She doesn't know what she is going to do with him. She has much work and cannot stay home to "control him." He pretends to "listen to her and to mind, then goes off and does as he pleases." She feels that "he has it in for her." He criticizes her for not having stayed with the father and refuses to believe that the father deserted the family. While he rarely talks or asks about the father, every now and then he brings up the subject and asks "all sorts of personal questions." Mrs. Mason says that she has needed to lie to him about some things he asks about. I asked her to explain this statement and she said, "Well, James wants to know if his father was any good? I once told him the truth, that his father wasn't, and he ran screaming from the room and called me all sorts of names." After that, James asked several times about what was wrong with his father and the mother would say "nothing, it's all my fault." On one occasion the sister answered for the mother and told James that the father couldn't earn a living for his family, so he took off. James wanted to know what kind of work the father had done. He had been a bartender and the mother didn't want him to know this, so she said, "he was a carpenter." Again James flew into a rage and said, "you dirty old liar, I know he was a bartender." She has no idea how he knew, and she tried to deny it.

I asked Mrs. Mason whether or not she had ever been happy in her marriage and she said that she had been. The marriage had gone very well until James was born. Somehow, the added responsibility of this second child seemed too much for her husband. He had complained of the expense of having two children, said he couldn't stand the noise at home and seemed to resent the attention that Mrs. Mason gave to the baby, although this had not been true with Helen. Mrs. Mason said that her husband "liked a good time; he did some social drinking, but never got drunk. He enjoyed a card game, having lots of friends." When she was "tied down" with two children, she felt that she couldn't entertain as much as the husband wanted her to and she refused to go out and leave the children. He then started going out alone and little by little they grew apart. She once told him that if he couldn't take the responsibility for being a husband and father, then he had "better get out." He said that he had been thinking of doing just this. In less than a month he was gone. She had not meant what she said, but when Mr. Mason indicated that he wanted to leave, "my pride wouldn't let me tell him and I pretended that I didn't care if he stayed or not." Again Mrs. Mason cried and said "you see, I really am responsible."

Mr. Mason apparently left the city, going to New Jersey to live near his parents. He wrote to the children several times and sent money. At one time he sent a thousand dollars and said he wanted this put in the bank for their education. Later he moved to Seattle and Mrs. Mason lost contact with him. When James was nine, an attorney visited Mrs. Mason and said that he was representing her husband, who was asking for a divorce. This was granted. Mrs. Mason was trained as a medical secretary and had no trouble finding work. During her years of separation, she kept the children in school and a day nursery. Later she had a high school girl come in during the time that she was away from home. Most of her off-work hours have been devoted to the children. She says that she has had very little "life of my own." Again I sympathized with her for the burden of responsibility that she has needed to carry. She commented, "I need no sympathy, I probably brought it on myself and now I'm paying."

James was not at home when I visited and I inquired about him. Mrs. Mason said that he had run away from home, some ten days ago. She learned through some neighbors that he was staying with a friend just a few blocks away, so she did not call the police. On the third day, he returned home, was sullen, would not talk about where he had been. He then became ill, vomited and "had the jitters." She put him to bed. The following day he was so weak that she did not have him go to school. She then took him to a doctor who examined him and told her that the boy needed rest and a special diet. She continued to keep him at home and in bed, but did not call the school "for fear you would insist that he come right back." When he recovered from his illness, some two days ago, he refused to return to school, saying, "nobody likes me there and I won't go."

This was the first time he had been so open about not going. She had insisted that he go to school today and he prepared himself for school, and said that he would go. She gave him a written excuse, prepared his lunch, and he took off. When he had not returned home by six o'clock, she called the friends where he had stayed before and found that he had been with them since 3 p.m. They asked that he stay for dinner and the evening and she had given her permission. The mother said, "James has a mind of his own and he's getting so big that I'm almost afraid to tell him what to do." I wondered if she might not be afraid of his leaving home for good? The mother was very thoughtful about this and said, "perhaps I am, I've never been able to think this out loud." I asked if she feared that he would follow in his father's footsteps and she then told me how very much James is like his father. He looks "like him and has the same disposition, sensitive and always getting his feelings hurt. The only difference being that the father liked people and James doesn't seem to want to make friends, except with the one family he visits."

Mrs. Mason asked if I should like to wait, while she went to get James and bring him home. I suggested that I return on Monday morning, at 9 a.m. to see him and to talk with him about returning to school. The mother seemed worried that he might leave home before I arrived, since she would need to leave early. I asked her to tell him of my planned visit and to ask him to remain home to see me and she agreed to this plan.

November 20, 1959
Interview with James. I called at the home at nine on Monday morning, as agreed. Mrs. Mason met me at the door, saying that she had stayed home from work to make sure James would be home to see me. She then excused herself and left for her job, saying that James was inside waiting for me.

When I walked in, James was seated at the breakfast table drinking coffee. He stood up and said, "Oh, hello, Mom said you were coming." I walked over and sat down at the table with him, saying that as he already knew, I was the social worker from the school and had come to help him get started back in school. He appeared to freeze up and had nothing to say. I said that I knew that he must be worried about being out of school, when he was supposed to go, and that I knew it was a hard thing to go back after missing so many days. Tears came to his eyes and he then turned his back on me and said, "I've been sick." I said that his mother had told me of his being ill, but that I also knew that he had stayed away from school for other reasons. He could tell me these when he wanted to. The important thing today was to get back into school and I was here to help him do this. He said, "I could do it myself if I wanted to." I agreed that he could, saying I supposed that part of my job was to help him want to. He gave a half laugh at this and his tension seemed to break somewhat with this humor. I then said, "How about getting your coat and notebook and heading over to school with me?" He made a half move to do this by standing up, then he looked me over carefully and said, "my mom said that I have to do what you say."

While getting into his coat, James said, "What are you, a cop or sumpin." I smiled and said that he must have been expecting a cop, after playing hookey for so long, but I really wasn't a cop but a man from the school who is hired to help kids having trouble in school and even trouble going to school. His comment was "That's a new one to me." James was very slow in getting ready and careful to try all the doors and windows to make sure they were locked, before we left. When we were almost in the car, he said that he had forgotten his pen, returned to the house for this and was gone for several minutes. He then returned with his hair carefully combed and wearing a shirt and tie, which he had not had on before.

Enroute to the school, James was very quiet and I did not make many efforts at conversation. He finally asked, as we neared the school, "Will I have to go in and see that old Mrs. Davis." I said that he would, but that I would go in with him and together we could make plans for his getting back into classes. He expressed his belief that she wouldn't have him back and I reassured him that she would, since she had been the one who asked me to come and see him. He guessed that she wanted him back so she could "give me the devil." I again said that we would face this together.

Mrs. Davis met us when we came into the building and invited us into her office. She paid very little attention to me and seemed to take charge of James, asking him, "How long have you been absent?" He told her that he had not been in school for over a week. She picked up his attendance record on her desk and said, "Ten days of absence! What do you have to say for yourself?" James held his head low and made no reply. Mrs. Davis said to me, "I don't know what we're going to do with this boy, he is always in and out of school!" I said that I knew this had been true but that I thought that I could work out a plan with James that would help him to be more regular in school, since he must have had some good reasons for staying away. Maybe we would need to work together on these reasons. Mrs. Davis said, "Well, I place him in your hands." She then looked at the class schedule and asked James where he was supposed to be this period. He said he belonged in "Social Studies." She then gave him a little slip and told him to go to his room. I excused myself for a minute and followed James into the hall, saying, "I know it's hard to come back," and asking him if he would be willing to meet in front of the school at noon. He replied "O.K."

and walked slowly down the hall, after I had given him a pat on the back.

Conference with principal (later). I returned to the office where I found Mrs. Davis very pessimistic about our achieving anything with James. I told her of my contact with his mother and that I had not yet had much opportunity to know James, though I would try to do so over the next few days. She said that the school could not continue "to put up with his being in and out," and that unless he was regular in his attendance something would need to be done about putting him where he would have to stay in school. She did agree, however, to my having some time to try and work with James. I told her that I would need her help all along the way and would keep her informed of what I was doing on the case.

Tentative evaluation. It is my impression that James is a very lonely boy, trying to put up a brave front and to find some place where he belongs and can feel comfortable with himself. There appears to be a strong neurotic component in his make-up, as evidenced by his ambivalence towards school, his swings in mood, and his obvious feelings of insecurity. He is intelligent, yet unable to work up to his capacity. He is a disturbed adolescent, whose problems are exacerbated. Social factors affecting this boy's behavior include: the absence of a meaningful adult male figure in his life, with whom he might identify and whom he might emulate; the ineffectiveness of the mother's discipline; the fact that, during the daytime hours, no responsible adult is in his home and the home itself holds little or no interest for him, and he has found few interests outside the home, partly because of his apparent inability to either make or sustain relationships.

Plan of treatment (tentative). To attempt to establish and maintain a meaningful relationship with this boy, which might enable him to gain confidence in an adult male and permit him to use this relationship to enhance his own self-esteem and his efforts to be himself.

Evaluation. James seems accessible to help. He needs to be understood so that he, in turn, can come to understand himself. He is making a feeble effort to "be on his own" and in a way that has been destructive to him. His effort must be reinforced and redirected with my help.

Interview with James (noon). I saw James during the noon hour, taking him to lunch with me in the school cafeteria. I asked him how things had gone for him this morning. With a shrug of the shoulders, he replied "O.K., I guess." He took very little food on his tray and had nothing to say to me while we were in line. He picked a table where we might be alone together and helped me with my plates. I did not try to make conversation and he busied himself eating, finishing what he had, almost before I had started.

When he finished he piled up his plates and took them to the window to be washed. He then returned and sat in the chair next to me, where I could not look at him without turning my head. He said very directly, "I just can't go to school, Mr. Burton." I asked him if he wanted to tell me why. He said, "It's all crazy and you wouldn't understand." I agreed that I might not understand, but would try to do so; I wondered, too, if he really knew himself. He was very pensive and finally said, "I just don't like it, it's not getting me anywhere." I asked did he know where he wanted to go? He talked of getting a job, "working in a grocery or something." I said that I thought he would make a good grocery boy. He asked me why I said "that." I told him that I knew from his school reports that he was very bright and could do many things, if he wanted to do them. He obviously warmed up to me with this statement, though he needed to deny that he was a bright boy, saying "Ah, I'm not so smart, my grades aren't too good!" I told him that I thought his grades didn't represent his ability; after all, hadn't he been out of school a lot? He said, "Yeh, I sure have." I told him that I was really surprised that he had made as good grades as he had, considering his absences. His comment was "I'm lucky, that's all." I said that I knew it was more than luck and that I knew that in many ways he had tried to make a go of school. He then told of "working in spurts. I kinda like my subjects, but the teachers and kids, some of them, get me down." I asked him to tell me about this. He said he couldn't. Could he remember just one example? He thought awhile and then said he couldn't except that they "are all stuck up." I agreed that both teachers and kids can seem stuck up. His reply was, "You sure agree with me a lot." I laughed and said that I guessed I did, maybe it was because I was so eager for him to like me. He smiled and said "You are O.K., I guess." I said that I would like to be more than just O.K. and maybe he could tell me how? He asked me could I "get him into shop?" I thought he had been taking shop, but he explained that he had never been able to take this subject, because it was an "elective" and used as a reward for students who were doing well in other things. I had not been aware of this school policy but agreed that I would check into the matter for him. I asked him why he might like to take shop and he couldn't seem to find a reason except that "it's easy to make things." I wondered who taught the course and he said "Mr. Blake." I asked if the kids especially liked this teacher and he said "Yes." Did he have any other men teachers? He didn't at present, but had one this past year and didn't like him because he favored the boys who went out for sports. James said he was "no good in sports and didn't want to play games anyhow." I told him that we had this in common. He looked amazed at my saying this.

James announced that it was time for him to go to his home room and thanked me for lunch. I said that I would like to see him again tomorrow and that, after that, maybe we could get together once or twice a week to see how things are going for him. He asked if we would have lunch tomorrow. I told him that I couldn't, but would meet him in front of the building after school.

November 21, 1959

Interview with James. I found James waiting for me in front of the school building. He seemed genuinely glad to see me but appeared anxious to get me away from the other students, possibly because he didn't want to be seen with me. We walked to my car where we sat and talked. I told him that I had talked with Mrs. Davis about the possibility of his entering the shop class. She had said that it was not possible for him to do so this late in the semester, but would consider his doing it next semester. He appeared to be very disappointed. I told him that I knew how disappointed he must be, since this is the one subject he so much wanted to take. I wondered if this disappointment might mean that he would again want to leave school? He asked me if he could be sure of getting in shop next semester, and I told him that I couldn't say for sure, but I would be willing to try to get him in. He said "I guess that's all you can do."

James thought he could get along better in school if he didn't need to be with the "same old group of teachers." I asked what he disliked about them? He just thinks he didn't get "a very good bunch." I inquired if he knew any of the other teachers and he said he had seen them and heard them talked about. He supposed though "that teachers are all alike." I said that I thought this was not necessarily true, that it seemed to me that teachers, like kids, were each different, that we had to know them pretty well to appreciate their difference.

I drove James to his home and let him out, asking him what things he usually did after school? He said that he "just fooled around the house" or went over to see his friends, the Penkowskies. He volunteered the information that they were his best friends. They are an older couple, living several blocks away. They came from Poland after the last war and don't know many people. James met them when he was once distributing some circulars and since that time they have befriended him. They have no children of their own and apparently give James a great deal of attention. They own a television set and let James watch "any program I want." I told him that I was glad he had these friends, because I knew he must get pretty lonesome at home, when his mother and sister are away. He said with some defensiveness, "I've got lots of friends but I don't see much of them." It was agreed that I would see James at the school this coming Friday.

November 25, 1959

Interview with James. I interviewed James at school. He has been regular in school all week. He reports that he is behind in his work and doesn't know what his teachers are talking about in most of his subjects. He has been given a lot of makeup work to do. He asked if I had seen any of his teachers, and, if so, what did they say about him. I told him that I had not talked to his teachers but would if he wanted me to. He said that he didn't. He said that his teachers had been treating him "just like I'm a criminal." In explaining this statement it was evident that he felt the teachers had shown him little warmth in welcoming him back to classes. I commented that his teachers had probably been mad at him for having missed so much school. He thought they shouldn't be, since he had been sick. I again pointed up the fact that all his absences had not been because of his being sick and they must know this. I agreed with him, however, that it was hard to come back and not feel welcome. Most of the interview was spent in discussing the work that needed to be made up.

November 26, 1959

Call from principal. Mrs. Davis called to say that James was absent. I agreed to go to his home and look for him.

Interview with James (later). James was home alone when I called. He opened the door for me but had little to say at first. He was sullen, looked as though he was worried and had not slept the night before. He threw himself in an arm chair and covered his eyes with his arm. I sat down on the stool in front of him and said that I knew he was upset about something. I was then quiet for quite a while. I then asked him if he was sick and he shook his head, no. Could he tell me what was troubling him? He then looked up at me with tears in his eyes and said, "I don't know, it's all crazy. I meant to go to school and couldn't." Could he be worried at not getting his make-up work done over the weekend? He said that he tried and couldn't work at home, couldn't think or write or anything. Had his mother been home to help him? She was home over the weekend and had nagged him to do his work but he couldn't. I asked him if I could see all that he had to do. He slowly got up and presented me with a number of books and papers, then sat down and explained all that needed to be done. It was pretty obvious that the burden of so much to be done at once had overwhelmed him. I wondered which one he was worried most about and he said math. He had two exercises in fractions to do, with no idea how to do them, since he had missed the instruction periods. I said that I would try to help him get these done and then maybe he would feel better about going back to school today. He thought that Mrs. Davis would never accept him back this time and I reassured him in this regard (though I too felt some doubts about the reception she would give him). Together we worked on the exercises. I was surprised how much James did know about the subject. When I worked along with him, he accomplished a great deal, was accurate in his figures, and showed good reasoning ability. I praised him for this as we went along. I noticed, however, that he became very fearful and upset when he made a mistake, then seemed to lose confidence in himself. He responds to support and feels deep failure over the slightest mistake. We finished the work in less than a half hour. He sighed with relief after the ordeal was over, then got up and went to the bathroom. When he returned, his hair was combed and he had his tie and coat on, and said that he was ready to go.

Enroute to school, James talked a lot about his friends the Penkowskies. He had visited them yesterday and had asked Mr. Penkowskie to help him with his lessons. He had been surprised to learn that his friend could not read English and therefore could not help him. He said that these people "would make some kid good parents." I asked if, in a way, they weren't kind of parents to him and he agreed that they were. I told him that I thought they were good friends for him to have. He said that he had thought of going over and being with them today, when he didn't go to school as "they don't seem to care whether I go to school or not." I asked if he thought they knew about education in this country and he wasn't sure that they did. The man had told James that he had never gone to school in Poland but had learned everything he knew from his mother. James thought he would like to be able to learn this way, but he guessed he couldn't since "my mom works all the time." I explained that we were lucky to have public schools in this country, that in many parts of the world only wealthy children get a chance to go to school. We got into quite a conversation about this.

When we reached the office Mrs. Davis was away and the clerk gave James an entering slip, at my request. He commented as he headed for class that he was "glad that old bag is absent." I arranged to see him again on Wednesday.

November 28 to December 20, 1959

Summary of interviews with James. James was seen twice each week. It was possible to arrange for office space in the school, so he was interviewed at school. The discussions focused around his everyday experiences in school and at home. He was protective about giving much of himself, rather keeping the discussion on the level of the things he had been doing. He had been regular in school, though the teachers had reported his being preoccupied while in class and showing wide swings of mood. His school work was irregular, some of superior quality and some failing. He seems to do better work for two of his teachers, Miss Wagner and Mrs. Andrio. Several times he has said that they are nice to him and that he "kind of likes them even if they are teachers." I have been careful to keep the interviews on the level that he sets, to listen to him and to answer any questions for him, without asking many. He has been guarded in his conversations about his mother and sister. During this period, I have not been able to see the mother, because she works during the day, but I have arranged to make an evening visit, soon after the Christmas holidays. James has had little to say about Christmas. Any mention of the day causes him to change the subject. He seemed badly depressed during the last two days of school, and this is possibly because the school makes so much of Christmas. He did say that he didn't want anything for Christmas this year, and implied that he was not deserving. I have felt that I need to give James a great deal of reassurance and support all along the way.

December 21, 1959

Interview with mother. Mrs. Mason telephoned to ask if she might come to the school to see me. I arranged a special appointment for her today. Mrs. Mason apologized for coming in during vacation period. I explained that while the children were on vacation, the attendance workers were not free for vacation until tomorrow. She said that she had been planning for some time to arrange to come to see me and to talk over a number of things. First she wanted to thank me for my interest in James and to say that I must have a great deal of meaning to him, since he talked a lot at home about me. It was partly this that made her want to see me, for it had made her do a lot of thinking. For one thing, she has come to realize how very much James has missed having his father or "at least the influence of some man." Then the fact that James has been trying so hard to get along in school and to attend regularly has made her feel that "perhaps I have not always done my part." After saying these things in such a direct way, Mrs. Mason seemed to become somewhat upset and could not go on with the other things that she must have planned to say.

I told her that I felt she had been doing a great deal of thinking about James and about herself and I knew that this could be upsetting, since they had had some real troubles. She said, "You will never know all that I have been through. Raising two children alone has not been easy." I agreed. I asked Mrs. Mason if she thought that James might not be considering me as being something of a father to him? She smiled and said, "You and Mr. Penkowskie are about the only two men he has ever known very well." I asked how she felt about my coming to know him in the way I have? She was thoughtful and then said, "I must confess that I've resented you a little, at least at first." I wondered if she could tell me why? She smiled and said, "Well you see, I've always taken full responsibility for James." I told her that I knew that my working with James must be threatening to her, for after all she had done a great deal for him and "on her own." She said "I guess I must really have it in for men." I could understand this with the bad experience that she had with marriage. She said that it wasn't just marriage, but first it was her own father, who was a "beast," then she has had some men bosses who were not easy to get along with. I told her that I wanted to be of help to her as well as to James and that I hoped that she would not always need to resent me. She said "Oh no, I don't even now, it isn't resentment, but a feeling that you have been able to do something for my son, where I have failed." I said that it could not have been all my doing, that she must have helped in any change.

Mrs. Mason told more about the thinking that she has been doing. She now realizes how lonely James must be to have to come home to an empty house. His sister is now working for the telephone company in one of the East division offices, and is only home on Sundays. She found it impractical to commute each day. James seems to have missed her greatly, though the two of them never got along very well. Mrs. Mason has been trying to get her daughter to transfer to the main office so that she might live at home and work on a shift that would permit her to be at home when James comes home from school. The daughter is considering this, but feels that she likes the experience of living away. Mrs. Mason said that she has given some thought to buying a television as a family Christmas present, feeling this might give James some interest at home. She wondered what I thought of this idea. I agreed that her idea might be a good one. She said that she doesn't care for television and has always thought it a bad thing for children, but "since everyone has one they must be all right." I asked if James had ever expressed a wish for one. She said that he had, some two years ago, in fact he hounded her for one. She had told him that she could not afford it though this was not her real reason for not getting it. James has not mentioned television for more than a year, though she knows that he goes to the Penkowskies to look at theirs, and now and then he watches television with some of the neighbor kids, though he is not friendly with many of them. I asked if James had expressed a wish for anything else for Christmas. She said, "You know, he is the most peculiar child I ever knew. He insists that he doesn't want anything for Christmas, and I can't understand it." I said that possibly he feels undeserving for having gotten himself in trouble with the school. She said that he "must have something on his mind, though I can't get him to say what it is." I said that James is a boy who keeps things to himself. She agreed saying "I never know what he is thinking." I told Mrs. Mason that I thought her plan to get a television was a good one, since James did need to have something to interest him at home, when she was away.

Mrs. Mason said that she felt better for having talked things over with me. She has never had anyone to consult with except her daughter and she sometimes misses this. I said that I had been glad to see her and would plan to see her again after the Christmas season. Before leaving, she laughed and said, "I thought I'd never be coming to a hooky cop for help." I replied that "these modern hooky cops" serve a lot of purpose and I was glad that she had come to see me.

January 3, 1960

Call from principal. I was notified by Mrs. Davis that James had failed to return to school following the vacation period.

Interview with James and his mother (later). I telephoned the Mason home. The mother answered and said that she was just getting ready to phone me. James was at home and refusing to go to school. She asked if I would come to the home and talk with them both. I agreed to do so, though I could not come until late afternoon. The mother said that she would remain home from work today to be with James and wait for me.

Called at the home. Mrs. Mason met me at the door and then stepped outside closing the door behind her in order to talk with me alone. She said that James had been acting strangely during the entire vacation period and she is very worried about him. Instead of being pleased with the television she got for Christmas, he appeared to be frightened. She tried to tell him that it was for him and he said, "No, it's yours, you keep it." He has watched it several evenings with her, but she doubts that he operates it when he is alone. On the day before New Year, she got a half-day off and came home early to find James seated in the living room with his trousers unbuttoned. He had apparently been masturbating. She was shocked by this and spoke harshly to him, saying something like "don't ever do that again." He began to cry and ran out of the house, not returning until almost bedtime. She asked him where he had been, but did not mention masturbation again. Since that time he has been unusually quiet and withdrawn and stays off to himself. She feels that a man needs to talk with him about "these things." She suggested that I go into the house and talk with James alone, while she goes to the store.

I found James in the living room resting on the couch, with his face to the wall. I sat down beside him and put my hand on his head. He turned to look at me, then turned away. I said that I knew he was awfully worried about something and maybe I could help him, since we had become friends. He mumbled something to the effect that he didn't need any help. I said that I thought he did, though he may not want it from me. He turned on his back and looked up at me for a long time without speaking. I sat quietly with him. He finally said "I suppose my mom told on me!" I said that his mother cared a great deal about him and that I cared about him, so it was all right for her to tell me. I thought he was worrying about something that was not so serious as he thought. He said "what did she tell you?" I repeated what she had said and he seemed confused by the word "masturbation" so I used the children's word, "jackoff." James looked very frightened and tears came to his eyes.

I said "Don't be afraid, James, most boys do that." He said in a feeble and doubtful voice, "Do they?" I explained that this was a part of his growing up and he shouldn't worry so much about it. He told me that he knew that some of the other kids do it, but they always hide out and do it. I said, "That is true and this is probably why you think it's so bad." He nodded his head in agreement. I asked him if he did it a lot and he first said "no," then said, "I guess I do it every day when my mom's not home." I wondered how long he had been worried about this and he said "Oh, a long time." A year? "Ever since I was in the 5th grade." I commented that that was sure a long time to stay worried and he agreed. I asked if he thought he could stop worrying about it and he wasn't so sure. Could he feel that he could talk to me when he is worried? He believed he could.

I observed the television and expressed my pleasure over the fact that he had it. He said that it wasn't his but his mom's but that he could use it if he wanted. I told him that I thought he should use it, since she had told me that she wanted him to have it and I thought this was a good idea. He said that his English teacher kept saying that television was a waste of time for children, that they should be reading and listening to good music instead. I said that different people had different ideas about television and that if he liked the programs, he should see them.

I asked James why he had not returned to school today since he had had a long vacation. He said he didn't know. He felt "sort of sick or something." I asked if he was feeling all right now. He agreed that he was. Did he intend to go to school tomorrow? He asked if he had to go and I said "You know the answer without my telling you." He half smiled and said "Will you be there?" I said that I wouldn't during the morning, but that I would tell the school that he was returning. He asked how many days were left in this semester. I said fourteen school days. He expressed some concern over the end-term exams and the fact that his report card would soon be made out. I said that while he may not have done so well in his subjects, he had certainly done better about going to school and I gave him credit for this. He said that it was because I made him go. I said that a lot of things inside of him tried to make him stay home and I thought that by the time we had talked more about these he would one day find it pretty easy to go. He made no answer. I told James goodbye and said I would see him on Wednesday. Before I got out the door he asked if I didn't want to see how the television worked. I stayed long enough to watch him tune in a station.

As I was driving away I met Mrs. Mason down the block, so I stopped and talked a few minutes with her. I told her of some of my conversation with James and how worried I thought he was. I suggested that she reassure him that what he had done was not so bad. She said that she would find this difficult to do, since she had been raised to feel that masturbation was a "sin." I talked with her about this and about how common a practice it is, especially for boys. She said "That's what comes for not having a man around to help raise a son." I agreed that children do need to have a relationship with both a man and woman. I agreed to see Mrs. Mason soon again and asked her to encourage James to return to school tomorrow.

January 5 to March 1, 1960

Summary of interviews with James, his teachers, and his mother. Because of a heavy caseload, I have been able to see James only once each week and to see his mother for one evening. James has been regular in school and doing somewhat better in his subjects.

The teachers report that James is showing greater interest and has started making gestures toward friendships with other boys. He seems to resent girls a great deal and does everything he can to avoid them.

James seems to like to come in for his interviews and talks very freely about many things. In one interview he asked me a lot of questions about God. He wondered if I believed in God and said that he wasn't sure, since people couldn't see Him. He asked if I thought God punished people for things and I said that I thought not, though a lot of people worry about His doing this. He said that one kid had told him a long time ago that God would shrivel up your penis if you played with it but he knew this wasn't true, since nothing had happened to his. He thinks that his home room teacher believes things like this because she is always talking about God. He related the incident of his being put out of class for his not believing.

Mrs. Davis arranged for James to be placed in a shop class at the beginning of second semester. James likes this man teacher and the teacher reports that he has real ability to make things with his hands. He is impatient when using the power tools and wants to complete his projects in a single class; however, he is overcoming some of this impatience. He made some bookends for me and I've been using them on my new desk.

At the end of February James asked to see me and told me that he had to tell me something if I would keep it a secret. I told him that I could not promise, since I did not know what it was, but that I felt he could trust me not to get him into trouble. He confessed that more than a year ago he had been involved in some destruction to school property. He had been on the school grounds after hours, playing with some other boys. They found a window open, climbed inside, emptied the teacher's desk drawers, spilled ink around and one of the boys had urinated in the corner of the room. James had never participated in any gang-type activity before. He had enjoyed doing it, "felt the other kids liked me." After it was over the other kids threatened to beat him up if he told. He became very anxious, couldn't sleep, and since that time has been afraid to be around other children, except when there is adult supervision. I reassured him that this had happened a long time ago and I thought that we could keep it our own secret. Since he had told me, he shouldn't need to worry about it any more. He said that he "even dreams about it and about getting caught."

In another interview, James confessed that "when I was a little kid," meaning a year or so ago, "I wrote some dirty things on the walls of the boys' room." Again I reassured him that this is something that many boys and girls do and that since he was no longer "a little kid" he probably wouldn't be doing it again. He expressed surprise that girls do it too. I had not meant to implicate them, but I felt my doing so made him feel more kindly toward them.

In several of the interviews I sensed how strongly James feared that he might be a sissie. This self-feeling had been reinforced by the jeers of other kids, when he would not participate in fights, and so on. I've been careful to point up his masculine interests and qualities. A doctor's certificate has been secured permitting James to go out for "sports" and he has been doing some bar work. He has very poor co-ordination, though he tries very hard.

Mrs. Mason seemed much more relaxed when I saw her. She reported that James has shown some real change at home. He is talking more with her, is using the television, and is even making some friends in the neighborhood. She says that she worries less about not being home, and because of this her work at the office does not seem such a burden.

March 1 to May 15, 1960

Summary of interviews with James and with homeroom teacher. Regular weekly interviews have been held with James. He has been attending school regularly with only two days of absence, due to an infection on his hand. He has developed an almost obsessive interest in his shop class. I feel that it is more because he likes his man teacher than because of the activity itself. He is still overly anxious about many things, but he is now able to talk about them when they happen and to resolve some of his anxiety.

I have talked any number of times with James' homeroom teacher whom he continues to resent. She really can't accept him as she should and I feel it is largely because of his one-time protest against "God." He needs her forgiveness badly, but I have told him not to expect it. His other teachers now speak favorably about him and none of them seem to resent having him in their classes.

I have been working with one of the social agencies to try and get James an opportunity for a week of summer camp experience. I have not yet talked to him about this, since I don't want him to be disappointed if it cannot be arranged. I feel that he should not go unless he wants to. His mother is willing for him to go to camp but she feels that she cannot afford to pay the full amount of the expense.

RECORD 5

USE OF AUTHORITY

Collaborative efforts of the school and the family to set limits for a child who was a problem at school and at home

(Selected interviews illustrate the part played by use of school structure and of the authority of the principal in helping a child change her behavior.)

ELIZABETH BERKLEY. . .9 years old, 3rd grade

Family members:	Parents: Mr. and Mrs. Berkley. Siblings: Two younger sisters, ages 5 and 6. Half-brother, age 19.
School personnel:	Mr. Boyd, principal, Mrs. Wilson, teacher, school psychologist, school social worker.
Reason for referral:	Aggressive behavior: "tattle-tale," disobedient, disrespectful of authority; in constant conflict with classmates; not learning and achieving up to ability. Referred by principal and teacher.

The social worker held weekly interviews with Elizabeth throughout the school year. She had monthly interviews with the mother and telephone contacts as needed. Regular conferences were held with the teacher, Mrs. Wilson. Reports were made to the principal who joined the teacher and social worker in conferences from time to time. The following interviews and conferences have been selected from the record to show the course of movement in helping the child.

October 8, 1959

Conference with principal and teacher. Mrs. Wilson had brought Elizabeth's misbehavior to the attention of the principal; he had decided to refer the case to me, after discussing such action with the parents. He related experiences former teachers had had with this child. She had been troublesome for the past year or more. Review of her educational record revealed that she had average ability and had been promoted each year of her school life although each teacher had expressed dissatisfaction with Elizabeth's use of school and of her ability. It was agreed that I would explore the situation with child and parents. Mrs. Wilson would make further effort to discover ways in classroom and school to engage Elizabeth more constructively. We set November 17 for our next conference.

January 22, 1960

Interview with Elizabeth. I confronted Elizabeth with my feeling that she was not doing anything with me although we had been meeting weekly since October and this was near the end of the first semester. I told her that I would have to bring this fact to the attention of the principal, the person in school who had asked me to help Elizabeth. I reminded her that she had stated that she "wanted to do better in school." This little 9-year-old child, who had been holding out and making every effort to present herself as an "adequate woman," began to yield a little and showed some feeling as she said she did want to do better in school.

January 29, 1960

Interview with mother. Mrs. Berkley from the beginning showed deep concern about the quality of relationship existing between herself and Elizabeth. She had been upset in most of our interviews. Today, she could hardly control herself for weeping and expressing her concern about the "battle of wills" she felt existed between her and Elizabeth. She said that not only does this go on with her, but Elizabeth is continually at war with her two younger sisters. I had to say, "And you let it be this way." Mrs. Berkley knew what I was saying and answered, "I know, but I have to hold so hard and tight to let this kid know that I am the mother." I thought this was so. No one else could do this for her, but Mrs. Berkley. She was so troubled about the child, she asked if a psychological examination could be made. I promised to discuss this with Mr. Boyd.

February 12, 1960

Interview with Elizabeth. Today seemed to be a point of crisis for Elizabeth in her relationship with me, and thus a turning point in our work together. For the first time she was able to meet me with any kind of depth of feeling in terms of response. We were working specifically on her problem in getting along with the teacher, with the children, with administrators, as well as with her mother, father, and sisters. I knew this was terribly hard for Elizabeth and could see that she was fighting to hold back tears, so I said to her directly, "Why do you keep holding your tears back? They were made to fall when you need them to fall. You are a little girl only 9 years old; you can cry." This seemed to unlock some kind of dam within her and she wept bitterly. It seemed to me that she yielded to herself in a way I had never seen her do before.

I spoke about knowing that she was mad with herself and with me and with her mother and daddy because we all said we expected her to do better in school, but she was not. She took up the reference to her mother, saying, "My mother never hugs me the way she does Mary and Alice." Elizabeth could finally say that she knew that she did not do much to make her mother feel like hugging her. She knew she had a part in that, too.

I spoke about the fact that Elizabeth frequently comes with her fingernails polished and her hair done in quite a teen-age style. I recognized that some days she would feel like a teenager and some days like a little girl the way she was telling me about her feelings today. She said that most days she felt like a little girl and really wanted to be her 9-year-old age. I thought she could be if she wanted, and not act like a woman trying to rule everything and everybody the way she sometimes tried to make us believe she wanted to do.

February 19, 1960

Conference with principal and teacher. We agreed that Elizabeth was not making the progress we had hoped for. It was decided that we would ask for a psychological evaluation of the child. Mrs. Berkley had expressed anxiety over Elizabeth's mental health. The report might also give us insight into the child's problems at this point.

March 7, 1960

Report of the psychologist. The essence of the psychologist's findings, based on the Bender Figure Drawings and Rorschach, were that this child was in need of limits being set so that she could operate safely and not try to rule adults as well as children. Parental and child roles in the family needed to be clarified and each appropriately carried. Elizabeth saw herself as a very unhappy, crying child and not really feeling it. She saw women as hostile with no outgoing feelings, and men as frightening and frightened. She viewed herself as a brother to her father. She felt her dependency needs rejected by the mother. However, even in view of this disturbance, Elizabeth showed capacity for feeling and relationship.

March 11, 1960

Conference with teacher and principal. We considered together the report from the psychologist. We finally agreed that Mr. Boyd would suspend Elizabeth on all occasions when she is presenting troublesome behavior to the teacher. It seemed to us this was a way we could help the child feel and realize, if she will, that she cannot rule the school. Mrs. Wilson is certainly a warm, caring, experienced teacher, but I believe she has some trouble providing the kind of strength that Elizabeth seems to be bidding for. The principal said he would take responsibility for giving Mrs. Wilson the extra support and help she might need in determining what was the limit the teacher had to take from this child.

Interview with mother. I discussed the psychological report in detail with Mrs. Berkley. She really let herself feel the impact of this and talked more freely about the father and his relationship with Elizabeth. Mr. Berkley had been an outstanding furrier and had had a big shop, but competition was such that he had had to go out of business. He was now working for someone else but felt keenly, "I'm not used to taking orders, I'm used to giving them." Recently he had said to Elizabeth, "Baby, daddy is no-where, he's nobody now." Mrs. Berkley agreed that she had to help her husband regain his sense of self-confidence and value; and, at the same time, she thought they would have to stop talking to Elizabeth as an equal and behave as parents. I agreed that I thought that was what Elizabeth was asking of them.

Mrs. Berkley wanted to discuss the psychological report with her husband and then see what they might do to work with the school in helping Elizabeth. She continued, "I know heretofore I have had to drive Elizabeth to do her homework; if that's what I have to do, that's what I have to do even if it means five nights a week. I just want to see what the father and I can do." I said, "I'm going to see if there is anything more we in the school can do to determine how to help this child know that she is expected to use her ability in school and to get along with other children and adults. There seems to be an urgency in this. For her to have had trouble in school from the first to the fourth grade is a long time."

March 18, 1960

Interview with Elizabeth. Today, Elizabeth seemed to be strug-gling with the limits set at home and school. She had been suspended for a day recently. She wanted to deny the meaning of this. Her father had told her he was giving her a time limit within which to do something better in school—until June. Her mother had said that she is sick of running to the school to see about her. We spoke of the fact that her mother has been "running to the school" ever since she was in the first grade. I said this was a long time. At first Elizabeth tried to deny this was a long time, but I held her to the fact that it is a long time for her and for everybody at home and school to be worried and stirred up over her, because she won't settle down and be a little girl and do the best work she can do in school.

In regard to the psychological examination, I discussed the report fully with Elizabeth and spoke as directly as I could about what the implications were. She responded by saying that she gets mad and scared and that she does not like being in the "dog house" at home and at school. I said forthrightly that she had to do something about herself now, that to continue to be "mad and scared" could make her sick eventually; that if she could only use her ability instead of dodging her work, she would feel lots better.

April 8, 1960

Interview with Elizabeth. She had always come in to the interview with a smile and sweet front, and again tried to make light of the fact that she had been suspended for five days after having "gone wild" in the classroom on March 31st. I said this was nothing to smile about, that it was serious and troubling to all concerned. She said she had done "pretty good" until just before Easter vacation. She was able to say, however, that it was probably not good enough. Before the end of the interview, Elizabeth was finally able to express some concern about her suspensions and about the "bad feeling" inside herself. She said, "With what mama and daddy and everybody at school is saying, and what I know too, I guess its me that's got to do better about school and I have to do it now." I agreed and said that we have only eight weeks in which to work on this. Can she bring all of her good intentions into action? She said she wanted to try.

Conference with teacher. Mrs. Wilson said that she was giving Elizabeth daily reports on her work and behavior. The principal required that Elizabeth let him know how she was doing each day. He held her to this kind of accountability. They felt she was beginning to make a little progress in both work and behavior in school.

April 29, 1960

Interview with Elizabeth. She brought a report of her good behavior and school work. I said how pleased I was to know that she really had changed and had decided to be different about herself and about school. She responded in a pleased, sweet manner, saying, "I have never felt this good in my life—no, never about school." We talked a little about what she felt had made the difference for her. She spoke about the part the principal, the teacher, and I had played, and about how mad her mother and father had been with her being suspended. She expressed strong feeling about this as she told me what her daddy said about her improving in school. She also spoke about how mad and angry she felt with herself sometimes for causing us all to bear down on her. She said she just got sick of being "mean and nasty" and having everybody else mad with her. She thought the things that made it hardest for her and made her feel the worst were the suspension and the principal telling her face to face that he was going to keep on suspending her until she made up her mind to do better in school.

Elizabeth said she was doing better at home, that she had really made up her mind to be a little girl and to let her mother be a mother. She was more childish in manner today and seemed not to have the false woman-like poise that had characterized her earlier manner. I said something about this. She said, "This is a real smile; no put-on today—I feel more like a little girl." She seemed spontaneous and outgoing, for the first time.

May 6, 1960

Interview with mother. Mrs. Berkley talked about Elizabeth's expressed feelings about her mother and father and about school. It seemed to have taken from about Thanksgiving until Easter before a turning point or change could be seen. There was one bad day, the day before the Easter holidays. But this seemed a natural time for restlessness with all children, we agreed.

Mrs. Berkley was very clear and direct in saying she knew that she and the father must continue to hold strict limits on Elizabeth. This is what will help her in her own growth. I knew we in the school had also had to set limits and hold Elizabeth to them. It had taken the principal, teacher, myself, and the mother and father in the home to bring Elizabeth to confront herself and decide to do something different.

Mrs. Berkley told me that Elizabeth had been loving and warm with her. At one time, the child had said to her, "Mama, would you cry if I told you something?" She went on then to tell her mother that she had loved Nanny (Mrs. Berkley's mother) better than she loved Mrs. Berkley. The mother told her she knew that. They then had a discussion about the fact that Nanny is dead and Mrs. Berkley is alive and is Elizabeth's mother and wants to be a real mother to her. She said the father had also come to realize that his role as father called for a different relationship with Elizabeth. They had had a private conference and she knew something had become different between father and child after that. Mrs. Berkley said Elizabeth is not only different in the home but that she now has friends among the other children. She gets along better with her sisters, also.

May 13, 1960

Interview with Elizabeth. This week Elizabeth again brought good reports of her behavior and school work. Her comment was, "I can't turn back, and if I bring bad reports I want you to be mad with me again." I commented on the reports that she must make to the principal. She said, "You know those little reports are baby stuff, but I do want to keep doing them. Then, come next September, I feel I can be like any other child. My mother will only have to come to school when other mothers come. I do my homework now. Mama doesn't have to drive me; I do my school work for Mrs. Wilson, and I'm getting along with the other children." The thing that seemed to stand out as most important was, "You know, Mrs. Wilson trusts me." Elizabeth went on to talk about how she has learned to let mama be mama, and said that she doesn't worry about grandma the way she used to. I said, "No one can ever take away what grandmother gave you." She replied, "I know my mother loves me now." She added that she felt so much better at home and at school.

Since Elizabeth was now doing so well, I said perhaps she would not need to come to see me much longer. She agreed, and I promised to discuss ending our interviews, with the teacher and principal.

Conference with teacher. I reported on the progress Elizabeth had made, as revealed in our last interview. Mrs. Wilson said that the child has seemed more like a little girl and that her manner with the teacher and children has been satisfactory. She said she had told Elizabeth that if the children picked on her, she should let her know. She wants to help Elizabeth sustain the progress she has made. I thought Mrs. Wilson's offer could be very supportive to Elizabeth. She had noticed that the little girls want to sit with Elizabeth now. Continued firmness with the child will be necessary, however. She spoke appreciatively of the support that Mr. Boyd has given her. He has constantly assured her that she does not have to put up with any foolishness on Elizabeth's part, and he has used suspension as discipline. Mrs. Wilson said that the change in Elizabeth is reflected in her attitude toward, and achievement in, her school work also. She is trying very hard and instead of Ds she rates "Excellent" on most of her papers now. Her work is neat, good, and correct.

We agreed that the case could be closed soon.

May 20, 1960

Ending interview with Elizabeth. We reviewed the problem and some of the difficulties we had had in our period of working together. We talked about the factors that seemed to have helped her change and want to be different. She thought our talking about the details and problems she was having in school—tattling, meddling, poor work—had really helped her know what she had to change in. She said, "I did not like you and everybody else being so mad with me and I didn't like myself very well. It feels so much better to be a darling rather then a pain in the neck!" She laughed in an impish, childish manner as she said this.

We talked about family change, girl friends, and her satisfaction at being loved and achieving. She likes having "changed and turned over a new leaf." She said it took time, though; "I started slow, and then toward the end I went fast." She was glad that soon after Easter she did have to make daily reports to the principal for a while. "That was baby stuff." I said that perhaps it was, but when she no longer needed to do this, the principal had recognized that she was expected to carry more responsibility alone for herself.

This last interview was the first time that Elizabeth volunteered to show me any of her school papers. She brought a notebook and on her own opened it and told me about the material there. The book was very neat, written in ink, and most of the papers were checked as correct. It was obvious that great care and thought had been put into keeping the notebook, over a six-weeks period. I said this was really proof of the good things I had heard about her from the principal, teacher, and other school personnel.

I told Elizabeth that I would be at the school on Fridays and would always be glad to see her, but that we need not have any regular appointments after today. This seemed to please her.

Case closed. Child's behavior and achievement in school have improved.

RECORD 6

PREVENTIVE SERVICE TO A CHILD IN KINDERGARTEN

Direct work with a child and his teacher to overcome
effects of the child's "accident" in kindergarten

BRUCE JONES......... 5½ years old, in kindergarten.

Family members: Parents: Mrs. Jones, housewife, and Mr. Jones, teacher.
                            Siblings: Melvin, 11, 7A grade.

School personnel: Mrs. Howe, teacher, School Social Worker.

Reason for referral: Child seemed emotionally disturbed; referred by teacher.

October 15, 1959

Conference with teacher. Mrs. Howe, Bruce's teacher, asked that Bruce be seen by school social worker because of rather sudden change in child's behavior. Bruce had been in kindergarten for five weeks. At first, he seemed to be a happy, congenial child in his new school experience and had worked well in his group. This was in spite of greatly impaired speech. For the last two weeks, Mrs. Howe said, she was concerned over Bruce's behavior. He seemed unhappy about being in school, he showed a reluctance to join in group activities, and he usually arrived late for school. A note from his mother, Mrs. Jones, indicated that Bruce was less and less willing to attend kindergarten. Mrs. Howe recalled that this change in behavior began immediately after Bruce had had "an accident" in school which necessitated his mother calling for him to take him home for the rest of the school session. Mrs. Howe felt that Bruce is a friendly, alert little fellow who needs to be helped over this hurdle.

I asked Mrs. Howe to tell me about the initial interview she had had with Mrs. Jones during the first week in September, before

233

Bruce entered kindergarten. Mrs. Howe said that no mention what-ever had been made of Bruce's severe speech impairment. The mother had made it clear that Bruce was eager to start school. In order to help prepare him for the new experience, Mrs. Jones had brought him to see his new room and to meet his teacher. Mention was made of an older brother, Melvin, who attends our school in the 7A grade. Mr. Jones is a school teacher.

I wondered how Mrs. Howe felt about my seeing Mrs. Jones before I talked with Bruce, explaining that it might help if I knew more of the boy's reactions at home and how the parents were handling matters. Mrs. Howe said she was all for this. I promised to set a time to see Bruce after talking with his mother. I would also arrange to see Mrs. Howe after I had seen Bruce.

Telephone call to mother. I called Mrs. Jones to arrange an ap-pointment, explaining the reason for my request. Mrs. Jones replied that she would like to make the appointment for that day. Since this was not possible because of my full schedule, we set a time for the following day.

October 16, 1959

First interview with mother. Mrs. Jones arrived fifteen minutes before her appointment time and waited, seated outside the office until I could see her. She was a tall, plump woman, carefully groomed. With much poise and a friendly approach, she showed no outward signs of an uncomfortable feeling. I said I wondered how she felt about coming to school—it seemed that she was greatly concerned. Mrs. Jones spoke freely, saying how disturbed she has been. She has been experiencing difficulty with Bruce for the last two weeks because he does not want to come to school. She related that two weeks ago, right after having had the misfortune of "the accident," Bruce arose each morning with varied ailments such as headache, stomach-ache, and so on, and begged to stay at home. Mrs. Jones wanted me to know that he was not going to put anything over on her. She ascertained he had no fever and let Bruce know that if he was too ill to go to school then he must go to bed and the doctor would be called. Then Bruce felt better and hurriedly got ready for school, leaving with Melvin, his brother.

Mrs. Jones felt that this was all a complete reversal of his atti-tude during the first three weeks of school. She wanted me to know how thoroughly both Mr. Jones and she had been preparing him for his first school experience and she added that things had been fine until the "accident." I asked if this sort of thing had been a problem at home and she assured me it had not, but, rather, was unusual. She was particularly distressed and annoyed this week because Bruce had brought home torn and scribbled papers instead of his drawings and boldly seemed to want to show them off. I explained that he must have been trying to tell her something. "Yes," she said, Bruce told her, "I guess you don't like this paper. I don't, but that's what I did." She said she told him it had once been a real nice paper, and he had made some pretty pictures; she wondered why he had scribbled all over it now. His answer was, "I wanted to."

I told Mrs. Jones of our concern over this behavior and it was here that she spoke of Bruce's speech difficulty, of an operation at one and one-half years, a defective palate (not cleft) and speech therapy which was delayed until he was 4½ years old. She had brought a letter from Temple Speech Clinic describing the difficulty and therapy. Bruce attends every Saturday morning.

I asked whether she felt that his speech had something to do with his school problem. She does not consider it as contributing to it, adding that Bruce knows he does not speak correctly and most children accept him although there are exceptions. "This must hurt a great deal," I injected. She felt so, but hurried on to say that Bruce takes it all in stride. He is thrilled to attend Saturday clinic and willingly practices at home, although she and her husband are careful not to "push him" too hard and too long. Melvin loves him, as she and Mr. Jones do. She added that Bruce is a lovable, self-reliant little fellow with a sense of humor.

I mentioned that we want his kindergarten experience to be a happy one and I wondered how she would feel if I talked to Bruce. I explained my job as school social worker and how the work proceeds with interviewing children, parents, and teachers, adding that because Bruce's teacher had noted a change in his attitude toward school, I wondered if we might help him by working together. Mrs. Jones hoped that I would talk to Bruce real soon and perhaps she could call me after my first meeting with him. "Maybe we can come up with something," she smiled. I arranged to see Bruce October 22 in the a.m., and she said she would call in the afternoon.

October 19 and October 21, 1959

Observation visits to kindergarten room. I had arranged with the teacher to make brief visits to Bruce's room so that he and the other children would come to know me better. They had seen me in the room on a number of occasions but I had not tarried long. Now, on each visit, I managed to speak to several children, including Bruce. It was during the second visit that Mrs. Howe told the children who I was—a helper to boys and girls. She mentioned the location of my room on the second floor.

Appendix

October 22, 1959

First interview with Bruce. I reached the kindergarten and Bruce accepted my explanation of wanting to talk to him in my room where it was more quiet. He came willingly. I said maybe he was wondering what I wanted to talk about. He didn't seem to hear me—he was so busy looking around and asking questions about the "big boys and girls on the second floor." On entering my room he looked around and in surprise asked, "Where's the boys?" As I pulled out a little chair for him, I tried to explain some of the ways I worked differently from his teacher and how I might be a helper to a little boy or a little girl. Sometimes things happen in school that make children unhappy. His teacher was wondering, I told him, if he still liked coming to school because she had seen him doing things that made her think he was not so happy about it— especially since the morning he had had that accident.

No, he didn't like to come much. I guessed it did make him feel kind of ashamed to have something like that happen to him in school. "I don't want to talk about it." I said it might be more fun to stay home with mother and play—"No! I am supposed to come to school—I am big enough." I identified with Bruce how grown up he must feel being in school and how hard it is doing new things in a big class and being with his teacher instead of mother. At this point he spotted the modeling clay and wished he could play with it. He began rolling it into two balls, then suddenly began whacking them flat saying, "Yesterday in school I made a boat—broke it up like this—mashed it." When I asked if it wasn't a good boat, Bruce nodded affirmatively and frowning as though I should understand said, "Sure—a good boat—but I wanted to." I suggested that maybe he was angry yesterday. His expression changed and also the subject, for he thought it was time to go. I wanted to know if he would like to come back in a few days. He offered, "I'll make another boat." As I said that maybe he will be able to tell me why he does not like to come to school, Bruce shrugged his shoulders and started off. We walked together back to his room.

Telephone call from mother. Mrs. Jones called to say that Bruce continues to bring home papers with nothing but scribbling; however, his morning aches and pains have disappeared. He and Melvin leave for school together. Mrs. Jones is annoyed that Bruce tells her he does "nothing" in school whereas formerly he talked of the singing, cutting, coloring, playing, and so on. She seemed more upset and showed more feeling, from the tone of her voice, than during our school interview.

I explained that I had seen Bruce for only about twenty minutes and it would take time to try to find an answer. Mrs. Jones had

236

hoped to be of greater assistance to me. I thanked her for her call and said I would see Bruce again on the 26th. I had arranged with Mrs. Howe to see him twice a week for three or four weeks. Mrs. Jones said that she would keep in touch.

October 26, 1959

Interview with Bruce. He seemed ready to come when I called for him. He found his way to the little table. I suggested he might like to use crayons and paper today but he preferred clay. I mentioned how hard it is to draw pictures, big pictures, and quickly, with a twinkle in his eye, he said he could draw them, not hard for him. He can write his name too. "Want to see me?" Taking the crayon he printed his name. "You must feel big to write," I told him, "and I'll bet Mrs. Howe is pleased too." He quickly answered, "I didn't show her." I thought maybe he did not like Mrs. Howe and at that he put down the crayon and looked me right in the eye declaring, "She makes me mad and the boys tease me." I wondered if it had anything to do with the accident he had had a few weeks ago. At this Bruce picked up the clay and began manipulating it, acting as though he had not heard me. I continued that I guessed he felt so badly that it was too hard to talk about. His eyes downcast, he said he was making a doghouse.

I told him I couldn't imagine why the boys teased him and before he realized what he was saying he blurted, "She's always telling me to go the bathroom—I am no baby." Some of the pieces began to fall into place for me. I recognized why Bruce felt extreme embarrassment and resentment at the mere mention of the word "bathroom." Punching and pulling the clay and finally whacking it on the table, Bruce broke loose with, "If she thinks I am a baby—I'll be like a baby—until she stops." For this I was not prepared, he took me completely unaware. He was angry and spoke so quickly it made understanding his speech more difficult. I accepted his feelings, saying I could understand why he felt like this, and that it would not be easy to forget it and show how big he was unless he really liked sometimes being a baby—scribbling, tearing paper—that was for him to decide.

Bruce declared positively, "I'm big! I am five and a half!" He sat upright to increase his height before me. I told him I would be talking to his teacher again. She may be glad to know how big he feels. He pushed the clay into a pile, left it, and arose to go, saying, "I'll make something for you next time." He asked if it was time to go—all the while walking out of the room. I said we would walk as far as the end of the hall together, then he might want to go the rest of the way by himself. This seemed to please him. He turned, waved, and quickly turned the corner and was gone.

Conference with teacher. We talked at lunch-time. Mrs. Howe was anxious to know the outcome of our meetings together. I related some facts of my interview with Mrs. Jones: the mother's distress over Bruce's not wanting to come to school and how she resolved this problem; the matter of scribbled, torn papers which he admittedly dislikes but continues to bring home and boldly shows off. Mrs. Howe could not recall when the scribbling began but she was aware of it. I told Mrs. Howe about Bruce's feelings about his accident and her subsequent reminders to him on the use of the bathroom, adding that I well understood her problem of training thirty-five new children every term. I related Bruce's resentment toward some boys' teasing and finally his remark showing why he chose acting "like a baby." A look of utter surprise came over Mrs. Howe's face as she gasped and laughed, "Why the little monkey!"

As we talked, Mrs. Howe came to see the pattern of Bruce's behavior and its implications. She decided to make the bathroom reminder a general one and refrain from individualizing it. I also shared Mrs. Jones's information regarding Bruce's speech difficulty, its history, and therapy. I was aware that Mrs. Howe had feelings of resentment toward the mother for not giving her this information. Mrs. Howe was willing for me to see Bruce twice a week.

October 29, 1959

Interview with Bruce. When I arrived at his room, Bruce was busily cutting out a paper Jack-O-Lantern. As I stood watching him, I asked if he wanted to come with me or finish cutting the face. Without hesitation he chose to complete his work. I waited no more than two minutes and with the last snip of his scissors he walked across the room to Mrs. Howe, placed the mask over his face, and sticking his tongue through the mouth opening, wiggled it and laughed. Mrs. Howe laughed, too.

We left together and this time I wondered if he could show me the way to my office, adding that sometime he could come by himself. He laughed, saying "Sure I can." Chattering and laughing, he walked along showing the way and pointing to my room at the top of the stairs. Clay and crayons were on the little table. "It's Hallowe'en. I'll make you a 'punkin' face." As he set about his task, I said I wondered if he felt the same way about school—that he didn't like it so much. Looking up as if to see the effect of his answer, he said, "I don't sometimes." I said that I supposed that some days he liked to come, and his reply was a brief "Huh-huh." When I asked about the boys who teased him, he seemed almost too absorbed in his "punkin" face to give more than an answer of "No more." I guessed it seemed like Mrs. Howe made it bad for him, telling him to go to the bathroom so much. His response was a quick nodding of his head. My comment was that Mrs. Howe meant to be kind and helpful just as I wanted to be. We understand that children do have accidents sometimes.

He hummed a tune as he cut and triumphantly held the finished face for approval, asking where I would put it. We both decided where it would hang. I wondered what he was going to do with the other pumpkin he made in class. "Take it home," he replied gleefully. "For Mommy or Melvin to wear?" With a big laugh, he roared, "No, it's for me!" I reminded him that it was time to return to his room and wondered if he wanted to talk with me next week again. Simply, "No," and he was on his way. We walked part way together and Bruce went the rest of the way alone.

October 30, 1959
Conference with teacher. That morning Bruce had brought Mrs. Howe a present of a small cut-out Jack-O-Lantern. The pleasure derived from this was mutual. Mrs. Howe had seen evidence of Bruce's participation in group activities. However, she felt concern over his bathroom problem. While she has not reminded him, she has desperately felt the urge to do so during these last few days because Bruce sits squirming and wiggling. I identified with Mrs. Howe in recognizing how difficult this is for her and how risky she must feel about it. I wondered what she had decided to do about it. She smiled and said she was puzzled but felt sure we could help the little fellow, now that we understood him better. I told of Bruce's decision against coming to see me next time. She felt that I should ask him again next week.

November 2, 1959
Bruce was absent all week due to cold. Mother notified by note.

November 9, 1959
Interview with Bruce. I reminded him of last week's decision and wondered if he had changed his mind. "Go upstairs?—all right." Off we went together. He talked freely. I said I was sure being sick was no fun but suggested that maybe being home with Mommy was better than being in school. Frowning and screwing up his mouth, he stated with emphasis that he wanted to come to school. He had to stay home—he had a fever. I supposed, then, he was glad to be here. He grinned and drawled "sure"—as if I should have known.

Going to the little table, he pulled the clay apart into two lumps, announcing, "Let's play clay—you make something too." As he worked, I said I thought he must feel pretty big when he takes care of himself without Mrs. Howe reminding him. He smiled. But I wondered if there was a little fun out of acting like a baby. "No—No!" His smile vanished and he worked intently making a little dog. I supposed he was still angry with Mrs. Howe. Looking surprised that I should imagine he was ever angry with her, he said he thought she was nice. Trying to explain at his level of understanding, I said that Mrs. Howe continued to remind all children until they remember to care for their own needs. There was no visible reaction. He talked of things he liked to do, color, sing.

Surprised when I told him his time was up, Bruce carefully picked up his dog to place on the shelf and, on second thought, decided to take it along to show Mrs. Howe. I said that maybe he might want to come only one or two times more because it seemed as though he was a happier boy in school. Saying he would come up again, he left it at that. I added that maybe he could decide next time. I walked to the stairs with him and Bruce went the rest of the way alone.

November 9, 1959

Telephone call from mother. Mrs. Jones reported that during Bruce's recent absence, he had repeatedly expressed regrets that he could not go to school. This pleased her and was reflected in the tone of her voice. The pleasure he exhibits from showing his drawings instead of scribbled papers, she felt, was indicative of his good feeling toward school. Mrs. Jones was appreciative of the school's efforts with Bruce.

I mentioned the nature of the most recent problem that became evident before his week's absence and wondered if it might have been a forerunner of his approaching illness. Mrs. Jones asked that I keep her informed if it persists and she will consult her physician. I explained that Mrs. Howe recognizes Bruce's changed attitude has made him a happier child in school. Again she expressed her thanks.

November 12, 1959

Conference with teacher. Mrs. Howe and I talked before school. She had chosen Bruce as the one responsible for taking care of the wagon during play-time in the yard. He was delighted. She had managed to have a private conference with him regarding another responsibility—the use of the bathroom. Only twice was it necessary to drop an unnoticed, whispered hint into his ear. Mrs. Howe felt that the understanding which came from the home was valuable in helping resolve Bruce's difficulty, together with our joint conferences which aided in gaining insight into the problem. I mentioned terminating conferences with Bruce, possibly next time, and this was agreeable.

November 16, 1959

Final interview with Bruce. Bruce was busy making a picture when I called for him and seemed not ready to come with me. I said I could not come back for him since this was the time I had saved for him. I said I knew it was hard to make up his mind, but he would have to decide. Putting down his crayons, he came along with me, talking of the nice things he does in the room. He talked of his friends—Alan, Joel, Fred, and his special friend, Howard. And I added, "Mrs. Howe," which brought a big laugh.

Once in the office he noticed some big Thanksgiving turkey decorations on my screen, hanging where he had put his "punkin" and he asked for it. He was satisfied to know it was safely put away in a drawer. Bruce made no attempt to use clay or crayons but merely glanced at pictures in a book, then quickly discarded it, saying Mrs. Howe told them a story out of her book. "School is fun I guess?" "Huh-huh," nodding his head. I suggested that this be our last time together. He seemed impatient and restless and let me know that he didn't want to be late going into the yard. He "took charge of the wagon." I said I knew he had a job to do and would make sure he was on time. He smiled and asked, "What time is it?" "Time to go," I answered. As we walked to the door, I said that this would be our last talk together. This was acceptable. He was preoccupied with thoughts of his responsibility—"his wagon." At the stairs he continued on his way alone, looking up long enough at the landing to grin and give me a wave of his hand.

Telephone call to mother. I called Mrs. Jones to tell her I would no longer be working with Bruce. I pointed out that both Mrs. Howe and I felt that Bruce's attitude toward school had changed. He was once more part of a group and enjoying his school experiences. The recent bathroom problem was improving and was not of great concern. Mrs. Jones was delighted, adding that at home Bruce was just as he had been in September. Again she expressed her gratitude to the school for the interest taken.

Case closed—satisfactory adjustment.

RECORD 7

REFERRAL TO A COMMUNITY AGENCY

School social worker's preparation of a mother and child to go to a child guidance clinic

---

MIKE SEBASTIAN ......9 years old, 4th grade

Family members: Parents: Mr. Sebastian, retired diplomat; Mrs. Sebastian, part-time in husband's office. Siblings: older brother.

School personnel: Mr. Gordon, Area School Social Work Supervisor; School Social Worker.

Reason for referral: Absence from school probably due to anxiety over separation from mother. Mother requested help.

Situation prior to referral to school social worker. Over a period of several months, the child found it increasingly difficult to separate from his mother, to enter school, or to remain in school once he had entered. Finally, he was not able to attend at all. The school personnel were anxious and concerned. Another school had been suggested but the child would not enter the school. Legal action on the basis of nonattendance had been discussed with both the mother and the child.

November 15, 1960

Telephone call from mother. Mrs. Sebastian telephoned the area office. She was distraught and anxious and asked for help. During the conversation it was learned that she had gone for one interview at the child guidance center. The area supervisor, Mr. Gordon, after clearance with the school social work administrator, was able to tell Mrs. Sebastian that a school social worker would be in touch with her.

Telephone call to child guidance clinic. As the school social worker assigned to the case, I decided to begin by calling the child guidance clinic. I found the Sebastians were known to them and that service would be reopened at the mother's request. The clinic was helpful in giving information that would be useful to me in the interview with the mother. We agreed that the purpose of my interview with the mother would be to try to help her to return to the clinic.

Telephone call to mother. I telephoned Mrs. Sebastian and made an appointment for a home call on the following day.

November 16, 1960

Interview with mother. Mrs. Sebastian answered the door promptly and admitted me to a well-kept, comfortable home. I noticed that she was attractive, alert, and seemed to be a warm, friendly person.

She sat on the edge of the chair with her hands clasped. I told her that Mr. Gordon, the area supervisor, had told me that she was having trouble getting Mike to school. Mrs. Sebastian nodded vigorously and said she just couldn't understand it—that he had never acted like this before. He gets good grades, has lots of friends, and seems to like his teacher. I said that I thought it must be pretty embarrassing to her to have him act this way. She said, "It sure is! At first everybody at the school was nice and patient but when things didn't get better—I can understand it— they talked about his interrupting the class and when I went to the school they began to look at me as if I were peculiar. I didn't feel right. I felt uncomfortable. We tried everything. The principal said if he was sick he'd vomit before going to school; maybe I should put him to bed, so I did but that didn't work. He didn't complain. He says he doesn't know why he can't go to school—that he wishes he knew why." I commented that I was willing to bet that she had the same wish. Mrs. Sebastian laughed and said, "Yes." She thought that Mike probably doesn't really know why. I agreed that it was hard to know. I told her that I had known other children with the same problem. She sighed and said, "I thought I was the only one! I'm so relieved to know that I'm not the only one. The principal told me that in all of his years of experience he had never seen a child act like Mike. Mike seems to like his school but we even tried another one just in case it was something about his school. He wouldn't even go in even though the principal and I pushed and pulled him. I don't know what to do. I wondered about a home teacher. What would you think about that?" I answered that I knew that it was embarrassing to her and having him at home would prevent the scenes at school although I did feel that it was important to help him get back into school as soon as possible. Mrs. Sebastian told me that she had been getting Mike ready for school every day and that this morning he left—got part way to school and vomited and then came back home. She just hadn't felt up to taking him. I asked where Mike was now. She replied that he was in the back yard working his garden.

She continued talking about Mike's abilities and interests in a positive way and again expressed her inability to understand why he can't go to school when he has so many interests and friends. I replied that it wasn't easy to figure out and that I thought it took an expert to help with it—someone like the people at the clinic. I explained that I knew Mrs. Sebastian had gone for one visit and I wondered what had gone into her decision not to go any more. She said that she really wanted to go but that she had not agreed with something that the psychiatric social worker had told her and that she didn't feel that she could just tell a person that you don't agree with them. I said that I could see how this might be true with neighbors and friends, but that I thought it was different at the clinic—that you could say how you felt. I told her that I had worked at the clinic and that I knew the psychiatric social worker to be the kind of person who would want and need to know how she really felt, just as I would want to know. I could see that it would not be easy for Mrs. Sebastian to do this and that it was hard to go and talk about the problem. She replied that she does want to do something about it—it worries her all the time— everything else is all right but this does worry her. I asked how her husband felt about it. She said that she had discussed not going back to the clinic with him and that he had agreed with her. She added that their older son is more her husband's child and Mike is hers.

Mr. Sebastian is a retired diplomat. He needs her help in his office but she has not been able to be there because she never knows when Mike might leave the school grounds. She worries about his being unsupervised at home or walking the long way to the office. I asked if Mike talks about her going to the office. She answered that he wants her to stay home but she is at home when he is there and that she can't have him telling her whether or not she can work. I nodded. Mrs. Sebastian mentioned that the family has been thinking about returning to Europe to live. She needs to work so that they will have money for the trip. She expressed her discontent with urban life and her interest in living on an island where they can have a simpler life.

I noticed that Mike had come in and was standing in the hall. Mrs. Sebastian said that she needed to do something, that she wondered about going back to the clinic. I said that if she decides to go back, she can phone and they will give her an appointment.

She asked if I had the phone number and explained that she would call right now. She asked if I would like to see Mike. I answered, "Yes, if he can tolerate it." Mrs. Sebastian tried to persuade Mike to come into the living room. He refused and eventually she raised her voice and pushed him. I got up and walked toward Mike. He ran into the back yard. I observed that he was a handsome, healthy-looking boy whose expression and actions were tense, anxious, and near panic. Mike hid behind the fence, but stayed close enough to see and remained within earshot. Mrs. Sebastian and I stayed on the porch. I talked to Mike across the length of the back yard saying that I had come to try to help him get back to school. I said that he probably was worried about not going to school and that his mother and I had been talking about his going to the clinic where he could see a doctor who would try to help him understand why he couldn't go to school. Mike watched me from his hiding place but made no response. I said that I was going back into the house but I would be there a while longer if he wanted to talk to me. Mrs. Sebastian stayed in the kitchen in order to call the clinic. I went to the living room. Mike suddenly ran into the living room, with his face averted. He snatched a model plane from the far end of the room and raced out again.

When Mrs. Sebastian finished the phone call, she made refreshments and asked Mike to take them to the living room. He was most reluctant to do so and after much urging he came in again with his face averted. He stayed away from the chair in which I was sitting. I thanked him for the refreshments and we were both silent. Mrs. Sebastian came in and said that she would be able to get a definite appointment tomorrow. Mike asked me if the doctor would give him a shot. He did not look at me as he asked this. I said no, that he was the kind of doctor who would talk with him as he and I were talking now. I thought Mike probably didn't know why he couldn't go to school but that I felt he wanted to go and that the doctor would help him. Mike nodded. I commented about his plane. Mrs. Sebastian said that both boys like models and she pointed out the large one on the table which the older boy had made. I admired the work and Mrs. Sebastian suggested that Mike show me his collections.

Mike brought his butterfly collection and extended it from a distance. I told him that I like butterflies too and that my brother, who is his age, collects them too. Mike's interaction became much freer at this point and he asked if my brother had a monarch. Later he showed me a picture of his brother. Mrs. Sebastian talked, with pride, about the brother's accomplishments. Mike said, "I hate him." Mrs. Sebastian said that he didn't really mean that. Mike also brought a picture of his grandmother with the comment that she had had a heart attack so that his father, who is her only child, would come to see her. Mike asked me to look at his garden and his pets. By this time, he no longer looked or seemed so anxious. He was expressive and responsive and seemed really to enjoy the interaction. He seemed intelligent and imaginative.

Upon returning to the house, I prepared to leave. Mike asked me if I would like some butterflies for my brother. I thought that he might want them for his own collection. He said that they were duplicates. I accepted them with thanks and he seemed pleased. He wondered if I would see him again. I said that it had been fun to talk with him and his mother. I didn't plan to be back because his mother would be going to the clinic and he would probably go soon so that they could help him get back to school. He looked disappointed. I added that I was at his school on Mondays and that I would see him there and talk with him again. He nodded. I gave Mrs. Sebastian my card; she understood that she could call me if she wished to. I told her that I would know through the school how things were going.

November 21, 1960

Telephone call to child guidance clinic. I telephoned the clinic and learned that Mrs. Sebastian had come in. I left word of my willingness to work further with the clinic on the school aspects of the problem.

RECORD 8

CONSULTATION TO A TEACHER

The teacher is helped to understand the dynamics of behavior of a seriously
disturbed little girl in kindergarten and to relieve some of the child's tensions

CAROL SMITH........	5 years old, in third month of kindergarten.
Family members:	Parents: Mr. and Mrs. Smith. Siblings: Two brothers, one older and one younger.
School personnel:	Miss Jones, teacher; school social worker.
Reason for referral:	Alternately overly aggressive or withdrawn behavior; fear of dirt, antagonism toward boys. Teacher requested help.

Teacher's statement of the problem. Miss
Jones said that Carol had two ways of responding to any suggestion
or request—belligerent and aggressive action to the teacher and
to the children, or a silent move to the bench at the side of the
room where she would sit for an hour or more, refusing to talk
or return to the group. Miss Jones, who at 35 was in her first
year of teaching, said that Carol was most difficult to handle. I
assured her that a child who behaved like Carol would be difficult
for any teacher to handle.

Miss Jones added other details of Carol's behavior, some of
which she had learned from talking with the child's mother. Carol
was unwilling to use toilets in large buildings. She would not
use a dish that had not just come out of a cupboard. Her food
must be placed in separate sections, two kinds could not touch.
She would not wear a dress with a wrinkle or a spot, even though
she had put it on an hour before. She would never sit on the
floor. She had more than the usual amount of friction with
her older and younger brothers. She screamed if a friend of her

brothers came into the house, saying they could not come in, that she hated boys. Carol told her mother that she liked school but did not like her teacher—that her teacher did not like her and made her lie on the floor on a mat.

Consultation to teacher. I told Miss Jones that from the description of Carol's behavior, she sounded like a child in need of psychotherapy. Even if the mother were interested in a plan of treatment by a child guidance clinic, and even if such treatment were immediately available, it was probable that it would be a long time before Carol would show real change.

The problem for the school was what could be done to help Carol now in her school adjustment. This was difficult, because of the neurotic-type symptoms, and even the most experienced teacher would be hard put to it to manage a child like Carol in a group. But the symptomalogy itself made a few concrete suggestions possible. If Carol felt strongly about taking her rest time on the floor, she might be permitted to rest on the bench. The teacher might arrange for Carol to be placed near girls rather than boys, most of the time. Miss Jones responded to these ideas by saying that since Carol was so very clean, she might well be put in charge of keeping the dolls' housekeeping corner in order. We agreed that these and other adjustments which the teacher might make in Carol's program were only palliative and that in the meantime, if possible, a treatment plan, with the help of a community agency, should be undertaken outside the school.

Two weeks later. Miss Jones reported that Carol had become somewhat easier to handle. She still withdrew to the side of the room some of the time, but she was less aggressive to the other children and no longer aggressive to the teacher. Carol was still not easy to live with, but she did not disrupt the whole class and seemed to try to do well more of the time. Miss Jones thought that until the child profits from treatment she was at least "containable" in a school situation.

Appendix B

Organization of the
Conference

background of conference

The fundamental responsibility for the planning and completion of the Conference on the Contribution of School Social Work to Social Work Education was carried by the Executive Committee of the School Social Work Section, National Association of Social Workers. More particularly, the Education Committee of the Section is deserving of credit. As early as September 1955 Florence Poole, then chairman of the Education Committee of NASSW [1] recommended considering a workshop "for preparing personnel for teaching school social work content in schools of social work." As planning proceeded, some shift in emphasis was reflected in the changing titles for the proposed conference.

In 1956 it was referred to as the "Institute for Classroom Teachers and Field Instructors in School Social Work." By the summer of 1957 Dr. Joseph P. Hourihan was appointed as the new chairman of the Education Committee. Subsequently the working title of the conference was referred to as "Teaching School Social Work." Finally the title was settled upon in August 1958 as being "The Contribution of School Social Work to Social Work Education." This was recognized as more accurately reflecting the conference focus on those elements which could be distilled from school social work practice for the benefit of social work education. It was expected that all social work students would profit from a greater appreciation for, and understanding of, the school as a social institution and the ways of working with children, parents, and schools.

The conference was made possible financially by a grant from the National Institute of Mental Health; this publication is one of the tangible manifestations of the grant. The consultation service provided by Dr. Milton Wittman of NIMH was invaluable to the Education Committee in its planning. In addition, the committee received consultation help from Mildred Sikkema of the Council on Social Work Education.

---

[1] The National Association of School Social Workers which shortly thereafter became the School Social Work Section of NASW when this association was formed.

253

selection of conference participants

It was planned that all schools of social work having field work placements in public schools would be invited to participate in the conference. Such schools were asked to suggest the names of classroom and field instructors who might be invited to attend and one each from both categories, class and field, where possible, was invited. The conference ultimately included one or more representatives from thirty-two schools or departments of social work.

education committee, school social work section, nasw

Joseph P. Hourihan, Chairman
Opal Boston
Louise Spence
Rose Green
Dorothy D. Hayes
Irene Hobbs
Florence Poole
Elsie Nesbit, ex officio
John C. Nebo, ex officio

organizational roster of the conference

Conference Leader Florence Poole, Professor, University of Illinois, Urbana, Illinois

Conference Editor Arlien Johnson, Ph.D., Dean Emeritus, School of Social Work, University of Southern California, Granada Hills, California

Speakers

Arlien Johnson, Ph.D., Dean Emeritus, School of Social Work, University of Southern California, Granada Hills, California

Elizabeth D. Keye, School Social Worker, Oak Park Public Schools, Oak Park, Michigan

Eleanor Loeb, Assistant Professor, School of Social Work, The University of Kansas, Lawrence, Kansas

Mildred Sikkema, Consultant on Education Standards, Council on Social Work Education, Inc., New York, New York

Ruth E. Smalley, D.S.W., Dean, School of Social Work, University of Pennsylvania, Philadelphia, Pennsylvania

Robert C. Taber, Director, Division of Pupil Personnel and Counseling, School District of Philadelphia, Pennsylvania

Jane Wille, Assistant to the Director, Illinois Office of Public Instruction, Park Ridge, Illinois

---

Consultants

John R. Altmeyer, M.D., Psychiatric Consultant, Health Department, Milwaukee, Wisconsin

J. McV. Hunt, Ph.D., Professor of Psychology, University of Illinois, Urbana, Illinois

Ruth Landes, Ph.D., Director, Adult Health Services Survey, Los Angeles City Health Department, Los Angeles, California

Florence Ray, Assistant Director, NASW, Group Work Section, New York, New York

Arnold Rose, Ph.D., Professor, Department of Sociology, University of Minnesota, Minneapolis, Minnesota

Representatives of Other Organizations

Marie McNabola, Training Specialist, Social Work Training Branch, NIMH, Bethesda, Maryland

Mildred Sikkema, Consultant on Education Standards, Council on Social Work Education, Inc., New York, New York

Workshop Leaders

Gordon J. Aldridge, Ph.D., Professor, School of Social Work, Michigan State University, East Lansing, Michigan

Tybell Bloom, School of Social Work, University of Pennsylvania, Philadelphia, Pennsylvania

Opal Boston, Supervisor, Social Service Branch, Indianapolis Public Schools, Indianapolis, Indiana

Rose Green, School of Social Work, University of Southern California, Los Angeles, California

Victor I. Howery, Ph.D., Dean, School of Social Work, University of Washington, Seattle, Washington

Workshop Recorders

Dorothy D. Hayes, Ph.D., Professor of Social Work and Chairman, Graduate Program in Social Work, School of Social Welfare, Florida State University, Tallahassee, Florida

Irene B. Hobbs, University of Southern California, Los Angeles, California (Area Supervisor, Child Welfare and Attendance, Los Angeles City Board of Education)

Louise M. Spence, Social Work Supervisor, Division of Children and Youth, Wisconsin Department of Public Welfare, Rhinelander, Wisconsin

Mary N. Taylor, Associate Professor, School of Social Work, University of Michigan, Ann Arbor, Michigan

Violet E. Tennant, Associate Professor of Social Work, Indiana University, Division of Social Service, Indianapolis, Indiana

NASW Staff

Bertram M. Beck, Associate Executive Director

Jerry L. Kelley, Assistant Director, School Social Work Section

SSW—1½M—5/62